CHRONICLES of GALAXY OSMARON

Jull, The Supreme Patriarch

'Only certain life-forms like the Lodorians can visualise in true conceptual terms. Humans and many animal life-forms with five senses are restricted by their strong reliance on the visual perception. Those intelligent creatures that have evolved and adopted to the oceans, have a better understanding of dimensional structures, even the simple things you take for granted. For instance, you appear to be bi-symmetrical; meaning you have two eyes, etcetera, and a line pass through your mirror image will reveal that symmetry. But have you ever asked why?'

Chronicles of Galaxy Osmaron Series

Chronicles of Galaxy Osmaron - I am Shadite

Chronicles of Galaxy Osmaron - The power of One

Chronicles of Galaxy Osmaron - Escape from Andromeda

Chronicles of Galaxy Osmaron - The Solarian Empire

Chronicles of Galaxy Osmaron - Fertilates

Chronicles of Galaxy Osmaron - Infilates

Chronicles of Galaxy Osmaron - Son of destiny

Chronicles of Galaxy Osmaron - Jull, The Supreme Patriarch

Chronicles of Galaxy Osmaron - Battle for Andromeda

Chronicles of Galaxy Osmaron - Battle for Osmaron

First Edition

Chronicles of Galaxy Osmaron

Jull, the Supreme Patriarch

The first stages before Battle for Andromeda

By

Adrian Graye

Nutralian Publishing
http://nutralianpublishing.com

nutralia
An imprint of Nutralian Publishing
5 Brayford Square, London E1 0SG
http://nutralianpublishing.com

This paperback edition 2012
B00005555

First published in Great Britain by
Amazon KDP 2024

Copyright © Adrian Graye 2012

The Author Adrian Graye asserts the moral right to
be identified as the author of this Work in accordance
with the Copyright, Design and Patents Act 1988.

ISBN 978-1-0687902-7-0

Printed and bound in Great Britain by Amazon KDP Publishing.

A CIP catalogue record for this title
is available from the British Library.

**All rights reserved. No part of this publication may be reproduced, stored
in a retrieval system, or transmitted, in any form or by any means,
electronic, mechanical, photocopying, recording or otherwise, without
the prior permission of the publishers.**

**This book is distributed subject to the conditions that it will not, by way
of trade or otherwise, be lent, resold, hired out, or otherwise circulated
without the publisher's prior consent in any form of binding or cover
other than that in which it is published and without similar conditions,
including these conditions being imposed on any subsequent purchaser.**

**All characters in this publication are fictitious and any
resemblance to real persons, living or dead is purely coincidental.**

This book is dedicated with love to Galicia and all its people. I consider that place to be the most spiritual on Earth. I can feel it in my bones.

&

To all those that believe in Universal Existence and respect the lowliest of life; for like babes, they are the beginning.

TABLE OF CONTENTS

PROLOGUE — xi

1. A refuge world — 13
2. George's visit to MIMIC — 18
3. Within Lower MIMIC — 24
4. The free world of Tyrrel 2 — 29
5. A moment of truth — 35
6. On Safari — 40
7. A wanted man — 49
8. Back at the Hearst Mansion — 57
9. A spiritual calendar — 66
10. Martian Base — 70
11. The third malady — 78
12. The moons of Endoh — 87
13. A visit to Lori III — 98
14. The loving hands of a god — 103
15. Lupher and Dracma — 111
16. Little good witch — 118
17. The Universal Healer — 125
18. Stellar convergence — 132

19	The main Federation worlds	138
20	Tarran - Planet of Cats	147
21	A stellar miracle	156
22	A visit to Polok II	161
23	A brand new dawn	174
24	Lodorians in preparation	179
25	A visit to Lodor	183
26	Nervia World	193
27	Beautiful Orban	198
28	The ancient Ancients	201
29	The fourth malady	204
30	Home sweet home	212
31	The fifth malady	224
32	The last maladies	230
33	A grand display	235
34	New Vogon	240
35	Home within Terminus City	243
36	The United Nations Conference	251
37	Earth in turmoil	259
38	The special cloak of office	264
39	A briefing before the first assault	271

40	Evil Dracma goes to Triangulum	279
41	Caefon in Andromeda	284
42	First Assault plans	291
43	As free as a bird	297
44	No prisoners are taken	301
45	The main assault	306
46	The Javols' den	311
47	The magic wand	318
48	Ceremonies and celebrations	322
	Epilogue	327
	The Chronicles of Galaxy Osmaron series	329

From the ANACHROMAGNON - The book of final light.

'If I lived to eternity I would become a god or I would be nothing.'

By Siend Seno of The Plains of Herron.

The human tree of life

Come with me and I will show you a tree.
It's like the human race, you will agree?
In autumn all its leaves will fall,
And again in spring, a renewal call.

I know your life is still quite young,
But look! this leaf here, how crinkled and brown.
You know it's the start of a summer long,
And yet, how dead is this leaf, quite wrong.

The tree itself looks healthy and strong,
And may hear many a new summer's song.
A cutter's axe or saw may rend,
A race of humans, extinction! The End?

An unwritten law to me is clear,
That there is a lot more than existence here.
For within this complex plan I see,
The pattern of another tree.

Although our autumn's three scores and ten,
Perhaps five billion in one fall, and then?
You could have travelled from some tree hence,
And are taking a path to another thence.

Have faith in God and mend all fences.
Be prepared, for a new journey commences,
A Great Spiritual Journey of Consequence,
Within a Cosmos of Magnificence.

Victor Roche

Prologue

Numerous swarms of rapacious Nano-bot Javols are currently on their way to our galaxy. They will arrive within 100 years. They are so numerous that they will blacken the skies of most worlds. Their sole purpose is to dominate and rear us like cattle for their own sustenance and entertainment. On arrival they will be hungry and starving and will feed on all life until many come close to extinction.

Only George Peterson, in the form of Jull the warrior Patriarch, with his new breed of soldiers and weapons, will hopefully save the day. During that most vicious conflict many will die and he must ensure we have a fighting chance.

By the time of their arrival the human population of Earth will be reduced to just 500 million. This new situation will give Earth enough time to rebuild her forests and wild life. However during that time the whole governing structure of Earth will be replaced by powerful AI minds like Headrons, Macrons and their policing androids. They will ensure that Earth never returns to the days of selfish and capitalist mankind in the form of Infilates.

Never again will mankind be given free reign to destroy a beautiful world in the name of greed. The days of Infilates are truly over.

George has quite a political fight on his hands with Earth's governments. Will he win that day?

A NEW SOCIETY ON EARTH

In the interim period, before the new Solarian empire, there will be a new society on Earth with no financial Banks.

No more manufactured money, in the form of notes and coins. Only his new credits and cards for transactions.

All cities and towns will contain recycling depots for everything. Those are run by Free-timers.

Every individual will work just 6 months in each year for full salary. Therefore double the people will be employed.

Every individual gives two months in each year freely to their local communities, for assisting the elderly, and the environment. During that time their communities allow them travelling expenses and food, plus a uniform. After that time they can be promoted to a higher officer grade (Grade One or higher officer with stripes). As incentive Grade One officers in any profession are given a special Credit Card for 5% discount on all transactions. Grade Two Officers get 7.5% discount, etc. Higher grade officers are elected to run their communities.

During this two month period of community help workers are called Free-timers. All Free-timers are compelled to wear uniforms during this time.

The last four months of each year belongs to the individual, for holidays and such like.

George's new caring society is very efficient and valued by all.

CHAPTER 1

A refuge world

The refuge world of Tyrrel 2 was one of great extremes. In orbit were 3 moons. One the size of Mars with a relatively dense atmosphere and two about half the size of Earth's moon without atmosphere. There were two orbiting stars. One twice as large as our sun and the other about half the size, but orbiting outside the system in an almost elliptical orbit. The most significant indigenous life were large furn-like trees and a type of rodent that lived off the pine-pods. They were useful for propagating the seeds of those plants. Small creatures and insects also existed to form a stable food chain. Despite its higher gravity, that world with its 5 great continents and 5 large oceans, including seas, lakes and islands, made it ideal as a refuge for life of all types.

When Lord Meron and his planetologist checked that world decades ago, they found no harmful bacteria or dangerous animal life. At that time all indigenous animals were non-predatory, living off plants or animal waste with almost no competition. That was until the later introduction of Robots, Androids, Dinosaurs and Titans. There were 5 great continents. The three populated but isolated ones were Solania with their main city of Solaris. That continent had been used for many of Earth's extinct and endangered life-forms. The continent of Tyrannia, capital Tyrannis, was populated with bio-engineered dinosaurs of every kind as were on Earth over 100 million years ago.

To the north was Titannia, it contained a wide variety of Titans, also bio-engineered. Titans were top of the food chain and preyed on the larger dinosaurs placed on their isolated continent. The continent of Feltwol was the bread basket of the Solarian Empire and the largest. There was also Cantoria, but that continent was left for overspills from the empire.

That world was left free to evolve in its many diverse ways. However most of the introduced engineered life-forms were given brain implants for more direct communication with their controlling Macrons.

Most creatures excluding the few indigenous life, were bio-engineered. Therefore it was a world of constantly changing habitats. A world where life was constantly evolving and adapting to fit its ever changing environments.

ROBOT CITY or REBEL CITY

Not all intelligent robots were subservient to controlling macrons. Some independent robots and androids had developed their own personalities and knew what they wanted to fulfill their existence, therefore it was not long before Solaris, capital of the continent of Solania, became the city of free robots. It was undoubtedly the largest city in the federation and was still being extended by robots. It was a free city for all, with its own android and robot police. Although that world was within the Solarian Federation, Solaris was all about freedom of existence so no one complained.

Nevertheless, Solaris was controlled democratically by city fathers and responsible city macrons that ensured that incredible city of over 50 million remained one of the most desirable within the Federation. Just on the outskirts of the city were large training camps for young people taken from Earth. Their trainers were mainly androids controlled by their macron. Then they would join the Federation Navy for more experience in space. Since that world was like a living ark, most endangered life would be delivered to its continents from other worlds in Galaxy Osmaron (our Milky Way Galaxy). Over the years that world had been terra formed for life as found on Earth, so it's oxygen and other levels had been maintained that way with large environmental machines. However gravity remained twice that on Earth.

Responsible for everyone on Tyrrel 2 was the clever scientist Doctor Hal Seaton (originally the Green Chameleon). He was now their ruler. He had fought on many occasions for their rights and many intelligent robots and androids admired and respected him. He had also introduced a range of games and sustenance in many forms to replenish their bodies and minds. Anyway, as far as Sarah was concerned he was the right person for that job, with his particular genius in bio-engineering and robotics. After all, he was the genius responsible for creating the Terminal Disease and also the Terminal Plague that wiped out over 5 billion Infilates in one fell swoop, giving Fertilates a better chance for survival. Although she didn't like the idea at the time, in hindsight it was necessary and a quick solution. Nevertheless since the death of his original body, as far as Empress Sarah was concerned the new resurrected Hal was a different person with a younger body and mind.

Hal's extended palace was on a hill that overlooked the human quarters of the city. At present the city's population was over 50 million, with about 5 million humans, excluding the Federation soldiers being trained. All young were educated in every possible field of technology. The difficult and labourious tasks being done by robots for a price. Unlike Eden, on Solaris everyone earned credits and competed equally for survival. Even so, robots and androids were respectful towards humans as their creators.

Dr. Hal Seaton was presently based on Tyrrel 2, with his occasional visits to Earth. He had grown to love that world with its many variations and freedoms. He now lived on a world without the silly politics of Earth or Eden, where everyone lived together in mutual happiness for the benefit of all. On that world the land areas were over twice that on Earth, so he could choose the best people and most suited places for his dangerous experiments.

MIMIC LABORATORIES

Dr. John Simmons now a youthful 25 year old was originally the 73 year old Professor Kane Powell. He had replaced his namesake Kane Powell with a younger body, complements of Lord Khan with the help of Solarian Megotron technology at Sol-Newtown Dome. Then he ceremoniously buried the old Kane Powell namesake in a coffin filled with sandbags. He was presently based on Earth and in charge of MIMIC Laboratories, just outside the city of New York, USA.

He was presently in charge of all anti-Javols bio weapons and was responsible for creating the dreaded Titans. They were meant to be his last line of defence in saving his precious planet, Earth. Professor Bengizara Khan (Ben) was responsible for all security on Earth, so all his developments were financed by Ben, being president of Solarian Banking. Earlier on, Ben realized several different types of weapons and ideas were necessary to win any prolonged war against Javols and could not rely on Solarian technology to save Earth, so unknown to Sarah and her Solarians he took another route. As far as he was concerned several methods were much better than one. After all, he was a military man and knew the score.

John had created what he and Hal called portal gateways between Earth and Tyrrel 2. Since most of the deadlier monsters and weapons would be stationed on Tyrrel 2, it was necessary to move them to Earth at a moments notice. Those secret gateways were installed in most underground facilities and domes along with anti-Javols warriors. Presently since the Terminal Antidote was not required, all that storage space was assigned to those warriors, all hibernating in their plastic containment suits. Those almost indestructible nano-bot warriors and Mind-Probes would be constantly produced and stored until the first invading Javols were sighted.

SOLARIAN BANKING ON EARTH

The whole structure of Solarian Banking had changed into a more military organization. Therefore all those branches were being secured and armed against Javols globally. Soon they were all upgraded with powerful anti-Javol portals of inter-stellar range. Although George Peterson (Son of Destiny) would soon be in charge, he had no knowledge of the Master Plan set in motion by Ben and his co-conspirators, Hal and John. Nevertheless, George was always on the side of Earth and of the Earth's Children Gang, so there was where his duties lay. Anyway, unbeknown to him, Ben was his grandfather, who would hopefully coerce him into taking a stand on the side of Earth.

With Infilate humans dying like flies mainly due to old age, it was not long before just 500 million plus Fertilates would be left on Earth to take control of the planet. Nevertheless, Solarian Banking under it's leadership would always have the real power to control Earth's populations. At that time in the near future, there would be no borders isolating separate countries. There would be just protectorate states with a lord protector in charge of his fief. All being controlled by a Supreme Lord Protector assisted by powerful Macrons. Even so, there would always be a parliament as on Eden, where everything would be discussed and voted for democratically. Hopefully it would be a world without greed, where everyone would live forever and share in a common wealth for the benefit of all.

After Ben's marriage he intended to spend his time protecting our galaxy Osmaron. At least his part of the galaxy embodied within the Solarian Arm. Nevertheless with all those inter-stellar portals, it was easy to move soldiers and weapons anywhere at short notice. In any event, he would always be based on Earth or a local system.

CHAPTER 2

George's visit to MIMIC

Professor Khan (Ben) wanted to introduce George to Hal and John. Since George was now the boss of Solarian banking he would be the one signing the cheques in future while he, Ben, remained in the background keeping an eye on new developments for the survival of Solaria. As far as Ben was concerned, Solarians including his daughter, Empress Sarah, were soft and much too relaxed for real bloody warfare. So once George was settled after his holidays on Eden and Mars he called to set a date.

'Lord Khan is on the line for you!' Cathy shouted.

'Yes! It's me!' George answered.

'Sorry about Vogon. Thank goodness those nasty people are now in Hell!'

'Yea! Thank goodness they wont be bothering us anymore!' George replied.

'I would like you to visit the MIMIC labs on Monday, if you are free! I would have liked to accompany you but will be unable to make it.'

'I should be free. What is it about?'

'It's about the defence of Earth. I have had some clever scientists working on anti-Javols weaponry. Now that you are in control of Solarian banking it's advantageous that you have a full picture of our organization and its diverse branches. Some of which are unknown, even to the Andromedans. We should never have all our eggs in one basket. If we are to win this terrible war we must be diverse!' Ben said.

'I understand! Can I take Cathy along?"

'You may take your whole gang along. They can all be suited up in the MIMIC labs before you visit for the demonstrations,' Ben said.

'Ok, Monday it is!'

'I shall send 3 limousines in the morning!' Ben insisted.

'Ok, I am looking forward!' George said and Ben ended the call.

Soon George called his gang together. Active members now numbered 13, including Parky, their butler.

'People, Lord Khan has invited us all to partake in demonstrations on Monday. Apparently they have been designing anti-Javol weaponry. But I think we should make a day of it. I have a funny suspicion it will be a day to remember!' George said. They were all excited in anticipation.

'Do we take along food and entertainment?' Cathy inquired, innocently.

'Three limousines are expected, so do as you like!' George replied. They were all under the impression of having a most exciting time, even a picnic perhaps.

As their limousines approached they could observe the MIMIC laboratories in the distance. Each part above ground level being made of green semi-transparent glass and in the form of 5 separate buildings which formed the letters MIMIC. Within the structures they could observe elevators and people moving about. The main reception area was in the centre of the M building.

'Wow! What a place!' Tim commented and the others were astonished.

The group of 13 gang members soon entered the foyer and were greeted by the female receptionist.

'Lord George, I presume?' she inquired. All Solarian councillors of status were lords in the truest sense.

'Please to meet you!' he greeted.

George and his group followed her to the reception area. There standing were Dr. Hal Seaton in his special suit. Not far behind were Dr. John Simmons and twenty of his best scientists. They were dressed in white overalls above their dark grey suits and blue ties. Hal was the first to come forward.

'At long last we meet in the flesh! It's such a great pleasure!' Hal greeted.

'Me to!' John said, full of excitement.

'I know a little about you, Dr. Seaton, but not much about John. Anyway, the pleasure is all mine!' George replied and firmly shook their hands.

'Lord Khan told me of your involvement in the creation of products to save our world. Being head of Solarian Banking, from now on I intend to increase funding to all those products created for our mutual survival. So just tell us what you need,' George said and they cheered.

While they sat to have refreshments, Dr. Hal Seaton followed to the rostrum. He was to inform them of the sacrifices made and great work they had achieved over the past decades in establishing a foothold to fight their mutual enemy.

'Before we visit the underground chambers to observe demonstrations, I would like to bring you up to date on our progress. Let me list the items, then you may ask specific questions relating to a particular project,' he said, but continued.

'We now have the following; The Satan's Bug. This is a virus that links with the Terminal Bacteria. It has no effect on humans or other primals and was specifically designed to target Javols. Once infected they literally burn up with extreme fever until they explode and die. This device is very contagious and will destroy swarms of those monsters. Therefore from now on we and other animals can be poisonous to all Javols.

'Our Anti-Javol Soldiers are also Mind Probes. They are the best warriors but can also download all information from a Javol's brain and take their place. That way we can duplicate their bases with our own. All our battalions have brain implants and are controlled by commanders. They are highly intelligent mini macrons that can make quick decisions during battle. Our warriors were designed to be more than twice as fast as Javols and are self-healing.

'The Self-Scanning Plasma Weapon or Plasma Gun can be made in several sizes and will cut a Javol to pieces in seconds. Assuming they remain stationery during that time. A suitable device with holder is readily available for demonstration.

'The Anti-Javols Suit is still under development. However the suit I am wearing is good enough for most purposes. It's bullet proof, can be made invisible, gravity can be controlled. Can be made disease proof with hood and nasal filter. It can also be used

in space for short periods in an emergency along with numerous other features. The utility belt also contains a range of canisters and tools for survival in the worst planetary environments.'

George and the others clapped. Then Hal turned to Dr. John Simmons who went to the rostrum as they cheered some more.

'Now a few words on our Titans. They are the worst predators in the universe and were specifically designed to hate and kill Javols. To maintain their kind we had to create a complete continent of the most ferocious dinosaurs on the world of Tyrrel 2.

'Our Krakens are over 100 feet tall, muscular and fast. Their thick skin will combine with our type of nano-bot swarms that can quickly spread disease among Javols. They were designed for destroying their largest swarms. When a Javol comes in contact with a Titan their skin will react to encase and destroy them. Their breath is concentrated with the deadliest disease. However humans and primals are immune.

'Our Medusas are somewhat different. They, like their other cousins, can fly to inflict maximum damage. They are nuclear powered and contain a single head with ten writhing serpents. Each serpent contains a powerful plasma projector. Their eyes are different and contain field projectors that will literally freeze a Javol into a solid mass of metal. Much like turning them into an immobile statue.

'Others like Minotaurs and Centaurs and their cousins with their special crossbows will assist the mayhem of wanton destruction. All our Titans contain brain implants and can be instructed or controlled by our war macrons. Titans are better used on worlds like Earth. However, we still have the problem of disease and vermin brought to our worlds by Javols. Therefore we are currently working on air-ships with powerful sprays to prevent their spread to populated areas. All titans are grown in incubators for a short period until released to their continent. Then they join their main social groups for mutual survival,'

George posed the first question.

'Your Satan's Bug. Can it be removed from an infected individual?'

'The Satan's Bug can only link with the Terminal Bacteria. So it can only be removed from those previously scanned by a Megotron before infection. It is estimated that the Terminal Carrier will eventually mutate and die. When that happens the virus will be unsupported and also die. However this will happen many decades in the future. We hope the Javols will be extinct by then. Since everyone will eventually be infected with no symptoms or effect, it will be impossible to exist on Earth without catching this bug,' John replied.

'What about Andromedans! Can they be infected?' Tim shouted from the back.

'They and other primals, being carbon based, are similar to us. However the disease can be tailor-made for a particular species, given the necessary DNA and other particulars. If they want to be infected they should visit Earth and not use portals. Then they may use portals on their return, to remove the bacteria. That way they can control the infection. However, Planet Eden will be well guarded. I was told that world is scheduled for encasement in an invisible shield or shroud, so they will be relatively safe from invasion. As far as I am concerned, Earth will bear the brunt. By so doing we will divert them away from others,' John said.

Soon all questions were answered and Hal returned to the rostrum.

'For safety reasons I would like each one of our visitors to use the special suits provided. We should now view the real action,' Hal said as George got up to commend him.

'I must say, Dr. Seaton and Dr. Simmons, you have both accomplish greatly. I never thought we on Earth had progressed so quickly. Now I know we have a fighting chance against those nasty monsters. Please carry on the good work!' George stressed.

'The real work was down at lower levels by our dedicated and hard working scientists, so we should also compliment them,' Hal said, so everyone stood up and clapped, while the twenty main scientist looked on with smiles.

'I think all you guys deserve Nobel prises, so I shall create a special fund including an honorary medallion or insignia of importance for those responsible. There will be one million dollars for those concerned, so please get me some names. As for you John, I will make you an important person in the near future, after I am settled in my new post. Who knows, perhaps I shall make you, Hal, the protector of Earth. Although you are a genius, you are also one with the necessary credentials. We need fearless people like you to take the lead, for a storm is already on the horizon. A storm that will shake all life in our galaxy to the very core. If we are to survive we cannot be complacent, so consider me on your side in future,' George said and they clapped again.

The gang members and others were soon changing into their special protective suits. In most cases they had to remove their clothes which they hung in the available lockers.

'My God! My suit is alive!' Tim yelled while observing the shimmering microbes as it adjusted to his smaller size. He did not wish to complain and be considered a weakling.

'They are composed of strongly linked nano-bots on a flexible bullet-proof layer. You are now a superman without the S logo. You will also carry a virus deadly to Javols, but quite harmless to humans,' John said and Tim became even more worried.

'You may control your suits manually or by implants. All controls are visible through your visor or specs while worn. There are also a small controller with communicator clipped to your belt. You may try it for a while. Gravity may be controlled by the G-Knob,' he said as Tim began to fly across the room.

'I really am superman without the S logo!' He exclaimed and landed close to Jerry almost knocking him off his feet.

'Careful with that thing!' Jerry yelled, being not too amused. The others began to laugh.

'Special implants are out of the question for now. We are awaiting suitable trainers in a week or so from Eden, so everyone should get acquainted with manual controls at this time,' George advised.

CHAPTER 3

Within Lower MIMIC

With their special protective suits, green for males and violet for women, they entered one of the large elevators and descended towards the lower labs several hundred feet below. That was where the demonstrations were held for safety reasons.

'There must be at lease 100 floors below ground level,' Jerry commented as the lift descended at great speed.

'To be precise, 125 floors. It was excavated by robots during the time of Dr. Jeffery Longhurst. I mean, when he was on Earth. It had not been used since his disappearance in outer-space. For security reasons only 2 elevators are used,' John said.

'Wow! What a place!' Tim exclaimed while floors flicked pass.

'I suppose it's the place that created hell for Javols!' George replied with satisfaction.

They soon arrived at the lowest basement and the elevator opened unto a ramp with four broad stairways. They were guided towards a local room. That place had a thick layer of bullet-proof glass, separating them from the occupants. Within the front area they could observe several metallic human-like figures about 8 feet tall. They appeared to be asleep on their feet. In front of that group were a larger and more vicious looking one with a reddish glow. He was built differently to the others. As they watched he came alive and yawned with outstretched arms.

'Are you being good, Trego?' Hal shouted.

'No, Doctor Hal. Always bad!' Trego flexed his metallic muscles and grinned profusely.

'We have some top visitors today, so get your guys on their feet for another demo. Firewater all around, please!' John said.

'On it, Maker!' he replied. They called John by that name. After all he was responsible for their design.

'All our warriors are assigned to a leader or commander. Every commander like Tregor will lead a battalion of 20 or more warriors. He is super intelligent and knows the personalities of everyone of his warriors, so they fight as a highly tuned regiment or group. Like us, he also has brain implants and will communicate directly with his soldiers and his war macron for instructions. For security reasons only he can communicate with his battalion. However we can communicate with him. All soldiers may function independently but can be overruled by their commander. Like Javols they can fabricate most things from raw materials. They can link together to form structures of themselves or Mind-Probes. However, as a Mind-Probe they become more independent to make decisions,' John said.

'Do they acquire human feelings and personalities eventually?' George inquired.

'They will. After all, personality is all about experience. They will also become conscious eventually and desire their own existence. Since they were designed by us humans, with similar senses and a notion of our likes and dislikes, they will naturally want to be like us for optimum happiness,' Hal replied.

'How long can they live for?' Cathy inquired.

'They can live forever. However, like us they need their special food for energy. Otherwise they go into a type of hibernation. They are not nuclear powered and use special revitalising chemicals in the form of a drink called Firewater. They can also drink water for revitalization, but it will only last a few hours. Firewater will last a day. They always carry surplus in their packs,' John replied.

'I like their design. Unlike Javols, that makes them more like us and limits their operations!' George said.

'Can they reproduce?' Tim asked.

'No! All our products, excluding dinosaurs, come off production lines or incubators. They cannot breed naturally. They do not have the necessary organs. However if an android wishes for a child, we may oblige and create one for them. It will be allowed to grow as a normal child and become part of their family. Such a program is now available within the city of Solaris,' Hal said.

'Solaris?'

'It's now the largest city in Solaria!' Hal said proudly.

'I've never heard of it!' Cathy replied.

'Not many have. It's on the world of Tyrrel 2. On the continent of Solania. In many ways it's like New York but ten times more massive. Solaris is a free city for everyone, even criminals and runaway robots and androids. However with an efficient android police force and a weapon's embargo, crime is low. The main law in Solaris is do as you please providing you don't inconvenience the other guy or cause him pain. There are no taxes, but everyone, including androids and robots, work for a living and get the things they want to fulfill their happiness.' Hal replied.

'If there are no taxes, how does your government work?' inquired Ann.

'They get it from an export levy. We export lots to other Solarian worlds. We are now one of their largest production worlds,' Hal replied with great pride.

'Stranger and stranger! I would love to visit that place some day!' Tim exclaimed.

'You will, soon enough!' Hal replied.

'Now we visit the Javols quarters,' John said. They soon arrived at another station.

'Each one of you, including myself, will require a plasma weapon. It's for your own safety,' John advised. They were handed each a pistol-like weapon with a conical barrel and rear bulge. It fitted snugly in it's shoulder holster.

'Not real Javols, are they?' Anne-Marie exclaimed with utter surprise.

'We had a special rig made with the aid of Solarians and went searching. Now we have several thousand down here for our experiments. We mainly use them to test the potency of our warriors,' Hal said.

'My God! Real Javols?' Tim exclaimed with curiosity.

'Don't worry, after over 3000 years in deep space they are well frozen and depleted of all energy. Not even their LPDs will work without repriming. They have to be revived and that takes lots of energy in the form of heat. Nevertheless they have on board all the chemicals they need for that purpose. We can only revive a few at a time,' Hal said and George swallowed hard.

'Those of you wishing to fight some Javols we have revived, wear your visors and nasal filters. It's always nice to know you fought a Javol and won. They are our worst enemy and it gives great confidence,' Hal said as all hands went up.

'They have a nasty microid spray that will kill if inhaled. It cannot penetrate your special visor. Anyway, they change colour just before, so you have warning. Just keep your distance and you'll be safe. No heroics, just shoot them down and cut them to bits. The mechanical contaminant spray will do the rest. Our spray nozzles are everywhere at this level,' John said.

'Only 3 Javols! You guys are not afraid?' Hal inquired.

'No! Only of what we might do to them!' George replied, full of confidence.

'That's what I like! Over confidence!' John said.

'You guys are all trained. This should be a piece of cake without implants, so encircle and let them have it. I will remain at the rear and observe. I don't want to get involved in case I transform into the worst monster from hell!' George said. They thought he was kidding and continued to the enclosed bay with 3 Javols hovering above. As they entered the Javols dived amidst a hail of plasma, but on seeing George they flew upwards toward the ceiling. For some strange reason they were overwhelmed by fear.

'How are we going to get them down from there?' Hal exclaimed.

'No problem! Let me do it!' George said and began to transform into their worst nightmare.

Jull spiralled towards them and in an instant they had dissolved into a harmless spray of dust, showering those beneath. Then without the Javols threat he transformed back into his usual George Peterson self.

'Sorry I deprived you guys of your fun. I am afraid I have that way with Javols!' George said and they were astonished.

'Please meet The Son of Destiny!' Andy shouted and everyone bowed.

'You are the chosen one! I never would have guessed!' John exclaimed with utter happiness and Hal could not move a limb while overwhelmed by such a surprise.

'Don't worry guys, I am on your side,' George said calmly and they continued.

'Now let's get back and see what our soldiers can do against Javols,' John said and they were once again on their way to Trego's enclosure.

'Trego please do us the honour with 3 Javols. Send one of your best to finish them, then extra firewater for everyone,' John said.

'You know, 3 is not enough for a proper test. Any one of my warriors can take on a dozen of those pigs,' Trego replied.

'I know, Pal. But we have to consider security and other problems in this place. Don't worry, very soon you will be free from this limited area for real training,' John apologised.

'One against 12 Javols. I would like to see that!' Tim was amused.

'As Trego had advised 3 Javols were not enough for his chosen warrior. He played with them for a while, kicking and punching them into each other. When he had enough he got into a spin and ripped them apart. He was self-healing, so their weapons had little effect. When he was finished the spray activated and their fragments formed into a dark sludge which escaped through the drains.

'That was quick and efficient!' Andy commented.

'Yea! Those guys are as fast as lightning. I could hardly observe his movements,' Cathy said.

'One day we will be able to move with such speed. That's why training is so necessary using Virtual Macron Trainers with implants,' George replied.

After their MIMIC demonstrations were over Hal took them to a lower area through a hidden trapdoor along with a trolley of their named protective suits. From there they entered a large cubicle. Hal entered a secret code and in an instant they were in a similar portal in the city of Solaris on Tyrrel 2. All those interstellar portals were designed with energy fields that killed Javols.

CHAPTER 4

The free world of Tyrrel 2

'Where are we? Cathy inquired with extreme curiosity.

'You are now on my world. This is in the basement of my palace!' Hal replied.

'We are now in the great city of Solaris?' George inquired with glee.

'Yes! I chose the best parts of the human quarters for myself. I built it on the top of a small plateau for the view. There are many such elevated areas in this part of Tyrrel 2,' Hal replied.

'It's a very lively city with every type of industry. Despite that, pollution levels are quite low. This city is nothing like Eden City. It's more like a giant New York with everything you can imagine. That's why it's called a Free City,' John said.

'I like that idea, it's so human. In that case, they must be similar to us on Earth,' Anne-Marie said in anticipation.

They soon entered a most beautiful palace of gold with every technology imaginable.

'My God! This place is so unique and beautiful. We could be in one of Sarah's palaces!' Cathy exclaimed.

Then they walked towards the veranda that encircled the palace. There were elevators at each quadrant on the side of the high almost circular rocky mound. They could have stood over 2 hundred feet above sea level. As they viewed into the distance they could observe plateau mounds upon mounds with similar palaces. In the lower valleys were all types of houses with the occasional palace at ground level. Just beyond a long stretch of water and in the misty distance was what remained of the assembly plants and living quarters of robots and androids. In the air were numerous flying ships darting here and there like fireflies.

'Wow! Two suns and I can see two moons!' Tim exclaimed.

'Two suns and three moons. The smaller sun is more like a large overheated world orbiting at a distance. We think it's the most beautiful world in the federation excluding Earth. The only problem here is the higher gravity. When you begin using your suits it can be adjusted to lower limits. Nevertheless, your bodies will get used to it in time. Oxygen levels are like on Earth,' John replied.

'I see what you mean, yet it's quite tolerable, providing we are not runners or jumpers. The ideal environment for the slimmer build. This world is ideal for training athletes to compete on Earth. Thank goodness we have young teenage bodies with little fat,' George said and they laughed. However, Anne-Marie and Pamela was not amused. They were over 40 with a little extra weight in unwanted places.

'Don't worry ladies, it will be your turn as soon as we get back to the mansion. That is providing we survive this intrepid vacation,' George said and they remained silent in anticipation.

'Will you be free for another 30 hours or so?' John inquired as he began passing around golden watches.

'As free as you want. I wouldn't leave now for all the tea in China! This is all new and magnificent!' George replied.

'These timepieces are tuned to this world with a 35 hour day. One larger moon period is just over 75 days. All watches are always set to the correct time by GPS, so no need to adjust. They contain a 100 year battery, about the same time on Earth. So no need to recharge for a while,' John said.

Tim stood on the balcony and took a telescope to his eyes and couldn't believe what he saw.

'My God! Roads and streets, and robots everywhere cleaning streets and making repairs!' He yelled.

'Please let me see!' Cathy grabbed it from him, then let him have it back.

'Yes! In this city all menial and labourious tasks are performed by robots and machines. Every thing here is modelled on Earth, so we have all kinds of cars for those enjoying that freedom. We have some of the most antique cars here with many auto clubs, including motorcycle fanatics. As the laws on Earth and elsewhere become stricter, they settle here instead. This new and free world is all about freedom,' Hal said.

'I like it! That's what true freedom is all about! Order is one thing but it must be balanced. I am getting to love this place!' George replied.

'You should! Since the android city knew you were coming, they had decided to hold celebrations in your honour. Therefore you are required in their part of the city to meet some powerful people!' Hal said.

'I am? In that case tell them I shall look forward to meeting them,' George replied.

'Ladies and others, who are not interested in more boring speeches may go shopping for clothes and presents in the most auspicious places,' John said and the women eyes lit up.

'Good idea! Take one of my robot ships, he knows all the best places and one of my androids can show you around. Place it all on my account. Here, everything is over ten times cheaper than on Earth. If you like, I can open an account for each of you in our main bank. Then you may visit whenever you want. But our meeting is set for the afternoon in 10 hours,' Hal advised.

'In the mean time I think we should see the city and do some shopping!' George said and they were happy everyone was together on their shopping spree.

'Are these flying craft safe?' Cathy inquired, while hesitating before getting on.

'They are a well proven design with multiple backups. They also follow set corridors in flight. Even so, our robots and androids always show off with new passengers,' John replied.

'We have all been scanned and there are Megotrons about, so don't worry!' George said and she was more worried. So were her mother, Pamela, and Anne-Marie who had not been scanned.

They were soon in the air and travelling at great speed. As they approached the other side of the city the structures became enormous.

'We process most food and domestic materials here for the Solarian Empire, including Eden. We are slowly becoming the industrial hub of the empire. Polaris on Melos 3 processes the androids and robots for the empire,' Hal said enthusiastically.

'Yet, pollution is so low. How do you accomplish those low levels?' George inquired.

'We recycle virtually everything. Here there are androids and robots specializing in every field. They get high bonuses for efficiency with many incentives. They are also given increased quotas when demand increases. That way they can afford their way of life,' Hal replied.

As they watched the massive city with its ginormous skyscrapers and interlinking sky-bridges, walkways and elevators, they were astounded. There were thousands of airships of every shape and size moving here and there, some even landing on large projecting ramps on the side of skyscrapers.

'This city makes New York look like a dollhouse. Everything here is so massive by comparison and so quick!' Tim exclaimed and everyone agreed.

Although there were portals and brain implants, they were seldom used. Everyone preferred the old ways, with Cell-phones, LPD based automobiles and air-ships. They only used the more advanced technologies when they had no other choice.

'So these androids and advanced robots over here are even more human than Earth humans?' Cathy inquired.

'They would like to think they are!' John replied with a smile of absurdity.

'This is like a Star-wars city, but so clean. How do they manage to exist together in such cleanliness, peace and harmony?' Tim inquired.

'Robots and Androids are very clean. Pollution are mainly created by Primals like us, because of our more complex biology and other requirements, and all weapons are banned,' John replied.

'Will such robots and androids take over the universe, eventually?' Cathy asked, with a somewhat worried demeanor.

'It's possible, but I think both kinds will always need each other, for all kinds of reasons. After all, we are nature's way. Primals like us will always be evolving throughout the universe, so we are here to stay, while in a sense, they are our children. The conscious ones realize their place as are our children and will always respect us for that,' Hal said and she was satisfied with that answer.

'I suppose Eden is a good example?' Tim interjected.

'It is!' John replied.

'By the way, John and myself will like to join your esteemed gang and be available in the future to defend our world Earth and worlds like this against our mutual enemy, the Javols,' Hal said.

'I thought you were already on board! Why don't you get your families involved as well. We have lots of space and they will be well protected!' George replied and they were satisfied with that answer.

Their vehicle soon parked on the side of a building. They took an elevator to ground level. The streets were filled with numerous stores displaying clothes, shoes and other products of incredible variety and sizes. There were even stores with wedding dresses on display. Golden and high technological jewellery were numerous and inexpensive. So were every variety of electrical equipment.

'Next time I get married I know where to go!' Pamela exclaimed. There were androids, and their families, robots and humans, all shopping like on Earth in a large department store.

'It's nice to wear clothes from a different world. Then no one can outshine you,' Tim said, while viewing the most outlandish jeans, t-shirts and other gear he could not have ever imagined. Not even in his wildest nightmares. He soon decided to add a full range to his wardrobe on Earth.

'I wonder if the electrics also work on Earth?' Anne-Marie inquired.

'They are dual as on Earth, with 120 volts for America and 240 for Europe. That's standard. There are also adaptors for conversion,' John replied.

The ladies were in their shopping paradise. They could not be held back by anyone, not even George with his special powers. George looked on with Ron, his little computer dangling by his side. Cathy always bought his clothes for him. She had the most impeccable fashion sense.

After their shopping spree, they had to order more transport for their goods and groceries. On arrival to the palace they decided to celebrate and have a party. That party was to acknowledge the home-coming of two new gang members, namely Dr. Hal Seaton and Dr. John Simmons. Although Hal was still single, Pamela had taking a liking to him and appeared interested. Nevertheless, with Pamela's future conversion in the Megotron, to a 25 year old woman, only time would tell.

CHAPTER 5

A moment of truth

After their party, it was time to visit the Grand Council of Solaris. For that important occasion George decided to take along a few gang members. Although Hal was responsible for the hole world, he left the city to govern themselves. Because of a signed treaty he could only be directly involved when asked. Anyway, Hal never liked too much active responsibility. He already had too much on his plate and responsibility was all about delegation and sharing. Why rock the boat when everything ran so perfectly. After all, those super-clever Macrons and their androids were so much better at intricate thinking than humans.

On that occasion George took along Cathy, Andy, Jerry, Hal and John. Just before 10 pm, Solaris time, the reception committee were already awaiting their arrival. For that grand occasion even macrons were represented by their human-like androids. One could not tell the difference. They all looked like perfect humans

in their attire and gowns, walking and talking with pride and dignity. They could speak every language in Osmaron. On that occasion they chose English.

On arrival George and the others went around the group of about 50, shaking hands and chatting until taken into their parliament building. Then Hal was guided to the rostrum for his introductions.

'I would like to introduce you all to one of our most important Solarian Councillors, Lord George Peterson, our Son of Destiny. He is well known to us by his interview on Gimbal and other escapades with his special gang,' Hal said and George made his way towards the rostrum amidst claps and cheers.

'Mr. Mayor, Fellow Councillors, Grand Mecrons, and others responsible for such a rich and free society. It's indeed a great pleasure being among such progressive people. I never thought such a uniquely free city could ever exist, but I have been proven wrong. These days it's nice to know such a refuge can exist for those not involved directly within the empire. Nevertheless you should always abide by principles we uphold through the noble efforts of our macrons.

'As you all know, we have two main rules in our federation, the first one being: To work enthusiastically and do our best for our society in the long term. The other: To follow our own paths of development and freedom, providing we do not cause pain or in any way inconvenience the other person. With those basic concepts in mind, we get rid of all those laws that impede us. Of course, some parts of our societies will be wilder than others, but variation is the way of the universe. That way we learn a lot more and grow. A child must experiment in the muck sometimes to develop a better immune system and learn the ways of its parents. I think freedom to pursue our ambitions to be the most important maxim of all.

'My main purpose in visiting your council today was to show you a video of death and destruction and to prepare you for a most deadly problem faced in our near future,' George said and nodded to Ron. The little computer began to display the video of the Javols invasion of Caefon and its destruction. They remained silent with trepidation and disgust.

'When do we expect them here?' Shouted someone from the rear.

'In about 50 of your years, so always be on your guard. You are not to worry, our special troops and Titan warriors will protect you. It's my duty to protect the whole of Solaria, so you may carry on as usual. However, all macrons may pass the images along and warn everyone within Solaria.

'Once more, I must thank you all for the privilege of allowing me this great honour,' George said. He was not in a mood for long speeches. Even so, he was given a standing ovation.

After they had left and were on their way home, George sensed trouble in his midst. Like his mother, Sarah, he was hyper-intuitive.

'So let's have it! You guys are never so tranquil, friendly and nice? Something is wrong, so what is it?' George inquired while glancing at Hal.

'We accidentally let some Javols loose on one of these continents!'

'Accidentally?' George was not amused.

'We found a specially sealed container, like a small spaceship and decided to take it to Tyrannia for our future experiments. We made sure all entrances were sealed externally. We hoped to release it's contents to test our Titans. However when we checked they had escaped. When we viewed the remote cameras, we could observe 4 Javols with a different one. He seemed to give the orders and was larger with strange markings,' John said.

'He was different because he was one of their forward commanders. He would be much larger with strange markings and with bluish lines throughout his form,' George said.

'And you let them go!' Andy inquired.

'We had no choice. They were too quick!' Hal replied.

'Well we have to hunt them down. They can communicate with their MasterMind via H-Wave and inform them of our technologies. Particularly of our weapons!'

'We don't have weapons on this world, other than what we brought with us. That is one of the reasons why the people here are so peaceful,' John said.

'Where are they now?'

'Last time we looked they were on Tyrannia. That continent is full of dinosaurs of all shapes and sizes. However, they haven't eaten since,' Hal said.

'They could have taken on board their ship everything necessary for their revival. Being a commander, he would have great privileges. Anyway, commanders cannot reproduce. They are too valuable,' George said.

'That's nice to know, but what about the other four?' Jerry inquired.

'We should keep tabs on their commander but kill the others. I might need him for propaganda in the future,' George said.

'I can feel a safari coming on!' Andy interjected.

'How can we tag him?' John inquired.

'Soon he will begin collecting bacteria and parasites. They will eat off the blood and dead flesh of his victims. His smell will give him away. Train a few good hunting dogs and muzzle them. Better yet, give them brain implants so you may communicate directly while hunting. They will be our locators. Call them Javol Locator Dogs, JLDs for short! We will need them in the future,' George said.

'Ok, Boss!' Hal replied and everyone realized who was in control.

'My God, we are now in real business!' John exclaimed.

'What about Trego and his keen warriors?' Andy inquired.

'We were afraid the might chase them away. Then they could start eating our dinosaurs and multiply. With all that food around they could become a worst nightmare to deal with. I think, in their present state it will take them a while to figure out the new environment before they decide to multiply,' Hal said.

'They could have received orders from their MasterMind,' Andy replied.

'What happens when they receive orders to kill and multiply! That's why we are so worried,' John said.

'They will not before linking with a larger group. Four units cannot multiply enough before we destroy them. So they will collect as much data as possible for their MasterMind,' George replied.

'In that case we stand a good chance!' Andy said.

'I tell you what, lets have a real safari. It might be our most incredible hunt of a lifetime, never to be repeated or forgotten. The women can make us a great picnic. Pity we are all vegetarians. Nevertheless it will not stop us from enjoying this hunt. To prove my point, let's take some armoured JLDs along, without implants this time. Trego and his guys could also do with some freedom. They could be our backup. That should add to the fun!' George exclaimed and they were all up for it.

'I haven't been on safari for quite a while?' Jerry said.

'You mean you've never been! That's settled then. It will sharpen our fighting skills. We could leave Anne-Marie and Pamela behind until they get scanned,' George said.

'I would prefer that, but they will want to come!' Hal replied.

'In that case, they will have to be scanned!' Andy insisted.

'I will take them the moment we get back!' John replied and Hal agreed.

CHAPTER 6

On Safari

The happy group sat down for dinner while assisted by several serving androids. It was a fully fledged vegetarian dish that everyone enjoyed with the most delicate of Solania's wine. When they were finished George stood up to speak.

'People, we are going on safari, so kill only when you are attacked or consider yourselves in greatest danger, but spare no Javols. We are to hunt all Javols with extreme prejudice. There are a few escapees that we can't allow to roam freely and multiply. There is also a commander. Leave that one for now. He can't multiply. Trego and his guys will watch our backs while our hunting dogs follow their scent,' George said and they were astonished.

'Free roaming Javols in Solaria. Now I have heard everything. This must be one for the books!' Tim was not happy.

'These are the original types so they should be easy to kill. Anyway, we have to sharpen our hunting and killing skills. It should be great fun!' George said, but they were not keen.

'Only communicate through visors. Don't make noises to attract the local dinosaurs. If they move towards you, ready your weapons and remain absolutely still. Kill only when they get too close. Remember, we are only after Javols. All our positions will be displayed on the map in our visors. Hunting dogs will be in blue, we in green and the enemy in red. Others in mauve, so watch your steps,' Hal said and they remained silent imagining the worse.

'Everyone, get suited up. We leave for Tyrannis in one hour, Earth time. We can get transport and guides from Tyrannis to the interior. It's a town of tourist and hotels. Most people go there to hunt dinosaurs. There are weekly quotas to fill. That way we keep their populations down by planned culling. There are cameras everywhere, so locating our quarry shouldn't be a problem. However there are many caves and Javols can camouflage to the point of invisibility, so always watch your backs. Never travel individually, always in twos or greater numbers and in line. The one on the rear should constantly check their rear viewer in their visor. Javols can't attack while invisible and need several seconds to transform into something else of an equivalent mass, so you will have enough warning,' Hal advised.

'What about Raptors and Rexes, wont they be dangerous?' Tim inquired.

'Raptors are clever and will have you investigated out of curiosity. Rexes are not interested, you are too small and not considered worthwhile. It's like us going after a small juicy fly. They will go after larger prey. If you get eaten and swallowed, use your weapons and cut your way out. It's a bit messy but quite acceptable,' John said, but Tim was not amused.

'Your protective suits are virtually impervious to such attacks, so have some faith!' George said.

'So they breed naturally on that continent?' Anne-Marie inquired.

'Yes! They have to breed in order to maintain a proper food chain or we would be forever making them. But they breed quickly. That's why we have to cull them. Hunting is big business on Tyrannia. Humans and other primals come from all over the empire to try their skills and take back images and memories of their exploits,' Hal said.

'Don't androids and robots hunt?' Cathy inquired.

'They can't. It's all to do with their initial programming. They must appreciate human life at any cost! They will only fight to defend us.' Hal replied and Cathy was pleased with that answer.

'There are 15 of us now, so that should be the body count when we return,' Hal said and they swallowed hard.

'We take the ground portal here to the one in our labs in Tyrannis. Don't worry, above ground is a beautiful five star hotel. It's one of ours, so no need to take food along!' John advised.

'Why do you guys look so worried? I am also coming along to watch your backs!' George said then the penny dropped.

'I suppose if ferocious Javols don't get us, there is always raptors and rexes to finish the job?' Tim said and everyone began to laugh hilariously.

From the small city of Tyrannis they took a large air transport with several reinforced jeeps to the interior. The freighter dropped them off and was soon on its way back.

'Now we are on our own, so make yourselves at home,' Hal said sarcastically. But they were not amused.

'Now we take the 3 jeeps to where they were last sighted,' John said, so they mounted and were on their way on the bumpy plateau. They soon came upon a deep ravine partly covered with trees and shrubs. They went across it, skidding for a while until they made it across a steep gradient to another plateau.

Each Jeep had mounted a powerful hunting rifle on top with telescopic sight. Hal, John and Andy took control of those weapons with keen eyes moving in every direction. Those weapons could only harm dinosaurs. Javols were immune from all such projectiles. The six dogs were caged and restless, waiting for action. Soon they came upon the Javols' craft but they were nowhere to be seen.

'There are several caves in the area, so we can use our dogs to track them. Maps will be automatically selected by your GPS coordinates, so you cannot get lost,' Hal advised.

'Let's do it!' Tim exclaimed, with serious determination.

'Ok, we split into 4 groups of 3, plus a soldier and dog each. Hal, Andy and myself will stay back in case you need help. The others, including Trego, can remain here incase we need more backup,' George said.

'I suppose we take the gloomy caves, while you guys remain on board having a laugh?' Tim inquired, but George and his group ignored his comments.

'Use your G controls to hover or move up or down. You can adjust for almost zero weight, when climbing. There is a built in infrared scanner that makes the environment visible to you, but not to others, including Javols,' Hal advised. They began to play with the controls until they got things right, then they were ready and determined.

George and his group wanted to place them in the thick of things to give them a taste of real danger. Only then could adrenalin flow to show real active determination and action in response to their dire situations. If anyone froze, that person would not be suitable when it came to fighting real Javols. So they were being tested.

THE CAVE

Tim and his group of 4 followed towards the left entrance. As they entered, only their images could be observed in their visors. However they did not lose communication. That cave separated into two branches, one horizontal and straight ahead. The other was more vertical with over 50% gradient. Tim decided to use his G-controls to check the higher level, but could observe nothing. They soon decided to follow along the more direct route deep into the cave. As they made their way they could observe numerous piles of skeletons, so they progressed slowly with weapons ready.

'These bones are relatively fresh. See how they are marked by a sharp object? I think our friends are here,' Tim advised, while observing a pile of fresh bones in detail.

Soon their dog began to bark but was held back by a line attached to their soldier. At the end of that cave they could observe a single Javol, so Anne-Marie immediately communicated to George and his group. They were presently on their way to the location.

'He must have seen us, but he does not charge. He must be afraid of us!' Pamela said.

'No! I think he is confident he can take us on and win!' Tim replied.

'Shall we wait for the others?' Anne-Marie asked.

'I say let's take the brute on by ourselves. There is only one of him and 4 of us. Our soldier, Rob, can stand back and take over only if we fail, so lets get him!' Tim yelled and rushed towards the Javol, but he simply knocked Tim off his feet, landing him into a large pile of bones. While in the bones, Tim struggled for a while but found difficulty getting a handhold or foothold.

After a while Tim became mad with frustration and began to fire his weapon at the large almost spherical object, with what appeared to be flexible limbs. Those limbs held implements for getting at his food. The energy from the first beam was so intense it went right through the Javol's centre.

There was one great explosion from the super-heated plasma that sprayed over Tim. However he had the commonsense to dive under the bones and was shielded. It was an instinctive move on his part. Nevertheless, his suit would have shielded him. Then the women began firing their weapons at the still moving remains until the whole place filled with putrid smoke and stank to high heavens. With their visors and air filters on they could not smell the environment, but did not wish to remain too close.

George and his group came running, but they soon realize they were too late. Tim soon crawled out from the pile of bones looking his usual innocent self.

'Tim did it again. He rushed that Javol and took him out!' Anne-Marie shouted.

'This needs celebrating. Tim we must celebrate your great victory when we get back to the hotel!' Hal said and George and his group agreed with fervour.

'They appear to be living on raptors. Now only 3 left!' John reminded and they left the cave.

'If they are eating so many, why is it they are not multiplying?' Hal inquired.

'Could be they do not have a high enough source of radiant energy. They also need to eat lots and lots to trigger the process. It could be they require one or the other or both. Or perhaps it's not considered appropriate at this time,' George replied.

SATAN'S BUG IN ACTION

'We found one!' Cathy shouted through their earpieces. As they left the cave their visors lit up. However on that encounter there were two. Those Javols had set a trap to catch their quarry. One flew down and grabbed Cathy by her shoulders, but soon realized he could not hold on while her nano-bots began eating into him.

The deadly virus on her suit had already invaded parts of his body and were growing wild. They were literally rusting him into a useless mass. He soon dropped her, but her anti-Gs kicked in too late and she hit the ground with a painful bump. Thank goodness she was wearing that suit at the time. Nevertheless, she collected her weapon, aimed and fired, until his remains had exploded into a white hot blob.

'And there was none!' she yelled with great satisfaction.

The other, realizing the dangers, flew away towards another cave.

'This virus of yours is quite effective! But sadly, not close enough to affect the other!' Hal commented.

'Perhaps it's a good thing it was contained!' John replied, while observing the super-hot and smoking fragments.

'Love, are you ok?' George inquired through visor as he hugged her.

'The suit protected my fall. No bruises, I hope?' she replied.

'Now there are two, we hope?' Tim reminded.

HIS WORST NIGHTMARE

They drove across another hill and soon found the main Javols hideout. It was in another cave. They could observe more piles of bones as they entered. That one was a long cave with many twists and turns. George approached their hideout with the others following behind. Their commander was furthest into the cave with his two Javols acting as guards. They must have sensed the deaths of their two comrades and decided to take a stand. Javols transmitted a death signal at their demise. However that depended on whatever time they had left during the dying process.

'Trego, you are wanted here! We found the other two plus their commander! I need a Mind-Probe for their commander. And I don't want you to miss any of the fun!' George shouted through his visor.

'On my way!' He shouted back.

Without warning the two Javols darted towards the group. Before they could connect two powerful beams flew over their heads at light speed.

'Down! Down!' Trego shouted through their visors. Soon everyone hit the floor. There was a massive explosion as the super heated mass of metal and other parts sprayed everyone. As they looked, there stood ahead of them was Trego with two smoking weapons in his hand. The group could not believe the speed and accuracy of their new companion.

'Now, that's a real Javols killer, if ever I saw one!' Andy commented.

'That's my boy! Very bad as usual!' Hal shouted.

'Too bad for words. I must get you a medal or insignia to show our appreciation,' George said.

'It was nothing, Master. Just flexing my muscles,' Trego replied as he outstretched his arms and flexed his metallic muscles.

'Another bloody comedian in the group!' Tim commented, while he dusted Javols' bits off his protective suit.

'Stay back people, this one is mine. For this guy we need a warrior as Mind-Probe,' George said.

Trego soon communicated to his soldiers and the soldier close to George was nominated. George decided to communicate with the Javols' commander, who was not amused and was full of hatred. Having observed the quick demise of his companions he decided to stay where he was and hold his ground.

'As you can see, you cannot win against us!' George shouted in his strange language, telepathically.

'A filthy clot will always be a filthy disgusting clot. You can never win against us, so get ready to fight and die!' The Javol replied, while vibrating his form.

'People, he just called us filthy clots!' George communicated to his group and they were not amused. Then the Javols commander transformed into the most bizarre form from hell. There it stood in almost jet black with dark brown markings. His head resembled that of a ram with long powerful horns, eyes glowing red. His giant body was almost human with powerful legs and feet that resembled that of a giant eagle with sharpest claws. He was indeed a creature from nightmarish hell.

'Now, what the hell are you?' George inquired calmly.

'I am your worst nightmare!' he exclaimed in a powerful human-like voice.

He blew a stream of microbes towards George along with sharp deadly poisonous spikes, almost knocking George off his feet. George soon regained his composure, but did not want to kill him, so he held his ground.

'Soldier, it's time!' George shouted.

'In a flash, the local soldier went forward. He lifted the monster above his head, spun him around and tossed him in a local corner. Then he held on tightly to him while the infection spread throughout his body. Slowly the soldier transformed into the original Javols commander with all his knowledge and identification codes. The commander's brain had been thoroughly copied. The monster soon began to vibrate and overheat. Then he exploded into another mess, to be blown away by the gang's plasma weapons.

'And there was none!' Tim shouted as he vaporized the last fragment.

'Now, his clone will work on our side. With his knowledge and codes he could be very useful to us in the future. We now have a way to communicate with their MasterMind and lead them down a blind alley,' George said and they were amazed by his planning.

'Now we have his exact duplicate, should I be afraid?' Tim inquired.

'Always be afraid, but have fun!' Andy replied as they left the area.

They were soon on their way out of the cave with Tim in the lead. As they approached the entrance Tim turned around and halted the group.

'My God! There are dinosaurs everywhere. They seem to be waiting for someone. I can see rexes, raptors and others everywhere. How are we going to get through,' he said.

The moment they were observed, the creatures began to yell and make loud deafening noises.

'Don't worry guys! They are here to thank us,' George said and walked directly towards them.

'I am afraid he has that way with animals!' Miranda exclaimed and they were surprised. Cathy soon rejoined him as they walked through the pack of dinosaurs together holding hands.

After their experience of that day the gang had earned the respect of everyone, including Trego, his almost indestructible warriors and wayward dinosaurs. Trego and his battalion were to remain in Solaris as city guardians during their future training. They were needed to train Georges special human warriors in the future.

When they returned to the hotel, it was drinks all around, in celebration of the gang's accomplishment in removing some dangerous Javols from Tyrrel 2. Hal and John were now convinced of George's powers and realized he was the chosen one to lead them in victory.

CHAPTER 7

A wanted man

After George's visit to the MIMIC labs and the free world of Tyrrel 2, he had a clearer idea of the methods and weapons needed in the war against Javols. He also realized he already had in place a great laboratory for his experimentation. Then there was the free world of Tyrrel 2 with portal links to Earth. He also realized that the genius Hal was the ideal person for taking a stance on the side of Earth against Javols and others. While John, with Hal and his occasional input could create even better weapons to fight Javols.

After it was known that George, the Son of Destiny, had returned from his honeymoon, he became a wanted man by the mass media and governments of Earth. That was because of his enormous popularity among Fertilates and Infilates alike. However, it was also because of his controversial speech on Satellite Gimbal, which was broadcasted throughout the planet and had made headline news in many countries.

Infilates were dying in their millions and considered him their only hope of survival. The volatile and insecure state of Earth's citizens made everything regarding their mutual survival very urgent, as violence between the separate groups were increasing. Infilates had nothing to lose and had many young criminal Fertilates under their control. Those they would incite to violence and bombs were commonly used to get their points across.

George knew that because of original agreements, the president of Solarian Banking was exempt from any of Earth's political affairs. Being completely immune from their jurisdiction, he could always tell them to take a hike, but he also realized that he couldn't let his people suffer the escalating conflicts for much longer.

An announcement soon appeared in the press, stating the extent of his new position as head of Solarian Banking and before long greater respect was shown by everyone. Those apparent orders by senior officials in Washington DC soon changed to requests and invitations. Soon they all knew George was President of Solarian Banking and the most powerful man on Earth.

Since his speech on Gimbal he had stirred up many a hornet's nest throughout Earth. Thereafter, all young Fertilates had chosen him and his gang as their only hope in an uncertain future. The whole world wanted to hear his opinion on many important issues and he decided to contact the United Nations and asked them to organize a convention for all world leaders and important people. It would be fully financed by Solarian Banking.

During that time he would state the facts regarding the future of Earth in the Greater Plan. He also decided to speak to the senate before that occasion and answer some of their urgent questions, but he had no intentions of mincing his words one way or another.

The UN Conference was set for six weeks time. The intervening period gave him a breathing space to sort out a few of his own problems regarding security and other necessary changes at the mansion in preparations for any forthcoming trouble.

President Donald Fraser came to visit him the following day with an army of security men. George realised the President of the USA had visited the mansion under extreme pressure from his senate and other powerful organisations, who had suddenly become worried for their financial future. He also expected dirty politics, even though he knew he could control them to a great extent.

'That was a very controversial speech you gave on Gimbal and many are still asking questions.'

'They should! That was the purpose of my speech!'

'The Senate wants to ask you some of their own, by way of an invitation, of course. You should also be aware that you are outside of our diplomatic jurisdiction, so we are powerless in influencing you one way or the other. We being bound by past agreements with your Solarian Banking organization. However, most of the young now consider you their leader,' a nervous Donald said.

'Do I have you on my side in these matters, as I have your father?' George asked.

'It's a very difficult situation for me to be in.'

'To me, that vague answer means no!'

'You know, I didn't want the job in the first place. But I can't do a job piecemeal and can't have two masters in the form of your organisation and my country, even though I think you are the future. If I resign, then you can have my services, but while I am in power and remain President of our country, I have to abide by our so-called democratic system,' Donald replied.

An urgent meeting was arranged for the following day and George was told that they would patiently listen to whatever he had to say.

George walked into the large room filled to the brim with almost every senator and politician in the land.

The moment he entered, the place became so quiet he could have heard a pin drop.

'What I have to say today will affect all future life on our planet. Therefore I would appreciate your undivided attention during my lecture... to be followed by a break and then you may feel free to ask me any of your questions.' They remained silent and worried.

'This here is Hercules and this is my Macron Ron. Ron, please start the show,' George said, and the lecture continued in much the same way as he had on a previous occasion.

'Now, this is planet Caefon, some three thousand years ago...' he continued.

When he was finished his audience were numbed by the savagery of the Javols, but were also amazed by the technology and knowledge at his disposal. Many left the room to clear their minds, take some refreshment or to even freshen up before the next psychological bout. But they returned to listen to more of what he had to say.

'Friends, this is the planet Eden, the way it is today and it is also one of my home planets, just a few light years from the Solar System. This is what Earth will look like in the near future; for this planet Earth is also part of the Solarian Empire. As you have seen, we have a great war to fight and many programs to complete before then. Some of which can be made a lot quicker with your assistance and cooperation. Even Infilates will benefit in that process and from what we have to offer. Perhaps this is the time for me to answer your questions?' George said.

'If, as you have indicated, this world is to be changed into a better one, will your people enforce the rule of democracy on Earth?' a senator asked.

'Freedom can only be fully enjoyed with a notion of responsibility. You cannot allow your children complete freedom at home, or even the freedom to vote for things of which they have very little knowledge. Neither could you ask ancient Romans to vote for the introduction of a television channel nor a reduction in the population growth rate. The survival of the Cosmos and Earth takes precedence above all else, including humanity and its outmoded notions of democracy. As far as I am concerned your type of democracy should have been left behind with the ancient Greeks. What you have is capitalism, not true democracy.

'The bulk of human population on Earth can still be considered to be little more than self-indulgent children when compared with Solarian standards. But even those weaknesses can be cured in time.

'I am very sorry, gentlemen and ladies, but your form of democracy has never worked. Even since the time of Socrates. It is a very divisive mechanism, based on the self-indulgent desires of humans. No other life-forms ever had a single vote in your so-called free-enterprise and democratic club for humans, which has only served to increase the rate of poverty and disparities between rich and poor. Not to mention all those extinctions of innocent life-forms.

'I shall introduce a truly moneyless society, where everyone starts off on an equal basis. In my society, everyone is freed from the bonds of self-interest and self-indulgence. I shall however uphold all personal interests by way of physical and mental self-improvement.

'Within just thirty years, the population of this country will be under forty million, with the wealth of a previous population of over four hundred million at their disposal. That population will be maintained and controlled within suitable limits over the next thousand years or so.

'Earth shall be divided into protectorate states and zones, with

fiefs and lords in charge of its habitats and peoples. In much the same way as you have seen on, Eden. Gone will be all your political borders and passports. Mankind will be free to go wherever he wishes, providing he doesn't harm the habitats of others.

'I am afraid, Friends, many of your jobs will be taken by super intelligent Headrons and Macron Computers, with sensors and androids sited throughout this planet. They will be programmed for the optimization of every aspect of life on Earth. In line with a broader survival scheme throughout Osmaron and beyond for the greater good.

'However, you should also appreciate that there will also be a much higher freedom within Osmaron, including the complete freedom from want.

'The future government of Earth will be truly autocratic, ruled by a Council of Lords who are themselves answerable to the Chancellor of Earth. Then the Empress of Solaria and finally the Grand Lord of Osmaron.

'During the intervening period, I shall assist you as best I can, before the Headrons and Macrons take control to remodel Earth's environments,' he replied.

'You speak of a heaven on Earth. I wonder if such a dream can ever be realized,' said a very stout politician.

'You look forward to a heaven elsewhere, only because you have a tendency to mess things up wherever you happen to be. I am sure you would do the same with a true heaven given half the chance. After all, you and your kind had many thousands of years to put things right with this world. A capacity you then had in abundance and one which you had seriously squandered without cause or necessity. That was, until you abused all of Earth's resources and its life-forms to a point of near extinction on all counts.

'Like little erratic children, you ravage, build and then you destroyed for no apparent reason. With little concern for those you trample on during the process. You have been placed on the balance of time and have been found wanting. You have not passed the test of time and are therefore not recommended to continue your inept processes of what you call politics in any of its forms. Because of those reasons, Earth is to change, and

luckily for its inhabitants, in a much better manner than before,' he replied.

'From what you imply, you must represent a much higher power. Are you alien in origin?' another senator asked.

'I was born on Earth and have been chosen by the Cosmos to lead Osmaron in the task ahead. Others within Osmaron have known of my coming and have prepared for that eventuality,' he replied.

'Do you have special powers?' asked another.

'Yes! And they grow on a continual basis. I have the ability to transform matter and energy, and to reorder certain sequences within certain space-time boundaries. But I only gain pleasure from the promotion of greater order within our universe. My strengths are by way of healing and in assisting the beauty in life.'

'The messiah!' Shouted someone in a local group nearby.

'I abhor using any forms of power for the purpose of destruction, although, I realise I shall have to use them to destroy our common enemies, the Javols,' he replied.

'If, as you have said, the Solarians and others are so advanced. Why do you need us to help against the... Javols?' another senator asked.

'Because if I didn't they would destroy your world with its many innocent people and other life-forms. I would like to make Earth great amongst those of Osmaron. I would like our planet and its system to be respected and become the leading power within Solaria and Osmaron. But you will have to earn that position through your own efforts and brilliance.'

'Where are these Javols now?' Another senator inquired.

'They are presently on their way! There are no easy rides or frivolities from now on, and you are expected to compensate for a most lurid and self-indulgent past. However, I can assure you that I shall always be standing in your corner, even though I shall be at times a very hard paymaster,' he replied.

'These protectorate lords and chancellors you speak of... Will they be people like us?' yet another asked.

'Yes! They will be honest and law-abiding people like you, who have worked their way up the ladder by sacrificing much for Solaria and its life-forms. Because it is only through giving that

one may gain. Most of the nitty-gritty and day to day tasks will be carried out by Headrons, Macrons and their androids and robots, which are programmed to maintain near-perfect environments over a thousand years or more. Even so, the Lords being closer to the people, can modify some programs to give greater benefit to their populations. Here, I mean all life-forms. This is by way of an improvement in their quality of life, education, health, sports, science and other topics beneficial to the different societies.

'All production and manufacturing, other than farming and food packaging, will be recited on dead habitable worlds within Solaria, thus removing almost all environmental pollutants from Earth.

'Further, Mars and Venus are to be transformed into clean, near Earth-type planets,' he replied.

'You mentioned population control, and we are very familiar with the Terminal problem and its repercussions. Will you use some such bacteria with anti drugs to control our populations in the future?' asked Donald.

'The lifespan of everyone on Earth is expected to rise well beyond five hundred years per individual within a relatively short time scale. Therefore, if we are to maintain Earth's population within the five-hundred million limit, strict control must be maintained. Children may be conceived only to replace those removed, either through death, resettlement or disappearance.

'Families breaking those rules will, as punishment, be sent to other worlds within Osmaron to assist in their conversions, but with the freedom to return to Earth on holidays. Many of those new worlds will be similar to Earth and will earn those families higher credits. Further after the Javols have been removed from Galaxy Andromeda there will be an inexhaustible number of worlds ready for populating.

'I am afraid, this is the only way to control population in a still copulating society, with a tendency to desire children for their own sake. Earth humans have always shown little concern for long term implications and population control.

'However, I can assure you that bacteria and drugs will never be used on our people again,' he replied.

'What happens if a good family breaks those rules through

ignorance or by accident,' Donald asked.

'They will then be brought before council. If found guilty, that family will not lose their privileges. Their value will be assessed in credits, to be transferred to their new location. It does not prevent them from occasionally visiting their home world and they can reapply for permanency or an exchange of residence with another wanting to earn higher credits on the new world.

'Many families may apply for such remote postings because of the promise of little population control and higher credits earned on worlds as beautiful as Earth.

'You should also take note, that the whole of Andromeda will be free for resettlement in the foreseeable future and we have ships capable of transporting millions on a daily basis. Not to mention the many other rich worlds within Galaxy Osmaron that are now linked through portals.

'Resettlement is not a problem. With proper engineering, virtually any suitable planet can be converted and transformed into a paradise like Eden. Nevertheless, every world must have a population limit, to save its eco-sphere and other life,' he replied.

They patiently listened to every answer and knew he wasn't the one to make false promises. But many were also worried about their political careers, existing wealth and commercial ventures.

Old habits died hard and it would take much encouragement and remuneration to make many of those wealthy politicians change their minds and give up the status quo, even to retire earlier than usual.

Many more questions were asked and answers given, until late into the night.

The USA President, Donald Fraser, decided to put those matters to the vote in George's absence. That was before the UN conference which was to be held in five weeks time.

CHAPTER 8

Back at the Hearst Mansion

Finally the mansion had been altered and decorated to the couples liking and it resembled an English palace. George and Cathy were avid collectors and had all types of rear paintings mounted on the walls throughout the mansion. The statues and sculptors were placed on pedestals in the main hall and passage ways.

He was worried that all such types of Earth's past would be forgotten after the predicted upheaval, so he saved what he could of the previous decades. He also intended to create a few of his own museums where human art, scientific and technological objects could be held to posterity. Those places would be on higher ground to avoid the rising waves.

'Darling what do you think of the main hall,' he asked Cathy, who was always particular when it came to clutter and untidiness. He knew if she didn't give an outright 'yak!' it would be acceptable.

'I think you have every European artists on that wall,' she replied, but smiled with satisfaction.

'Well, it's meant to be the European room. However, I think I've overdone it, and even now, not enough space to mount them all. Anyway, Parky has a good eye for such things and reckons it looks ok,' George said. She glanced again at the four main walls, but could find nothing wrong with his choices and their positions.

'You could have electronic frames made and place the originals in secured vaults,' she advised. He realised she was not pleased.

'Thanks for the advise! Too many of them and I also hate clutter. I think in future I shall have each electronic frame programmed with many originals. Then I can change selections on a daily basis,' he replied.

'This is a great idea, and it will save space. Now you can have thousands in a small place. The Macron can run a random selection program on a daily basis,' she said and he agreed.

The following day George got out of bed later than everyone. After his intense and long meeting with those politicians he felt quite drained. He also wanted to catch up on the many lost hours of sleep since Eden and elsewhere.

Eden was such a beautiful and exciting place, that its environments tended to keep everyone awake until very late. Further, the highly advanced Andromedans with their special diets tended to require less sleep than Earth humans. So they assumed everyone was as tough and resilient as they were in those regards. Nevertheless he couldn't get over the loss of Vogon, his favourite spaceship. Clive was currently looking for her replacement planet-wide. Then there was his gang's escapade with Hal and John hunting Javols on safari in Tyrannia. That was another great world with a great future within the empire. He should call Hal and John to thank them and give them an open invitation to the Mansion.

'Today is my day, to rest, relax and enjoy,' he said to himself, as he gave a long contorted stretch while glancing beyond the rear of the mansion. Then he took the cell-phone and dialled a number.

'Hal, it's me!'

'Hi, George, what's cooking?'

'Not much, only the usual politics with our stubborn politicians,' George replied.

'I know what you mean!'

'Anyway, I called to say thank you for a great adventure and to give you and open invitation to my mansion. It's time you took your place as a well regarded gang member. Also I am to give you one of our insignias. I will call John shortly,' George said.

'That's great! I will visit you shortly. Just another meeting with our Solaris administrators. Since your speech they got a little worried about security. They just need a convincing lecture on important matters,' Hal replied.

'If you need me, just shout!'

'Will do!' Hal replied and George called John.

It was just ten a.m. and the sun was a beautiful glow in the almost clear blue sky. Birds were singing and he could observe two horses in the distance frolicking with each other. Finally, his stomach growled and signalled time for breakfast.

'My still beautiful world! I swear to you that one of these days you will be restored to your former self,' he said to no one.

'Ah, Darling! There you are. I have made a progress list, and another for possible future appointments, subject to your perusal, Sire,' Cathy said in jest.

'Yes, Mam! But if not too much trouble, can I have some breakfast and coffee before we get started?' he asked, in a seemingly subordinate manner.

'Darling, could you just have coffee in the study and breakfast afterwards. If you don't mind.'

'Why, My Love!'

We have visitors!' she replied, happily.

'Ok, in that case I shall wait for you in the study and you can also get yourself a cup. I don't feel like drinking on my own today,' he said.

He went into the large study that was situated on the ground floor towards the rear of the building. Then he pulled the curtains to let the glorious light through and sat behind his desk as Cathy walked in.

'Wouldn't you like to live forever on a day like this, my love?' he asked.

'I never thought anyone could be so happy. But these days I feel so good when I am with you. Just our friendship, contentment and security. I suppose they must be the most important ingredients in any relationship. A type of responsible partnership,' she said, and kissed him on the cheek.

'I think the pure air of Eden has something to do with it. It must be some kind of withdrawal symptoms I'm having, because I've never felt this good before. Not so pure and complete within myself,' he replied.

'Even so, I think we are quite suited to each other,' she said.

'I suppose it's also because we allow each other their own space and freedom. You know your responsibilities and only ask me for advice when you find yourself in uncharted territory, but so do I as well. That way, we both grow and develop as a couple of individuals, with an even stronger bond with mutual respect for each other.'

'You are philosophising again!' she reminded.

'You know, I think the best relationship must be by two individuals that accept their mutual differences and often agree to differ. Relationships where both try to follow or copy the other by coercion, blackmail or sex, seldom ever work,' he replied.

'Here goes the Philosopher again... Anyway, Darling, the portal has been fitted and the robots have ported back to Mars in order to test and adjust its range. Venusa says the shuttle Cleopatra on Mars has been unearthed and is being converted for passenger use. Two of your special weapons are ready for testing... but the special cloak is still being developed, whatever that means.'

'I know what that means. Please continue!'

'We have received invitations for uncle Ben's wedding and he wants you to be his best-man. Clair had her final test yesterday and the cancer is completely gone, so that makes you a healer of the grade one class. I have also received a comprehensive list from Caefon Dome. I think we should complete that project as soon as possible.'

'Agreed!'

'Finally, we have to organize several visits to Solarian Banking's head and regional offices, worldwide, in order to introduce you and your deputies. Perhaps starting with Sol-Newtown. May I suggest a small introductory speech followed by a buffet and perhaps giving a complete holiday within the dome on that day?' she said while reading off her list.

'You know, you have become super efficient since you had those Brain Implants fitted. You must have already gotten used to them.'

'Since receiving the trainers from Eden the learning process had become much simpler, so I am getting there!' she replied.

'Anyway, we shall visit Mars in a few days, to observe progress, so please inform Venusa of that visit. Also, tell uncle Ben that I joyfully accept his invitation as best-man. Andy can take over the Caefon Dome project as its administrator. Perhaps his wife, Joan, can assist him.'

'Ok Boss!'

'Finally, set our visit to Sol-Newtown for a mutually convenient date within the next few days or so. Also, tell Jerry and Andy that I would like to see them immediately,' he said and she left with her hand-held computer with confidence in her stride. But Cathy had also absorbed the information within her powerful brain implants.

Both men Andy and Jerry, soon entered the room.

'Would you both like some coffee?' he inquired. They nodded yes as he typed a code for the kitchen, followed by '3 cups coffee please, immediately,' and Parky soon entered.

'Sorry, Sire, but the kitchen staff is preparing lunch,' he said.

'That's all right,' George replied, realising there was no coffee.

'Gentlemen, would you please be seated? Andy, I would like you to take over the Caefon Dome project as its chief administrator for now. But you can have it as your special baby in the future, if you wish.'

'I would like that!'

'Try to get some of your specials to join us on Mars if you can. We desperately need experienced fighters to train our soldiers. I must also contact your director, Chad and Carl in Europe. Your father, and his special people can also get involved in the recruitment and training program.'

'That will be great!'

'Jerry, while I am busy elsewhere, you are to take control of Solarian Banking and try to sort our miner problems at this end with the assistance of Barry and Ann. Why not have Miranda as your personal secretary, she is always very good at that sort of thing.'

'I agree! Thanks! I shall do my best!'

'I want you to start planning for an interplanetary trade fair to coincide with the UN Conference. I know I haven't given you much time to arrange things, but just try your best. Use special androids if you have to. There is no restriction of such technologies within Solarian Banking and our security will be quite adequate. Here is a list of urgent requirements.' George sent the list via brain implants.

'Sometime during this week, we are to visit Sol-Newtown and after that, there is uncle Ben's wedding. So please stay close to base and talk to Cathy about any queries regarding those matters. She is organising everything.'

'We shall, Sire!'

'We have lots to do, so please get to know the machinery you are dealing with inside and out. That way we may become much more efficient and learn to use our new brain implants in that manner as well.'

'Yep! I am getting there!' Jerry replied.

'Finally, the implants we acquired on Eden carries much power, so try and use the portable trainers provided, so that the menu options become second nature. But don't try too hard, we'll get there eventually. Any questions?' he said.

'Many of my specials would love to join, but their absence here on Earth would leave the territories wide open to Infilate gangs. Commander Chad and Carl have decided to begin another recruiting campaign here and in Europe, but it will take several months. In the mean time, we can use Warland for our training purposes,' Andy replied.

'Yes! I understand. However, the infilate population is dropping fast. Only the few young Fertilate rebels are causing the problem and they will be dealt with soon. Your men can be ported to Mars on certain days, so perhaps they can work for us on a part time basis to begin with, until the Infilate threat is removed. Why don't you put some formula to them, backed by a salary they can't refuse? You make those decisions and let me know of the outcome.'

'Will do, Sire!'

'I have only just recovered from the cumulative loss of sleep since Eden, but I feel like god himself. I hope you guys feel the same since Eden?' he said.

'We do!' they nodded.

'Are you guys happy with everything?'

'I am looking forward to my new duties, and it's nice to see Anne-Marie, the kids and Clair together at last. Dad should be joining us in a few days. He is also very excited with the outcome of your recent meeting. But he wants it to be a surprise. I just have to get myself in the right mood for business. I'm also still drunk from the effects of Eden and the new implants don't help. You know, after all this time, I think I am still a little shell-shocked from that kidnapping ordeal and later the loss of Vogon. But I can feel the bad taste of those ordeals just departing.' Jerry said.

'Good!'

'So in reply to your original question, I am "revving to go",' Jerry replied. They always preferred that phrase to the one of "rearing to go". It tended to more closely match their efforts.

'I am afraid if we are to stay on top, we shall have to start delegating. Here is where ones trusted wife, husband or friend, in the form of a secretary, works best. I have always considered women to be the best administrators, despite the fact they sometimes prefer us to be top dog. So guys, take my advice and let your women be your guides,' George advised.

There was a fluctuation in power as lights dimmed, with a slight tremor and suddenly they became concerned for their safety, thinking the disturbance to be the start of an earthquake. Suddenly Cathy and the others rushed into the study without even knocking.

'Sorry, Darling, but a strange feeling came over us and we began to hear voices in our heads. I hope you don't mind the interruption, but we are scared for our lives,' she said.

'So much for administrative skills if we down our tools at the least indication of trouble,' he said, while glancing towards the rear of the building close to Vogon's landing pad.

'There is your great threat, Ladies. Six new visitors from Eden,' he said. They all went towards the window to watch The Ship melt into its shimmering stairway.

'Goodness gracious! That's the little ship from Andromeda. The one they call The Ship. What is it doing here at this time?' Cathy asked, looking absolutely confused.

'We have some more Visitors, Darling?' George said, watching the six young Ancients walk down the glimmering stairway. Jon gave a voice command and the stairway and entrance melted back into the body of The Ship.

'Wow! That's some ship. Makes me shiver just seeing that happen. How bloody strange?' Andy replied, glancing at George for an explanation, but they were already on their way out of the study.

'Let's go and meet our guests, Dear!' he said and the now happier Cathy pulled him along followed by the others.

Jon, Lira, Merol, Julia, Ecrol and Petra looked as happy as ever and they knew each other beyond formal invitations and greetings.

'Life on Eden is very quiet at this time and we felt we were missing out on some real action since your recent safari hunt. So here we are to join you. If you will have us, that is. We left the children behind to take care of business in our absence. Venusa and Martia are to join us shortly, and Bawaki wants us to visit her world soon for recruitment purposes,' Lira said.

'Vicious Cat-Women fighting Javols. That will be one to see!' Tim murmured.

'Goodness! You are the greatest surprise we've had since our return from safari killing Javols on Tyrrel 2. We couldn't be more pleased to see you and your famous ship,' George replied, as they moved in the direction of the lounge.

'The Ship is now also a member of The Gang. He insists and when he makes up his mind we have to follow,' Jon said.

'Well, we are also pleased to have him as a member,' George replied.

'You should visit him and tell him so yourself. He will like that very much,' Petra said. George immediately excused himself and walked back towards The Ship.

'Dear Ship,' he said, tapping at one of its sturdy legs. 'I gladly accept you as one of my senior gang members.' There was a silent moment and then the words.

'Dearest Lord of Osmaron and Son of Goh, I humbly accept my new appointments, to do in future as you command.'

The Ship said those words and George walked proudly away to join his guests.

'You ladies have not yet learnt to use your implant's communication modes?' Julia inquired.

'We tried to communicate before arrival, but was unable to get any response,' Lira said.

'You mean... you were the voices we heard in our heads... The implants also have those powers?' Cathy inquired with surprise.

'Yes, but you have to learn when and how to switch them on and off, much like a complex communications centre with many different codes to access its different modes, for security and privacy. After all, we shouldn't eavesdrop, interrupt or interfere with others. But it's quite simple when you know how. So while we are here, why don't we teach everyone, including the men, the art of implant communication, mind linking, memory assimilation and data processing in the world of Virtual Reality.'

'Wow!' Cathy exclaimed.

'Through such methods this whole world could become Eden or any other world you wish to model through your Macron. Therefore, I can guaranty that when we are finished, you will be new and more efficient individuals. You can always return to normal by pulling the master switch. However, the implant is transparent to all other mind functions, so you'll seldom be conscious of its presence while working in the background,' Lira said.

'I never thought it was possible to create Virtual Worlds with these implants. Now I can have a Virtual Meal and never gain weight again,' Cathy replied.

'Providing it's not a Virtual Coffee when the kitchen staff is busy,' George reminded and she gave a curious look which made him worry for planting that thought in her head.

'Folks, the day is still quite young. So why don't we visit uncle Ben's place and do some pole fishing at the little river, providing we throw them back into the water after they are weighed. I always wanted to visit that place. In particular the spots Sarah and Dr Longhurst used to visit. We can test our portal as well and tomorrow we can all visit Mars on a picnic. I want to assess progress and show you some new toys then. Hal and John should be joining us later.'

'That will be great!' Jon replied.

'Shall we?' George demanded and they all agreed to go after lunch.

'So, let's get a picnic together and select a few bottles of wine!' An enthusiastic Cathy was already on her way to the kitchen, followed by the women. Parky, the butler, was always responsible for those special tasks.

CHAPTER 9

A spiritual calendar

Suddenly, the Hurst's Mansion was bustling with every variety of human life and many changes were being made to accommodate her new occupants. There were also much noise coming from the top floor while Ron's meditation room was being constructed for the installation of more highly advanced technology. He wanted the virtual image projectors to operate in such a manner, that the whole room could be transformed at a moment's notice into different scenic environments depending on the wishes of those involved.

Most of that technology was introduced from Eden for George's benefit, but could also be used for others with or without brain implants. Relevant subliminals and sensual stimulation through smell, etcetera, could also be supplied by selection. Nevertheless, Ron could create most of those images from within himself without the need for a powerful Macron.

'Our room is taking shape and those two androids from Eden seems to know their job expertly. Have you given any more thought to my problem since last we met?' George asked Ron, the little computer.

'Yes, Master. I am afraid that according to my calculations, you are due for another one of your attacks the day after tomorrow. However, I am not sure of the precise time.

'I have compiled a list of all such events. It's now at three weeks and four days, our time, from your last and could change with planets in close proximity, gravitational and other anomalies, certain field strengths, rotational period, atmospheric pressure and other dynamics. However, in your case such variations will not significantly alter the time of its occurrence.

'Anyway, if you remain on Earth and things remain as they are, we expect the following sequence of events.

'The next one is 25 days from the last and the one after that is

16 days, and so on. The numerical reduction follow a sequence which is inversely proportion to your acquired powers, whatever that represents.

'This sequence goes like this: thirteen, eleven, nine, seven, five, three, one and perhaps zero, if we are to decide they are mostly odd numbers... As you see, zero has no effect in the times your attacks occur, but takes your final powers upwards to a point of infinity. It gives you a power equivalent to that of the whole Cosmos, even to shift galaxies by thought. But even the limit of one, is quite an enormous value.

'We shall know within a period of one day, from day-one on the chart what relationship it follows, if indeed it does. I am continuing my calculations and will have more relevant data for you soon. This phenomenon may relate to the thirteen main dimensions within our Cosmos. That first time when you had the nosebleed, which was triggered by my Subliminals, was the thirteenth. You could also be traversing the dimensions one at a time while synchronising with each in the process.

'As you see, all of your past attacks fall precisely on the predicted days as indicated on my list,' Ron said.

'This is indeed quite strange and appear to be very predictable, but not quite prime numbers,' George said, while trying to see a pattern in the numbers.

'It seems to follow a set pattern and what do you think the sum of all these dimensions are?'

'It seams like 13+11+9+7+5+3+1 and zero is 49 then 36. Since two have passed since, that leaves just 9+7+5+3+1, ignoring zero is 25 and 7+5+3+1 is 16, so you appear to be right. As you said, it seems to take place in a predictable manner.

'I see! So I only have another 32 days before I find myself in ultimate oblivion. You might have to help me get back to normality within this third dimension, if I get lost somewhere along the way in that strange plenum.'

'You do! And I shall always be ready to assist, whenever I can!'

'Can you somehow save a normal part of me through my implants, so that I can have those powers and still be like I am now?' George said. He was not pleased with a process he had little control over.

'If you don't mind, I shall spend all of my future moments contemplating those problems. With minor breaks, of course, to control the construction androids and your visits,' Ron said.

'Please remind me to take the following days off our schedules and I shall have to take you along with me in future. Just in case.'

'No problem!'

'Thank goodness the UN Conference is in five weeks time. I just hope I am able to make it in human form and in a visible manner,' George said, humorously, leaving Ron to his own desires.

He then called Cathy into his study.

'Love, do you find my attacks strange?' he asked, while she gazed at him in a curious manner.

'You haven't had another, have you?' she inquired.

'No, Love. I shall have five more in due course though. Perhaps six, before they completely stop.'

'You will?'

'Yes! Do you know why I have them?'

'I assumed you were slightly anaemic at the time and had taken a tonic from Doctor Martin,' she replied.

'You are my wife and that gives you a right to know the true nature of my illness, for want of a better word.'

'What do you mean?'

'Come here and let me show you a chart. See here, I have had two such major attacks already. What else do you see?' he inquired.

'You are due for... one, day after tomorrow. Why is it like that, Darling and how do you know when?' she asked.

'My Dear, I have been chosen by the Cosmos to save all life from the evil rapacious Javols and others. The attacks give me greater powers to fight them. Like a powerful charger it saturates my being with a special type of power and energy. That's the reason why I go limp.'

'Really?' she remained sceptical.

'So far, I have been charged from the strange substance of the thirteenth and eleventh, next it will be the ninth dimension, and so on.'

'Is it dangerous?'

'No, not dangerous. So you must not worry anymore for me. Ron tells me that it should not change me physically. It's just a force of the mind, like gravity, even spiritual, but of a much higher level in order to control all lower dimensional orders.'

'I only worry for you. Is there anything I can do?'

'I don't think you can do much. Anyway, apparently, during each episode I take a little of something from each dimension and after each attack the time is shortened to the total sum of the remaining odd dimensions. The shorter time is probably because of the power buildup from my previous attacks. I must remain here at the mansion each time and Clair is also involved spiritually. But I don't know in what way yet,' he replied.

'If that is the case, how can I not worry. You could fall and harm yourself. What if you were swimming in the pool?' she replied.

'Dearest, I have decided to transform Ron's room for the sole purpose of meditation and that's where I shall be on each of those days. You now have the chart, so you can remind me on those occasions and ensure that they don't clash with any important appointments. Now come here,' he said, as he embraced and kissed her.

'It's all very strange to me, Darling, and I am worried, in case things don't work out the way we expect them to. So I shall keep my fingers crossed in future and do a little praying for us both,' she said and left, still quite concerned for his safety.

CHAPTER 10

Martian Base

That day, in anticipation of a their new adventure to Mars everyone got up early. They prepared for an extended trip to Mars and decided to leave via the large basement portal at the mansion. Although just a medium size one, it could transport twenty-five humans on each trip and they decided to give it the full test. With such devices there was always a large safety margin. That was mainly because such android and robot created technologies did not depend on costs as would be in any capitalist society.

Several meals had been prepared and it was also decided to take the microid Hercules, one of their primorph guards, and Parky, their chief butler, along to assist. Ulysses would guard the mansion during their absence. They wanted their staff at the mansion to experience those broader aspects of life. Therefore George always took them along with him on such missions.

Ulysses had already visited Mars on a previous occasion. They filled two trolleys with everything necessary, squeezed into the portal around the trolleys. Then a code was selected and suddenly they arrived at the basement station on Mars. Another code was selected and they found themselves within Venusa's ship.

'Please visit my Mind-room,' the voice said and George selected yet another code. They found themselves in a large room with many lights, to be greeted by two beautiful women.

'I am Venusa and this is my twin sister, Martia. We are the human parts of our ship's minds and created to be exactly human, with flesh, blood and bones like you,' she said proudly.

'We would like to join your gang and assist in whatever way we can,' Martia said. Then Venusa's ship spoke.

'Our human forms are linked to us through special long range implants. That way, we are able to visualise and feel in your human terms. So it will also give us great pleasure, being able to live our normal lives among you as well.'

'That will be fine, we are all just one fun-loving family anyway and would like such beautiful ladies on board. Anyway, how is our projects coming along?' George said.

'Two of your weapons have been made and tested. The special cloak along with others, are now being constructed and our ships are being converted into military types.

'The tunnel to Caefon Dome has been drilled and one hundred robots have been assigned to construct the large station there. Next will be the LPD train and the construction of fun lay-byes on-route. We are soon to include museums, wax houses, a circus, a theatre, planetarium and others.

'As you can see, the city complex and training facilities are also being constructed,' Venusa said while a large part of the room became a holographic display showing images of the work as it progressed. Their Mind Rooms could also become a virtualized stage where events could be made real. Those images could also be downloaded to implants.

'We have decided to use hexagonal structures, which offer the best compromise in perimeter to width ratios. That type of construction is necessary for optimum thermal insulation, fabrication, construction and for any future linear expansion of the base in the foreseeable future within this rarified atmosphere.

'As you will appreciate, once a dome is constructed it cannot be further expanded and putting circular domes together always leave unused areas where they meet which we think is wasteful on space and materials.

'These hexagonal structures also simplify the addition of shutters, doorways and docks,' the ship said.

'Ah! It's like one massive honeycomb of living apartments. I like the idea very much!' George exclaimed and the ships were happy that he accepted their own original ideas in such matters.

'Both you guys are geniuses and I am happy to accept you all as top ranking gang members,' George added with pride.

'Most of the miners in Caefon Dome have decided to mine for us freely, thus releasing many of our robots and androids to carry on the construction program here and elsewhere,' Venusa said.

'How did you manage that?' George inquired.

'Our namesakes Venusa and Martia went over to make another

drop of groceries and clothes toward certain city improvements, which were to commence immediately. After that, they came forward in their droves to assist us. Anyway, they have great experience in such matters and also have a say in any changes we make to their environment,' the ship said.

'Take a note for me of those actively involved in the program. Andy and I would like to make it up to them later on. But if they are all involved... then that's a different story. Is there a portal fitted in Caefon Dome?' George asked.

'Yes, just under the main square. But access to the surface is still makeshift and will remain that way until the escalators have been fitted. I am sure you can use it in single file, but you should wear protective helmets, incase of falling debris,' Martia said.

'Why don't we visit the weapons research and development unit first and observe some of your ideas in use?' Venusa asked and they went towards the nearest portal.

The large laboratory contained many blinking blocks, spherical, circular and donut like structures. Many of which were constantly rotating. The androids in that area had very large heads and small flexible hands and fingers. But it was thought, they were also microids with the ability to transform into most forms during the course of their duties.

'Please follow me this way.... These are the two weapons I mentioned earlier,' Venusa said.

'Guys, from our recent experience on Tyrrel 2, you all know that normal humans, without the necessary armour and weaponry, are unable to wage war against Javols on a one to one basis. They are made of strong metals, and with the unique ability to transform into most types of animals and weapons, except explosive types like guns and bombs. Even so, they have the technologies and installations for developing the most advanced weapons for use against us.

'They can also spray deadly microid dust that can take a human body apart in seconds. We on the other hand are human, made of flesh, blood and bones. So because of those and other reasons, we have to fight them with a new type of technology. Foremost, to protect ourselves and then, to do them the most damage possible. The purpose of our future operations is to kill Javols until there is none left to kill. Even so, they must not be allowed

to copy our technologies, so built in to these weapons are anti-Javols technology.

'Guys, this one I have christened the Mazon. It's a hand gun which is made in two parts, an ultrasonic scanner at one kilowatt output and a maser at ten kilowatts.

'Soon, Hal's plasma weapons will be modified and upgraded to our latest specs. I found them, along with the suit, ideal for fighting Javols. Nevertheless, we need vectorization for travelling through matter. Those suits will be ideal for our human soldiers.

'With our present weapon, the small spherical protrusion at the base of the handgrip is a small nuclear power pack. Both beams are focussed together into a single one, with auto feedback from the target. It optimises both beams' intensity and frequencies for maximum damage and penetration depth. There is also a small transceiver on a special mine-probe frequency for duplication purposes. When it's properly synced to their molecular structure, it can shatter them to bits. However that process can take many seconds. Plasmas are always the best for quick results, but we also loose their minds. We need a slow kill to copy their memories, if we intend using mind-probes for duplication.

'This weapon has an optimum killing range of twenty metres. So one has to be at close range to cause any real damage to Javols and even then, Javols only die during transformation. If one is cut in two the separate parts will rejoin and by then it will be pissed-off and attack with more ferocity. So their whole body must be effected by our weapons and they have to be induced into changing part of their structure before the individual microids begin to reject each other and fall apart like powder. Then their whole system fragments into a black sludge that stinks even more then the live Javols. Unlike plasmas, this weapon is safe, being harmless to humans and primals,' George said. Then he went forward, lifted a white silvery piece of material and began to extend it.

'One way of inducing such a change is to place a neutral net over them. That net prevents them from communicating with other Javols and induces them to escape. Since they abhor being contained in small spaces, that need will override any other considerations while its over them. Then in order to escape they have to transform. Therefore, they must be blasted before the net

is fired. This one is called the Javols Net for obvious reasons.

'*This weapon over here is the Gravitron. It is capable of generating a very intense gravitational beam, like an intense gravity laser plus intense EMP (electro-magnetic pulse). the share intensity can rip any body apart, including humans. By adjusting the beam-width and mode, one can lift an object in the air, but you must also remember that the body will also be attracting or repelling you by an equivalent amount, so make sure you are firmly anchored when using it in the rescue mode. The EMP part can be used separately through implants. For security, these can only be implant operated.*

'*In the kill mode, you simply select, KILL, then point and press the trigger in your minds. Here again, it's fields are synchronized and optimized for Javols' molecular bonds. It also has a built-in optional safety feature for humans and animals when it's in the kill mode. The radiation emitted by primal life is over ten times per unit area more than an equivalent active Javol. So all these weapons can tell the difference. Even so, nothing is guaranteed, so always know your target before you pull the trigger.*

'*There are other weapons like direct and indirect Javol poisons, Satan's Bugs, Hal's Plasmas, Subliminals and other types of hand-grenades and mines. Powerful Plasma Cannons, Homing Torpedoes. Planet Destroyers are used by the larger ships. However, we try not to destroy planets.*

'*The planet destroyers are giant back-to-back gravitrons that can suck and channel the matter from stars onto planets. I hope we never have to use those.*

'*Most of the smaller weapons are almost completely harmless to humans, property and other primal life-forms. In the case of the Mazon, prolonged exposure can cause intense temperature buildup, but any pain will cause such targets to scream and move away quickly. However, it is not so with Javols. Their nervous systems, for want of a better description, are much more crudely structured. Their concept of pain is not the same as ours.*

'*The cannon version is mounted on a servo tripod and can neutralise a small installation at a distance of several kilometres, with the beam optimised to the target size.*

'*The beautiful thing with this weapon, is that it cannot be seen or felt by any Javol until the damage is done. But they are quite resourceful and might soon devise detectors to sniff out such weapons. That is why careful planning is so necessary if we are to remain invisible for many years while fighting the enemy from within. Obviously, we still carry normal hand guns for killing humans and other Javol sympathizers. But they are useless against Javols. Some Javols may also appear to be humans, animals, boulders, pillars and even trees.*

'One more thing and may I stress this point. Cutting a Javol in half or even smaller chunks doesn't necessarily kill the monster. Those pieces can rejoin to form the whole with little change to the individual.

'There is another unit called the Javol's Detector Probe... that small device will detect a Javol in any form within a hundred metres or so.' George explained while they listened attentively.

They held and handled the strange weapons and realized that the Javols' wars were going to be different to any other known within the Solar System. They also felt with considerable apprehension, how they would fend during their first assault. Nevertheless many had received great confidence from their recent encounters while on safari on Tyrrel 2.

'Now, we come to special protective clothing. This one fitted on this human dummy, I call the Phasor Cloak. It's still being developed, but when finished will become your protection. It can also be used for stealth and transport. The whole thing is designed like a deep-sea diver's suit, to fit onto the body tightly, including an optional helmet for the head and a utility belt for the waist.

'A small protective net-filter with visor falls over the face to allow you to breathe normally, but at the same time to keep microids and dust out. The large hood at the front of the helmet will fall about your face to seal your body off, in case you find yourself in deep space or within a pressurized environment. There is also an oxygen supply of twelve hours on your utility belt, which you can fit into your nasal cavities before you activate the helmet and hood, if worn.

'Once activated, the suit is resistant to most types of impacts and cannot be easily penetrated by any normal projectiles, lasers, and so on. That also means, it can withstand extreme

pressures and climatic variations. But its greatest advantages are in its ability to make you invisible, and that is not all. By using your phasing controls, your body and the cloak becomes impervious to all normally vectored matter and you will be able to travel through any type of matter in three dimensions. But that part is still in the development stages. In effect it takes you out of this material universe and shunts you into another created by the suit's technology. Further, when linked to your brain implants every action can be speeded up a hundred fold, making you observe the world about you in slow motion.

'With special sensors and implants you are able to see your other invisible companions while using similar suits. But there is one drawback, and that is... you cannot use any weapons while in the invisible or mobile modes. So you have to select your targets, surprise them, fire, net them, become invisible and wait to witness their destruction and replacement. That way, they will not be any the wiser. Such battle sequences can easily be programmed within your brain implants.

'Those are just our first field weapons. I am sure we'll design many others, even to suit our personal requirements. That will happen after our first missions,' George said.

'Incredible! Truly incredible! When do you think we'll begin the fight?' Andy exclaimed with extreme surprise.

'We are to set up base in Lower Cantor in just two months time, then we can mine the local interstellar space within Andromeda with our battleships. That mission we'll complete ourselves. It will give us a little experience and teach us how to coordinate and use our weapons against more modern Javols. It will also show up any weaknesses in our weapons and strategy, not to mention those of our enemies.'

'Wow! As soon as that?' Tim said looking worried.

'Before that time, we shall have to screen all our local installations well away from our theatre of operations, so that we can play with them and find their weaknesses. There are also the recent Javol mutants. But we won't meet any of them for a while yet,' George replied.

'Will it be a very dangerous operation?' Cathy asked.

'Yes, but we'll all have life-protectors and other safety features including many powerful weapons that will be installed at Lower

Cantor.'

'That's some consolation!' Miranda replied.

'You shouldn't worry unduly. The Gang always fights in twos and males and females are usually matched and trained together as a single unit. That way, one can keep guard, while the other uses the net. Further, they may become invisible, alternatively, to confuse the enemy. And don't forget, we have powerful brain implants that can be linked to our suits and weapons, making us virtually indestructible,' he replied.

'We could do with some of my specials on that first mission, if they are to train our future soldiers,' Andy said.

'That is a great idea. See what you can do. They can use Hal's special suits for now, without the Satan's Bug. We don't want to infect those in Andromeda, only the invaders,' George replied.

They returned to have lunch, then visited Caefon Dome on Mars by portal. George was greeted haughtily by David Anderson and the Mayor, and he introduced Andy as their new administrator. Then he explained the long term plans for jobs and the new city and base that was being built. It was to give employment to many miners throughout its length and breath, and at high credits comparable with salaries on Earth.

After having tea with the Mayor and his associates, they went back on board Venusa's ship.

'You are both welcomed to live with us at the mansion from today onwards?' George said to Venusa and Martia.

'Let's take the portal from my ship in future. I shall now complete the programming. This one can be used as primary default,' she said, as they both entered the cubicle for home.

CHAPTER 11

The third malady

President Donald Fraser visited the mansion late that night with his usual security detachment. He intended to accept George's invitation and spend a few restful days with his wife, Anne-Marie, and children, including his granddaughter Clair. He realized it was a turning point in the history of his nation, but those changes were everywhere on the planet. Unrest and insecurity abounded as Infilate people died in their millions and the waters continued to rise and engulf more coastal cities.

Deserts spread throughout Africa and South America, left famine in their wake and many poor and starving refugees wandered the continents aimlessly. At that time the only safe places on Earth were the large environmental Domes and they were sealed from the outside. The only entry being through hidden portals in their basements. Those were used for the distribution of foodstuffs and other essential resources. The larger domes contained self-sufficient cities of Fertilates who followed their masters dictates to the letter.

Early the following morning Donald and George got together for a few private words in the study.

'You know, what you said the other day at our meeting makes a lot of sense, but my people still have many doubts and reservations about you and your plans for Earth. Many still have lots to lose and will not give up their wealth without a fight, so they need to have guarantees. There are also many nations on this planet that will have to be pulled together for the common-good and that is an almost impossible task.' Donald said.

'Nothing is impossible!'

'Further, they are not sure that you can wield those changes and satisfy everyone in the process. Even so, you've got a vote of 57 percent in the house. It's not a lot, but it proves you have a majority support and I think the international tide is turning in your favour. In particular, since your Gimbal speech.' Donald continued.

'That's encouraging!' George replied.

'While most of the minority of wealthy Fertilates are on your side, the Infilate cities are getting worse, despite their increasing death rate. Disease and crime is rampant, aided by some stray unsatisfied Fertilate criminals, who have little faith in their limited future. I'm sure most of the oldies are now controlled by those young criminal Fertilates, who think there are rich pickings in those places. Those greedy few, like vultures, have muscled in on the rich elderly and dying to claim their wealth.'

'Yep! This situation is predictable. Our Specials will take them out eventually. Very soon those few will be alone. Anyway, to where shall they go when all infilates are gone.' George replied.

'Anyway, despite everything, I would like you to know that you have my vote, even though I am not yet a member of your gang. Also, I can see from the important people about, that you are growing from strength to strength,' Donald said.

'Well, thank you, Donald, for those observations and for your vote of confidence. I had that meeting with you guys to test the waters, so to speak, before the UN Conference. Now, at least, I know what stance to acquire. But I am afraid, most matters are not fully in my control at this moment in time. Even the Cosmos has its own way of doing things and today happens to be another one of those strange baptismal days for me.'

'Really?' Donald was not sure what he meant.

'And by the way, you are now one of us. I have great plans for you! Nevertheless, I must leave you now to complete my meditations. But I am sure we'll be able to get together sometime later today, after my meditations,' George replied, and left for Ron's room.

Before he went upstairs, he had a haughty breakfast; not knowing how long he would have to wait. The small room had been recently completed to Ron's exact specifications. Virtual image projectors were fitted on every wall, including the floor and ceiling and the room was filled with a strange mist. Its sole purpose was to act as a strong reflective medium for whatever images were to be projected unto them. But George could equally have had those images through his brain implants and directly into his brain. Yet, he preferred to do things the more natural way and visualize those changes through his own eyes.

'Do you have a specific image in mind, master?' Ron asked.

'Let me have the first invasion of Caefon by the Javols. Place me in the middle of one of those pleasant landscapes in Cantor, just before their swarms appear,' he said. Suddenly all the walls became part of a beautiful near violet scene stretching to infinity, with many children playing in the park he had chosen.

He had adopted a yoga position for his meditations, but with his eyes open, as if meditating on the scenes about him. Javols were soon flying overhead, but for some odd reason ignored him and went instead for a mother and her young child. One of the Javols snatched both and began to dissect their bodies in mid air amidst desperate screams from both mother and child. Until their struggles and screams suddenly ceased. Then all that was left falling and floating downwards were blood-ridden clothes and small lumps of fatty tissue along with a partly dissected skeleton. The Javols usually discarded those body parts, since they contained very small amounts of the chemicals they required.

The whole scene became even more gory and nightmarish, with Javols changing into all types of monstrous forms, perhaps created to put even more fear into their quarry. They tended to get much satisfaction by observing their victims at their worst.

It was not long before he went even deeper into that nightmare that suddenly changed into the dreams he had on the two previous occasions. When they ended, he had a third and even stranger dream. Then he awoke in a very peaceful Cantor, now walking in a tranquil garden all by himself.

The image terminated and Ron began to speak.

'How was your experience?' he asked, both now in a beautiful overgrown garden in virtual space.

'I had the two previous dreams as well, but that new one was very different. I felt I could become anything and all things. The whole universe... every atom and still be conscious.

'By thinking of a place - a rock on a mountain - I could be there and be the rock on that mountain. As the rock's entity or spirit, to

feel exactly like the rock. I could be in a tree and feel every part of that tree as if I was the tree. Then I could spread myself thinly throughout the whole Cosmos, to permeate and feel everything as if everything was me. Everything changing its structure in the process to follow my will.

'It's the strangest thing I have ever felt,' George said.

'Perhaps that's the quality of the ninth dimension. The ability to become all things. In that case, the eleventh could be the ability to control all things and the thirteenth the main key to open all those dimensions, itself giving the ability to achieve all things,' Ron said.

Suddenly, there was a knock on the door.

'Darling! Can I come in?' shouted Cathy.

'Yes! Please enter!' he shouted back.

'Clair has just recited another one of her strange poems as if in a trance. I have recorded it in my implant. Have you had another attack, Darling?' she inquired.

'Yes, but it was quite mild. Nothing to worry about,' he replied.

'She always tend to have those moments during your attacks, as if you are both linked in some strange manner... Let me recite the poem through my implants:

It was on a dark night. I could have been on a meadow green,
In sleeping, I was covered and could not have clearly seen.
Except for girls casting flowers in the misty wind,
To cover the field for reasons I could not find.

A little girl came close to me,
And opened up my palm, as if to free.
But instead she placed a little key,
And said: 'Be careful let none see,

For this a key of spirit strong,
So keep it safe, for demons long.
No human's ever before have won,
Of wisdom, power, greatness. None!

Around we spread these flowers wide,
To keep all evil from your side.
Now we must leave, so clasp your key,
And from henceforth, be a power free.

The girls then quietly slid away,
And I was left, now start of day.
I opened up my palm to see,
No form of symmetry. No glowing key?

'What does it all mean?' she inquired.

'Could it be a warning of some kind, or could it mean that I had already received the key that first time?' George inquired.

'The poem simply tells you that the little girl Clair has another key which completes the whole. The key is herself and she is the one chosen to guide you on that final spiritual journey.

'We should keep her safely in the mansion, with us, until your attacks are over. You both could be in danger from outside forces if she is the key. Therefore, the mention of demons.

'I am not sure what the flowers represents, but the gardens around the mansion are now in full bloom. So it could simply mean that we remain here, where the flowers are spread widely,' Ron advised.

'I find all this dimensional stuff quite difficult to absorb,' George replied.

'Only certain life-forms like the Lodorians and Octans can visualise in true conceptual terms. Humans and many animal life-forms are restricted by their strong reliance on the visual perception. Those intelligent creatures that have evolved and adopted to the oceans, have a better understanding of dimensional structures, even the simple things you take for granted. For instance, you appear to be bi-symmetrical; meaning you have two eyes, et cetera, and a line pass through your mirror image will reveal that symmetry. But have you ever

asked why?

'Why in a perceived three-dimensional universe with time as its norm of action, you and all other animals that roam on a plane have those attributes. Aquatic creatures on the other hand have greater variety, like the octopus, squid, Jelly fish, crustaceans and many others. But even so, most life-forms tend to have sensors like vision and hearing in pairs, to give them the greater advantage of parallax. Therefore, although perception is really in 2-D, they trick themselves through their minds into believing that they observe in 3-D, even though they can never be true 3-D observers, yet that way they may get very close to the absolute.

'It's the way you have adapted in order to handle the three-dimensional world with time adding a fourth, by way of hunting and searching for resources to enhance your survival causation. Therefore, we can loosely say that perception is always one dimension lower than the real dimensional plane of the life-forms's existence, less time of course, which makes it four.

'So what we call 3-D is really 4-D, since matter and all other detectable substances could not exist without time. Without time we would have a point of singularity which is just a single point without any space. That point represents the universe itself within 5-D. So the whole of our universe would shrink to nothing, a singularity, and no substance would ever exist except within its domains.

'Using that type of argument, a life-form from within the fifth dimension will perceive its world in 4-D, et cetera, and one within the first dimension - if we are to visualise in that manner - will have zero perception. All universes are 5-D and perceived in 4-D. They occupy no time, although they have 4-D within them. A line of zero thickness has no symmetry and always takes an odd number of points greater than one to cause the mirror intersection in the first place. But here we are not talking about the causal substance of the plains, just their attributes.

'What if, those attributes controlled causal order within those planes and dimensions. Matter, which we accept as solid, may be just a stretching of causation within its own Cyberspace, real

to us but completely unreal to a so-called ghost. Yet, the ghost world may be equally real to another ghost although unreal to us. Since we are on poems, let me recite another:

We occupy organisms, to live and breathe as one,
To observe light in all its colours and enjoy sounds of music all alone.
We sense feelings and emotions with conviction and conscience,
To think, create and invent, in art and in science.

All this from an aggregate of microcosmic cells to form a macrocosmic being?
Because of an urge to survive from some strange primordial beginning?
A union of conscious spirit, mind and cell,
And in death, where will my Identity Spirit dwell?

Within a Cosmos of infinite proportions,
For how long shall I remain devoid of senses and emotions?
Will I be once again conceived to another race?
Into a different land of time and space?

For what is reality or even solid mass.
Is a ghost within its own universe as real as shining glass?
Perhaps within a Greater Computer Mind,
We are all just players of a different kind.

Appearances can be deceptive, for mass reduces to nothing,
And only when matter with matter touch we think there is something.
A form of Causal Order imposed upon a sea of Chaos Prime.
A self sustaining battle till the very end of time.

For time itself, whether forward or backwards be, is just another player,
And our laws of science here may not relate within another cosmic layer.

But I am sure, that any death to me will not be long,
For within a Cosmos of Infinity, a space time traveller I belong.

'All I can advise, is that life within any new dimension takes a lifetime to learn, and only by those specifically born into that dimension and suitably evolved to attain such knowledge.

'A creature with 4-d perception will be able to see around corners and can be everywhere at once, but even with those unique abilities, would find it extremely difficult to exist within our dimension.

'How can anyone see everything at once and absorb such information or relate such information to a 3-D world? There is also a singularity that contains all things, much like a universe of infinity within most black holes. Such a black hole could be just a few metres across when viewed externally by an observer and yet contain an infinite space within.

'Within the third dimension, due mainly to causation, everything is spread out to infinity by time and each identifiable object appears to be separate, because of its different causal history. However, when causation is removed space itself ceases to exist - as in the case of someone travelling at the speed of light within normal space time.

'If one could attain that speed without altering one's inertial frame, one would find both destination and source objects approaching. Then they become one, as their velocities get close to that of light. That would occur until everything assumes the same relative position within that Hyper-Space.

'Well, within the fifth dimension all primal substances and attributes are singular. Therefore, all stars and planets within our third dimension really occupy the same singularity within the fifth, although spread out within the third by time. Because of those reasons we may travel to any two points within a universe instantly while within the fifth dimension, but always limited by time in the fourth.

'For all we know, our complete universe could be contained within such a tiny black hole, within some other primordial universe, and all galactic black holes may contain complete *universes, each one living a separate type of existence with its own modus operandi. Even so, the super plane above must contain just seven egg-holes, to give rise to these seven main primal universes in our plane of universes or multiverse. That's assuming that all universes are a type of living cosmic organism,'* Ron advised.

'Do you understand Ron's argument?' George asked Cathy, who was contemplating profoundly on those deep thoughts as if daydreaming. But she soon shook her head as if to take herself back to reality.

'Sorry, Darling. Did you say something?' she inquired, profoundly.

'Nothing of supreme importance!' he replied and they both left Ron to his own devices.

CHAPTER 12

The moons of Endoh

George had decided to take a short break from his demanding duties. Having been left in the shadow of his latest strange experience, he wanted to meditate on some of the new ideas Ron had given him.

As always, the mansion was bustling with human life, which made it difficult for him to meditate or focus. He soon found himself feeling uncomfortable so decided to give up all duties for the day. He was to join Cathy and the others, including the six young Andromedans from Eden in the lounge for a drink.

'Jon, have you heard of the moons of Endoh or observed any strange hexagonal structures during your travels?' George asked, while sipping his Blue Bermuda cocktail.

'Yes, we once came upon a world with many such structures and dangerous aliens called Hexolytes and Drondytes. The Ship knows more about that topic than I. Why don't we visit him now and ask him your questions? Perhaps, he can even take us to where you wish to go to find such information. But he is only designed to transpose twelve humans, although several androids may be included on any single trip,' Jon replied.

Soon the door bell rang and Andy entered.

'Some of my specials have arrived, Sire. Just twenty for now. I have told them to remain here overnight. They can always pitch a tent on the grounds,' Andy said, awaiting a decision from George.

'Make them comfortable. They can use a marque or pitch a tent. In the mean time, why not invite them in here to have a drink with us,' George replied.

Andy soon went towards the front, shouted an order and the soldiers followed him indoors.

'Specials! At ease!' he shouted and they saluted George on their way and went to get their drinks.

'I would like us to go on an exploratory trip with the

Andromedan ship tomorrow, and Jon, I would like you and your Caefon gang members to join me in that venture. The crew also includes, you Andy, Joan, Tim, Carol, my wife and myself. I am also going to take along Ron and Hercules. They might come in handy if we have any unforseen problems. Ulysses can stay behind this time to take care of security about the mansion in our absence. Now, where in Osmaron are those confounded moons of Endoh?' he said, while beckoning the others to come closer to hear more of what he had to say.

'Now people, officially we are all on holidays from this moment on, so I want no mention of work by anyone for the next few days. Therefore, I shall ask the kitchen staff to prepare some food for twelve passengers on a two-day mission to a place or places unknown. We can also take along some entertainment and video cameras if we intend to have a picnic on the way back. Guys, we leave for the middle of the galaxy or wherever I can find my special moons, tomorrow!' he said. Then walked out and proceeded towards Ron's meditation room.

They wondered what new game was afoot and the soldiers thought he had gone off his head or perhaps even that he had too much to drink. But Andy never liked his boss looking ridiculous in front of his men, so he called them together.

'Guys, I must talk to you in confidence. You see that strange looking tank out there on three strong legs. Well, it's an intergalactic space ship that has travelled to Andromeda several times in the past. Take it from me, it can make the trip in just a single day. If you doubt me, come and see us off tomorrow morning. But keep it under your hats for now. Because it's top secret,' Andy said, touching his nose several times in his usual manner with a broad grin and then walked away amidst hilarious laughter and shouts of 'Andromeda eh, and pigs will fly,' from his Specials.

'I told you, he and the boss had a great sense of humour,' said an older captain and the happy group of Specials settled down to their routines.

That morning Jon went close to The Ship and uttered a command and to the amazement of the Specials its side melted into a shimmering stairway and they suddenly realized it was probably even capable of taking its crew all the way to Andromeda in a day.

Soon everything they thought necessary for their supposedly short trip was loaded on board The Ship, including the strange casket that held the Cloak of Aron which appeared to be much taller than George.

'Where are we going to this time, Darling?' Cathy asked, looking sympathetic to his recent afflictions, whatever they were.

'We are to locate one of the three moons of Endoh and I am not sure where they are,' he replied.

'Why don't you ask The Ship?' Lira said.

'Why do you always call him The Ship? It sounds so impersonal. I must give him a new name if I am to communicate with him on a one to one basis.'

'Good idea?' Lira replied.

'Let me see... Micol, Seno, Melor, Sefran. Yes, I shall call him Micol after one of your greatest ancestors,' George said and turning towards the large screen.

'My glorious ship, I now christen you with the name of Micol. From henceforth so shall you be called,' he said.

'Thank you for that great honour, Master. Now I am truly a person,' The Ship replied.

'Now, Micol, could you advise me on the whereabouts of Endoh?'

'There are three Endohs, my Lord. One towards the centre of our galaxy, and the others, similarly situated within the Triangulum and Andromedan galaxies, thus forming an astronomical triangle. I suppose you require the main portal,' Micol asked.

'Only if it is necessary for our purpose,' George replied.

'That portal is still operational and is within Triangulum. But both moons are interlinked. The Andromedan installations have been disassembled by the Javols. It will have to be replaced. The

operation of just two bases does significantly reduce the total power of the system when measured on a galactic scale, perhaps by a factor of seven. One of three cubed over two squared,' he replied.

'Can the Javols use it to their own advantage?' George asked.

'No, my Lord. By dismantling their system, all of the rear strange energies and forces would have quickly dissipated into the near vacuum of causal matter. The enclosed cylinders were specially designed to contain them and any hairline fracture could have been disastrous,' The Ship, now Micol said.

'Shall we visit our Osmaron base first, then we can assess the situation there?' George replied.

'In that case, you may now assume a relaxed position within your bunks ready to be transposed.'
'Move, People!' George shouted.
'All causal matter must now be transposed!' Micol said and the sirens went as the large screen displayed their new mode of travel.

They quickly returned to their bunks and the canopies descended, sealing them in. Suddenly came the brilliance and everything shown brightly, even their bodies glowed and they were floating in a sea of energy, with strange visions and dreams of tomorrow. Soon the brilliance was gone, the canopies lifted and there on the large screen was the planet Endoh and its three moons.

Its sun was now a neutron star since the nova explosion many billions of years before. There were gaseous clouds everywhere. They were caused by so many dead and dying stars in the vicinity. That whole volume of space was being illuminated by so much radiation in that central part of the galaxy.

The beauty extended far and wide in every direction, as colours formed into bizarre images and energetic matter and energy reflected, absorbed and radiated over most of the electromagnetic spectrum. To them it was like looking onto the face of God.

The background radiation, at the galactic centre, was always visibly present everywhere.

'We are just within the galactic nucleus of Osmaron, This is the throbbing heart of our galaxy with its massive black hole,' Micol said.

'Why so close to the centre?' George asked, as the others gazed at the grand spectacle on the large screen with wonderment.

'I suppose it's the last place anyone would search, and installations in here are well hidden from view by the dense dust clouds.

'Here is the moon in question. It forms a twin orbiter and it appears to be in tact, protected by its outermost companion. They both circle Endoh in twenty point six Earth days.

'When its sun exploded, its outermost companion may have acted as an umbrella, to shield it from the initial shock waves and super heated gases. As you can see, most of Endoh's atmosphere was blown away by the event.

'It's now a dead planet within a twilight zone,' Micol said.

'How beautiful is this area of the galaxy. So many different images and colours,' Cathy said, intently admiring the great spectacle.

'Don't let that fool you. Out here the radiation will kill any normal person in a day. It is also the most chaotic part, where matter and energy is constantly in turmoil,' George said.

'This is the heart of Osmaron. All heavy and strange substances would be at their densest at the nucleus. They have been collected here since the beginning of time and assisted by the great cycler at its centre. This also makes it an ideal place for the construction of those ancient bases.

'I suppose, it's the reason why the Javols' MasterMind have established itself at a similar location within Andromeda,' Micol replied.

'It's regrettable, it's so far from Solaria and Earth,' Andy said.
'Could we get our portals to work over such a great distance?'

George asked.

'You will need to create a similar base within Solaria. For these are intergalactic portals of great range. Each galaxy must contain its own duplex. All we have to do is choose a moon of the correct dimensions and then we can simply transpose a complete installation on the prepared surface of suitable curvature.

'I think a suitable moon does exist within the Lori system, around Lori III which is habitable, although very massive by Earth's standards,' Micol replied.

'Can we visit the cave, without damaging anything or triggering some ancient booby traps?' George asked Micol.

'Some sensitive areas on the surface of the moon might be, but the inner cave was used for refuge and will not be mined,' he replied. Then he hovered about the moon checking those massive installations, many of which were covered by debris. Finally he transposed inside the cave, with more hexagonal structures and systems of containment tanks.

'What are all these hexagonal structures used for?' Jon asked.

'Most are used to hold systems of containment tanks, others are used to hold elementals separately,' Micol replied.

'What are these elementals?' Lira asked.

'They are creatures much like our androids, but constructed from strange energies and forces. They are what you would call demons. Some are hostile and others are friendly, signified by the special coding on their tanks. Many are not able to exist naturally within this universe now, because it has evolved significantly since their confinement to perpetual containment billions of years ago. Like a fresh water fish, finding itself at the bottom of a deep saline ocean. They would soon suffocate and dissolve into the changed ocean of our space-time-continuum,' Micol replied.

'But they could still be useful or dangerous to us?' George asked.

'Yes, my Lord, they may still have a sting in their tail at their moment of death. A last destructive act before they dissolve into our space-time continuum. So they must remain where they are for now,' Micol advised.

'Would you like to observe one of those creatures and the others can tune in, via their implants?' Micol said.

'I would love to, if at all possible,' George replied.

'In that case, you will have to go outside and climb the metal ladder onto the blue and yellow striped container over there. Just at the top of the step ladder is a transparent window through which you may observe the creature,' Micol suggested, but George suddenly became conscious of many dangers while exposed to that strange environment.

'Are there enough oxygen and pressure without using a spacesuit?' he asked.

'Yes, My Lord. This was originally designed for humans like yourself. Hence, the sealed cave, where oxygen and other elements are constantly replenished and filtered to exact proportions, even better than mother Earth,' Micol replied. Nevertheless as space travellers they were always prepared in their space clothes, which made them immune from radiation.

'Ok, let's get on with it!' George insisted, as the ship transposed and landed in the large cave and transformed into its stairs and entrance. George walked across to the large hexagonal tank and climbed the ladder. As he glanced through the little transparent window all he could observe was a glowing mist. But even as he watched the glowing mist was changing into a form. He couldn't believe his gaze, for in front of his eyes an exact duplicate of himself was sitting in the middle of the tank. The being had transformed itself into his exact likeness.

'How incredible!' he said, but hurriedly returned to the ship.

'We must find some way to preserve them to posterity, because we might never see their like again. They might even be able to assist us one day against the Javols,' George said.

'Could the Javols have such creatures at their command?' Andy asked, having seen the creature through George's implant.

'Yes, but they would in all probability be controlling the Javols. They may even form the Javols' MasterMind, because it behaves very much like them and in a highly intelligent fashion,' Micol replied.

'You mean to say that when the Javols took over our third moon-base in Andromeda, they tried to eat one of those beings, which could have taken over a few to form their MasterMind?' George inquired.

'Several of those beings could have possessed those initial Javols. That is one of the ways in which they could survive. But we can find out about such information if we revive the master computer of this base.

'However, you will have to take the power off standby, and place it on full capacity. There are no mechanical switches here, so you'll have to use the Cloak of Aron. Think deeply of what you want to do in simple Sunolinguistics and it will be done,' Micol advised.

'Will it be dangerous to you all?' George asked Micol. Remembering the warnings given to him by his little computer.

'No, My Lord. The cloak will not allow any damage to this base. So we'll all be completely safe. But just in case, try it on... at that area in the distance yonder,' Micol said, as if slightly apprehensive of undesirable future possibilities.

'Darling, are you sure it's safe?' Cathy complained.

'Yes, Love. Anyway I have to try and this time is as good as any,' he replied.

George had a feeling that everything was perfectly safe, so he asked Hercules to help transport the large heavy casket to the assigned area, which was towards the rear of one of the larger domes. Then they left him on his own.

George released the cover clips and lifted the large cover. Then he removed the four sections of the cloak from its transparent bag. He tried holding the rear upper half, while attempting to fit the front upper half unto his body, expecting both to somehow connect, but nothing happened.

He attempted, until his arm muscles were exhausted. So he placed them back within the casket in order to rethink a new strategy.

'How can anyone wear such a cloak, cut down the sides with everything in two halves, even the sleeves? Perhaps I should spread both rear parts on a bed or in the casket, lie on top of them and then slide the upper parts over my body. Clothes designed to be put on in a lying down position. How strange.' He uttered those words, while fixing himself inside the casket. It was much longer than his height and about a three quarters of a metre wide.

The moment the uppermost parts touched, the interior of that strange casket began to glow and the different sections of the cloak knitted tightly together about his person.

'Not a casket at all. Some power source. Perhaps even another portal, but for laying into,' he said to himself.

He composed himself and got out of the casket. He thought a command in English but nothing happened. Then he corrected his absentmindedness and thought correctly in Sunolingua and it was done. The whole cave came to life with all those gas-like lamps, dormant for billions of years, suddenly coming alive and everything sighed into activity.

'I am Jull, son of Aron and also your new master. I have returned to take control!' he commanded and suddenly the whole place became super charged with static energy as that part of the moon began to repair and replenish itself after so many millennia of neglect.

There were massive electrical discharges everywhere, to the extent that Micol had to seal his entrance to protect the fragile humans within.

After about fifteen minutes the transformation ceased. Another thought was transmitted and the moon within distant Triangulum was undergoing a similar transformation. Then everything went silent on both worlds.

He thought again and the suit leapt from his body and sealed itself within the casket and the lid automatically clipped into place.

'God! The power of those ancient patriarchs. I did not realize I could operate the whole process through my implants,' he mumbled to himself. Then he thought a command to Micol and he formed his stairs and entrance, with Hercules following to assist with the heavy casket. Nevertheless, the others remained safely inside Micol until George said it was safe to do otherwise.

Yet, George still didn't realise that he had also acquired a natural ability to control such powers, even without the help of the strange Cloak of Aron.

'Perhaps I should have thought the casket into Micol,' he said as an after thought, still not realising that it could have been done if he really wanted it to happen.

'Micol, I have also received a list of demons from the master computer. I shall now transfer that information to you through my implants,' George said.

'The two held at the Andromedan base were their leaders Lupher and Dracma. They were left there in isolation because it was the furthest distance from their home world, Triangulum. They are the worst and most powerful of all Hexolytes and are presently in control of the Javols. Originally designed by Dracos of Pol II within Triangulum. They shortly became their masters, by some strange quirk of faith and assisted Dracos in the creation of the other more recent Hexolytes. But they should have died since? They may have evolved into stronger entities over the aeons.

'They may also have undergone some form of conversion or possession with Javols. Hence the reason why they remain so close to the Andromedan nucleus. Here, they can receive an abundance of the strange energies they hunger for and also gain universal power through the Javols.

'A new lease of life for almost extinct entities.

'If that is the case, I am afraid we have an enormous task ahead of us, if we are to defeat the Javols and their supreme masters,'

Micol said.

CHAPTER 13

A visit to Lori III

George's companions and most of all, brave Cathy his wife, felt worried for him while in that strange cave on Endoh's second moon. Therefore they were very relieved when they were finally on their way back to Solaria and Earth.

'May I suggest we return home via the Lori system, which is also within Solaria.
We can then visit the moon and carry out the required measurements before returning to Earth,' Micol advised.

'That is a very good idea, Micol?' George replied to The Ship.

'You may now return to your bunks in order to be transposed to Lori III. All causal matter must now be transposed!' Micol said. Warning buzzers sounded.

The brilliance came, then their canopies lifted. Suddenly they found themselves watching a tri-planetary system on the large screen.

'There are just three main planets orbiting this star. Lori III, which is the closest to the star, is over twice the size of Earth. But she is placed much further away and is in a balanced orbit about her parent star. Even so, all three worlds are quite massive by Earth's standards.
'The outermost worlds are gas giants and much too massive and extreme climatically to support primal life as we know it.
'Lori III has nine moons and the others, several of their own moons. As you may observe, one of its moons also has several of its own and is larger than Mars with a reasonable atmosphere, although somewhat erratic, being frequently eclipsed by the mother planet. All moons are in balanced orbits about their parent planet, hence there is a minimum mutual tidal action.

'Lori III's gravitational field is just over twice that of Earth, over its much larger surface area. Most of its inhabitants are what you would call reptilian.

'The smaller grass eating crustaceans form one of the main links in the food chain on land,' the ship, Micol, further advised.

The northern part of the planet was presently in early spring. Green and mauve patches could be observed within the most northern and southern hemispheres. Those fertile areas were well away from the equatorial desert band that completely encircled the planet, giving it the appearance of two almost equivalent semi-spheres from space. Even the clouds were distributed in a symmetrical manner. Therefore, that band or ring may have had some effect on its weather pattern.

Here again, there were no very large oceans as on Earth. Just numerous seas and lakes on a single planetary continent.

'We once landed close to that northern sea and met some of its friendly natives.

'Shall we pay them a second visit?' Micol asked.

'Why don't we? After all, we are supposed to be on holiday and I would like to observe another different intelligent life-form. Can they be recruited? I mean, be trained to take care of their world in the name of Solaria?' George asked.

'I think they are practical enough for that responsibility,' Micol replied.

'How strange and harsh a world,' Cathy exclaimed while observing the extensive browns and greys from space.

'Yes, My Dear. But we can only do with what we have been given and some of us have little choice in the matter. That is why the more fortunate of us must sacrifice certain things in order to help the unfortunate and dispossessed,' George replied. Cathy realized he was always right in such cases and was slowly becoming like him in such matters.

'One of the equatorial moons could have exploded in the distant past, or perhaps a collision between two moons at that time,' Jon said.

'You mean to say, these creatures could have used powerful nuclear weapons in the past?' an intuitive Cathy asked.

'No! Not its present populations. But their predecessors could have used such weapons during a limited thermonuclear war,' Jon replied.

'Who would their predecessors have been?' asked Joan.

'We are not sure, but we think they could have been the Drondytes and Hexolytes. Both interplanetary predator species have always competed vehemently for domination of subspecies, with a mutual dislike for each other, even to a point of mutual entrapment and destruction,' Jon replied.

'Yes, Jon, I think your assessment of the situation to be correct. The Hexolytes were never a primal species, but began life as a complex elemental. They were designed by Dracos many billions of years ago. They soon overpowered the alien Dracos and took over his home world. The Hexolytes, under their new rulers Lupher and Dracma then used him and his people to develop a completely new technology of portals, special cloaks and weapons to reap havoc on all primal life. Some say they could live and feast on the pains and sufferings of others and the more the suffering the more enjoyable their meal.

'They carried many weapons for the sole purpose of reaping the most pain and suffering from their captives. But they also preyed on their enemies, the Drondytes,' Micol said.

'What a sick race of demonic monsters. Thank goodness they are not still around,' Cathy replied.

'Do you think they are all gone from this world?' Joan asked.

'It's difficult to say. Shall we visit the lower hemisphere and see for ourselves?' Micol replied.

They transposed and materialised close to another one of those seas. But there were no buildings or signs of intelligent life anywhere. Just large sand pits and small mounds. They were amidst the mauve grass-covered meadows that were being grazed by many small crab-like creatures. They appeared to be quite slow and docile. More like small cows and sheep, but crablike.

'What do you think?' asked George.

'Sonar checks have revealed large underground channels leading to larger mounds, which are used to carry stale air and unwanted gasses from the lower levels. The whole place is honeycombed and riddled with these burrows, but there are no underground cities or large caves, just family units occupying an area of the planet to themselves, much like farmers.

'On assessment, these sandy areas appear to be the exit and entry points for Drondye descendants. They must sleep during the warm hours and come up during the night to harvest their crustacean cattle. They must all live within the planet and visit its surface for food, meditation and play. But some of their food could also be grown in special chambers underground.

'The sand pits must be their sealed doorways. Their construction make it very difficult for any of the local predators to enter, without suffocation. Further, their scent cannot be followed easily through sand.

'A unique species, evolved to survive in a completely different way and yet are quite intelligent,' Micol said, with an air of excitement.

Then the ship displayed images of those creatures on the main screen. They were like king cobras with hypnotising eyes and horns on their heads, but with the body of a crocodile and with small human-like hands. They could also walk upright and balance on powerful tails. On their yellow chests were poisonous horns for stinging their prey.

'What a bloody monster and what powerful hypnotising eyes. An awesome creature!' Andy exclaimed while turning his head away from the beast of all beasts.

'Should we try to communicate with them?' George asked.

'No, Siend, they have nothing to offer us and are better left to their own desires for now. The northern Hichie tribes are less ferocious, indigenous to this world and are amenable to training. These species here should never be allowed to visit the northern

hemisphere because they will consume the others. Anyway, for now they are unable to cross the desert area because of the deadly sand snakes that roam its band in abundance,' Micol added.

'In that case, we should carry on with our present program in locating and assessing the moon for conversion,' George advised.

They left that area and began to circle the planet once more to select the moon. Then they made all essential measurements from the air.

'It's perfect for our Solarian Base in these parts. All we have to do now is clear an area of about twenty-five square miles, which is the size of Endoh's Base,' said Micol in an exciting manner.

'I hope our conversion will not cause much damage to this beautiful heavenly body and seriously affect the world below,' George inquired.

'No, My Lord. It will only change a small surface area on this moon. However, those on the world below may be disturbed by those changes, which will be visible to many,' he replied.

'In that case, send a signal to Lord Malik of Polok II, and it will be done,' Jon advised Micol.

'Consider it done!' Micol replied and the H-wave signal was sent.

CHAPTER 14

The loving hands of a god

They soon left the large moon and decided to visit the northern regions of the main world to observe its indigenous life.

'Be warned. The area of this planet we now visit is highly laden with the smell of ammonia and other noxious gases. Although not at all dangerous, it may take a little while until one is acclimatised.

'After landing, your weights will be more than double and the oxygen content is slightly less than on Earth, so you are to walk slowly and take deep breaths. Here, hydrogen and nitrogen are in abundance and form the main bulk of its atmosphere,' Micol advised.

The ship soon landed in much the same place as it had on a previous occasion. After materialising many of the local dinosaur-like creatures disappeared within their underground homes.

'Where is Ooh-Kaa your tribal chief? I would like to talk with him!' The Ship, Micol, resounded.

The creature that appeared was trembling on her tough webbed feet and her hand claws, also webbed for digging in soil, was equally shaking.

'He... and many... of our males have gone hunting... towards the rich northern lands. Master... they will be there for two long weeks and one week to travel back. I am sorry... great one, for not having been more helpful. Please do not take my life because of my foolish incompetence. I have many young children to nurse,' she replied, in her strange high frequency screeches and grunts that Micol clearly understood while translating and transmitting every sentence via implants to his crew.

'Such a beautiful and polite race. I wonder if we were like them at the dawn of our history?' Cathy asked, although not expecting an answer.

'What is your name?' asked Micol.

'I am Wi-Kaa, one of the wives of Ooh-Kaa and have borne him many young over many seasons,' she replied.

'Well, Wi-Kaa, thank you for your assistance and please return to your duties,' Micol said, as the ship suddenly disappeared, leaving the poor creature even more nervous than she had ever been.

They decided to go in search of the hunters. Micol knew that the female meant a total of three weeks, one to go the other to hunt and finally for their journey home. But the rotational rate of the planet was two point eight times that of Earth. Therefore, one week was really two point eight weeks. But here again, their week was closely linked to their fastest moon which took twelve days to traverse its orbit. So on Lori III, one week was really equal to thirty three-point-six days and the hunting trip was expected to take them over one hundred Earth days.

'I have found them on my scanners. Ooh-Kaa is over there, with his visible tribal markings chasing the hunt,' Micol said.

'The one they are chasing looks more like an extinct Australian iguana, but with webbed feet. They are not having much luck with those clumsy and useless stone spears. Don't they have any metals on this planet?' Cathy inquired.

'In abundance. But they are still prehistoric and have not yet learnt to use metals. They still think fire to be lightning from the gods.
'I suppose, in a way they are right. Fire only gets started on this world when there is lightning. While on Earth there are many forests, more oxygen and a constant supply of dried wood and leaves. On this world only large cacti and mauve grass exist, with a high capacity for storing water. Further, dead leaves contain much sugar and are quickly devoured by the lower life-forms and

bacteria. Therefore, there was never any great stores of coal, oil or gas deposits and fire has never been used as a tool by anyone.

'If anything, they have always treated such rear occurrences with respect and desire to be left well alone.

'How can any species develop metallic tools before first learning to control fire? But even that is not all. The heat must be hot enough to melt the iron ore, to which is added, other elements like carbon for hardness, etcetera. You know, on Earth iron came after bronze and copper. Those discoveries were over periods of thousands of years, and here we are, wanting them to jump several ages in one.

'However, they have a high intelligence and a general understanding of many things. I think they are now on the brink of one of those great evolutionary jumps, but unfortunately, unlike Earth, this planet is void of suitable plants. To really get started on that path they require plants with dense shoots that are suitable for making handles, even bows and arrows.

'This world has such limited resources for them to take that all important jump. For those reasons, they appear to be permanently stuck technologically in the stone age,' Micol said.

'Perhaps we should give them a little push in the right direction. Not enough to cause drastic changes in their living pattern, but enough to allow them that vital new step. More like a parent helping the little child to take its first step. After all, it's our responsibility to help the weaker in this universe of ours,' Cathy advised.

'Yes, Dear, once again you are absolutely correct. I would like us to return immediately to Venusa's ship and have some primitive bows and arrows constructed out of the raw elements of this planet. We should also locate a suitable deposit of flint to construct a fire box, which they can use for starting fires. We can also collect cotton and birch shoots and seeds from Earth, which they can use in time for weaving clothes and the wood can also be used for their spears and arrows.'

'Are you sure, Darling? Wont that change the evolving pattern on this world?' Cathy inquired.

'They are being held back unfairly. Within The Greater Purpose it's our duty to remove all such restraints to a more natural evolution,' George said and they agreed.

'Since there are no birds on this world, they can improvise for feathers, and so on. We must now find a dense deposit of iron ore and take a large chunk back with us. Part of it we'll place across their trail,' George said, and Micol began scouring the surface for any local deposits.

It was not long before a suitable rock was found, and Hercules went out to chip large chunks off the outcrop. When they had enough, they went to collect samples of plants and mauve grass. Then they climbed back on board.

'Folks, we have work to do,' George said, while they returned to their bunks. From there they were transposed to the Admin Dome on Mars and then to Venusa's ship.

'I apologise for this intrusion, Venusa, but we have an urgent mission. Micol will shortly update you with the facts. We are to return urgently to plant these weapons and equipment along their trail before they complete that part of their journey,' George said.

'For this particular exercise we can use a synthetic wood until suitable seeds are brought from Earth and planted on that world. An android will be immediately sent through portal to Europe to collect plants and seeds. Propagation will be a major problem on a planet like Lori III, without insects, bats or birds. In time, we might have to introduce a safe insect to assist the process, if random air currents are not enough.'

'Understand!'

'You should plant the first seeds very close together for now, with the special nutrients provided and hope they take root in the untested soil,' Venusa's ship said.

'Let's do it! This way, we can try and try again until we succeed! But try and see if anything can be bio-engineered and cross matched with our own plants for those planetary conditions. Also, give some thought to suitable insects,' George said, and Venusa's ship scheduled the new program in motion.

Just within one hour, they had exactly what they required and were once again on their way to Lori III to search for the hunting group.

'There they are! They seem to have been successful with their last chase. Those two leading members appear to be holding full skins. But there is still fifteen left without a catch. Do they use salt to preserve the meat on these long trips?' Cathy said.

'Animal tissue is preserved for a much longer time on this world due mainly to the lower oxygen levels and absence of that type of quick acting bacteria. Further, the more natural bacteria have evolved to consume the sugars from dead plants of which there are always numerous amounts,' Micol replied.

'Let's travel for another five miles ahead of them, and place the small kiln and other devices on their trail,' George advised.

When Micol landed, George and Hercules got out, carrying the bulk of the equipment. They were soon followed by Cathy and the other crew members who wanted to stretch their legs on a different world, but found the higher gravity did the stretching instead.

When they left the ship they were immediately greeted by the strong stench of the planet, much like a urination pool, and they became aware of their much heavier bodies. Slowly, they progressed towards a rocky mound. They deposited some of the raw iron ore and not too far away Hercules prepared the ground and fitted the small kiln with an iron safety grill on top.

A crude anvil, a hammer and blower were also included. Its purpose was to concentrate the oxygen on the heated metal. The seeds and three young shoots were then planted throughout that area. The whole area was laid out as a blacksmith's workshop, with many tools and weapons, some only partly completed.

When they were ready to leave, the ship checked the position of the hunters and the fire was lit with the addition of several delayed fire crackers to draw their attention.

Then metal knives, spears and arrow heads were generously spread all around the kiln. That was to give the impression that someone was making those weapons.

They were pleased with their handiwork. The trap was set and Micol transposed into the lower clouds to observe their reaction.

'I hope the oxygen levels on this world is high enough to melt iron or we might have to use a different alloy?' George said.

'The stronger blower and coal we brought from Earth should be enough,' Cathy replied. Nevertheless they had numerous options for choice.

The first hunter on the scene was Ooh-Kaa and observing the exploding flames, signalled his males to be silent while he bravely progressed slowly towards the strange fire.

The explosions had stopped and there was no one in the vicinity to challenge him. He observed the beautifully made spears that were resting against the large rock and the temptation was too great for him to resist, so he quickly went across to collect one. He nervously glanced around incase it was a trap. But nothing happened.

Ooh-Kaa gave a few grunts and hand signals to his fellow hunters, meaning for them to stand guard around the area, which they did. Then he went up to the fire, touched it and instantly screamed in pain. Ooh-Kaa took hold of the spear, checked its balance and threw it towards a large cactus tree and it went straight through its thick outer skin. He went to retrieve it, but when he observed the blade, it was still in perfect condition.

Then he threw it at the rock and observed, but the spear was still in tact, with no visible damage to its tip. He went towards the bows and arrows which made very little sense to him. He removed an arrow from the quiver and threw it like he did the spear, but it was too small to throw by hand. Ooh-Kaa immediately concluded that it was somehow linked to the bows which had similar coloured markings.

He picked up the bow and aligned an arrow with the markings, then he pulled the string back as far as he could and then released. To the amazement of all his hunters the arrow flew all by itself to a distance of about twenty metres and stuck into the ground.

He was dumbfounded by the cleverness of whom or what hunter had made those weapons. But he had also seen strange gods from the skies in the past. That was soon after he had become leader of his tribe and many sun cycles ago. He concluded that everything was possible where he was concerned.

Ooh-Kaa shouted to his youngest son, who immediately came forward and began to communicate in their strange language.

'Father, it's a set of special spears made of a hard but pliable material, which unlike rock chippings, can be reshaped and re-sharpened. This here appears to be a natural deposit of that substance. But I have seen this material closer to home, in the valleys.'

'Really son?'

'You see, it can be made flexible and into a liquid when heated by lightning-strike-fire. And this small tool here creates several lightening-strike-fires to start the large heat to melt the substance. We need much lightning-strike-fire to melt it, with these other substances here. But all these I can make from our own local resources,' he said.

'Son, I know you are the most industrious of us all. Can you really make these weapons?' Ooh-Kaa asked.

'Yes, father!' he replied with certainty.

'I am sure I can, if everything is here,'

'Son. I think the gods are with us on this trip. So get the group together and we shall say a prayer and sacrifice our hunt to the lightning fire of the gods.'

They formed around the fire and began to dance and chant, while he placed bits of meat from his bag unto the grill. While the meat burnt, its sweet odour was pleasing to them and they went closer to the fire, to observe the process in operation. After all, here they were using God's weapons, including his lightning heat.

His young son said a short prayer and took a small piece of cooked meat from the grill. Unlike raw meat, its taste was very pleasing and he blinked his large slitted orange eyes several times. Partly because of the hot meat, but primarily because of the delightful taste. The others, observing his expressions of enjoyment, did likewise, until all the meat was eaten.

'Father,' he said.

'This marks a turning point in the future of our tribe. Because now, we have acquired weapons and knowledge of a most superior nature. Such knowledge, I am sure, no one of our tribes has yet learnt. Not even the dragons beyond the Snake's Desert. We should take the spears for now and hide the other parts well away from this place, to be collected on our return journey. Let me fill the lightning fire with sand. It will kill its powers for now,' he said.

He dowsed the fire with sand and to everyone's amazement the fire went out and the place became cool once more. They hid the items and took the metal knives and spears. They were soon on track and travelling to the land of the iguanas, with metal spears in hand, but this time with proper hunting weapons.

'What a bloody little genius!' Cathy shouted.

'Dear, I think you have finally found your vocation in life and close to our local moon base. You can always visit them in person or appear like a god from the skies. I can imagine you suddenly making an appearance with lightning, thunder and brimstone... while assisting in their development,' George said, jokingly.

'But Darling, It took the little one such a short time to decipher the whole process, even creating some new ideas of his own in the process. All they needed was a little kick in the right direction,' she replied.

'Can you imagine a little dinosaur like him in pants?' Andy said and they all began to laugh.

For a while they viewed the whole situation on the screen and when they were certain that their mission was successful, he gave the order.

'Folks, let's return home. Perhaps we can still have that picnic at Empress Sarah's place, if it's still day when we return,' he said and the ship and everyone prepared to be transposed to Sarah's house, on its original spot at the rear of her manor.

CHAPTER 15

Lupher and Dracma

Endoh's third moon-base within Andromeda was presently the domain and headquarters of the Javols. It was just over three thousand years since the time of their creation and their installations there had spread far and wide. With the aid of their MasterMind, they had moved many planets together to form a giant stellar system with numerous worlds. Many were inhabited, with orbiting radiation shields where necessary. Shielding from the galactic nucleus and its intense radiation were for the benefit of their Primal slaves..

The system so formed was different to any of the more naturally evolved stellar systems. Since Javols never required sunlight most of those worlds were dead and always showed the same face to their sun while their other hemispheres were held in darkness. Nevertheless, being close to the nucleus of that galaxy made everything shine brightly from the high ambient levels and background radiation. All of the uninhabitable worlds were linked together and filled with numerous installations.

While George searched for the Moons of Endoh he soon found the installations of the ancient moon-base in Andromeda to be almost completely destroyed by the Javols on their first visit. However since that time it had been extended, and was now mostly used for the control of their Master Mind and the storage of essential supplies.

The mother planet seemed almost identical to the Endoh of Osmaron. It was thought that all three of the Endoran systems were quite similar. With the three moons having almost identical rotational periods and masses. Their parent neutron stars also appeared to have had identical masses and ages. The Ancient Patriarchs or Masters of the universe, had a great belief in symmetry and were always precise in their selections.

Most of the Javol's headquarters had since extended to a nearby planet, which was more abundant in natural resources, although with a somewhat depleted atmosphere. However, Javols were not like primal humans that needed to evolve under almost precise planetary conditions. They could easily have felt equally comfortable on a small moon with zero atmosphere.

However they required a living world for their primal captives and that location was more suitable for their Timit slaves and other primal life-forms necessary in their expansion programs. It also made their leaders feel less isolated, despite the existence of so many installations, meteor defences, administration computers and powerful communications equipment. Even so, they never liked automatons in the form of robots or androids, so there were always many primal slaves to control those systems.

That part of Andromeda was just within its nucleus and not two distant from the enormous swirling black hole they called Mecladon. The name meant fire-dragon in one of the ancient dialects.

Here, the sky was perpetually bright, with all that background radiation almost as it was at the centre of Galaxy Osmaron. It was estimated that the volume of space around that Endoh was at least five times brighter than anywhere in Osmaron. Further, Andromeda was a lot more massive than Osmaron and Triangulum put together. The higher intensity was mainly due to the stellar density and destruction of so many stellar bodies and systems, as they were pulled into that powerful black hole Cycler called Mecladon. But here, the skies were even more beautiful, with many more supernovas, gaseous and dust nebulae. It was also flowing with elemental energy in abundance. There was more than enough of the elemental substances to maintain demonic beings like Dracma and Lupher within a comfortable living manner, although not able to leave that area and freely roam beyond the nucleus.

Anyway, presently there was insufficient life for them to prey upon within that galaxy at any distance from its nucleus. All having been devoured by those rapacious Javols in the previous three thousand years of their ravenous harvesting. Nevertheless, their masters had kept a few species like the near-human Timit to breed and prey upon.

Their master's current restrictive situation had left them with the only choice of escape and they could only have engineered a clever plan with the unknowing assistance of their near metallic subjects, the Javols. Therefore, although now Masters of the Javols, they were also in a type of prison from which they could see no escape.

Dracma and Lupher had since adopted one of their powerful near-human forms of previous existence aeons before. Being mainly Javol in form, they were able to transform to almost any shape of an equivalent mass. However, unlike the Javols they preferred a single form which reminded them of their past and they had permanently adapted to that one.

In their present forms they were over two point five metres tall, with just two fingers and one thumb, and with near cloven hooves for feet. Their noses were broad with golden rings. Two horns on foreheads were adorned with jewels. With slit reptilian eyes, both stood together on the high railed balcony, looking out towards the core of the massive swirling nucleus a few light years away. Since they were identical twins, it was difficult to tell one from the other. Lupher was currently munching on a Timit's leg. They were not happy and wanted to find a way out of their present intolerable situation.

'So many aeons of unfulfilled dreams. So many aeons of natural development lost. I feel drained of all spiritual consequence and elemental substance. Even with the occasional meagre rations of living Thoraxi and Praille failures... and the occasional Timit pleasure.' Lupher said.

'We could have been still held in one of Aron's perpetual prisons! If not for their stupidity and curiosity,' Dracma replied.

'Sometimes I think that would have been a better destiny! Now we are stuck permanently to this place always gasping for breath.'

'Why do they always use us to punish their failed scientists, even unto death? And they treat us like their gods during those sacrificial punishments.' Lupher was not pleased. He had just vanquished many good scientists because of another timely failure.

'Since they have destroyed the Thoraxi world, there can be no replacements.' Dracma said

'It's regrettable, those fools destroyed Aron's moon with all its technologies. Such a ridiculous waste. Those are losses from which we shall never recover. You know, that cave contained much information relating to our own survival.'

'Brother, if only we had a scientist like Father Dracos to build us new portals and cloaks... to even find a way to depart these crude Javol bodies with their insatiable desire to eat and replicate... Such incompetence and hungry idiots, always eating, eating, eating... like Crotamoss, always eating.' Dracma said.

'I do believe... it would have been a lot better as a captive within one of Aron's dark tanks for aeons than amongst these idiots for a day. They leave us so little of the painful pleasures to feast upon. Yet, they are free to roam and take those pleasures themselves and in so doing have destroyed our only means of escape... by eating every primal scientist and engineer within the Galaxy.' Dracma replied, while drinking a large mug of Timit's blood.

'Nice bouquet! It's much better when we starve the fat ones for a day or so.' He drank it in one gulf and burped. 'That really hit the spot.'

'I prefer starving the slim ones! Thank awful badness we had prevented these idiotic Javols from advancing too quickly on their own, and travel to the local galaxies to do likewise. You know, there might still be many competent scientists left within Triangulum and Osmaron who can help us. But we have to somehow make contact with those civilisations without compromising our positions here in the process.' Lupher replied.

'That will be difficult! You, as usual, had the brilliant idea to take control over them by showing them a better way through MasterMind and they are not even aware of our gross difference in intelligence and mind. But neither can we eat and duplicate like them, for splitting our entities would cause us sudden death and neither can we be exposed to excessive stellar radiation. Nor absorb more than our daily rations if we are to remain single individuals.'

'I would be a lot more comfortable and grossly eviler, if we could leave these semi-metallic bodies and be contained within one of our master's cloaks, with all its powerful attachments.' Lupher said.

'They get nothing out of those they eat. No pain, no suffering, no sadism, nothing. Just plain physical nutrients, to fill their insatiable appetites. Why don't they plant a tree or graze Cattlelac like the primals have done since their beginnings? Why waste all that elemental substance?' Dracma complained. But Lupher knew how he felt and decided to listen to his barking for a while. If anything, it broke the monotony of his boredom and was almost music to his ear.

Lupher gazed at the massive energy capture dishes orbiting above the now dead planet. One that always remained in that precise position in the sky, despite the slowly moving canopy of dusty images and numerous stars, and decided to add a few of his own important words on the topic.

'Everything has changed significantly since the days of Drondye. The universe have since become a cleaner, tidier, simplistic and a much more boring place.

'You know, Father Dracos was one of the most clever scientist the universe had ever known and he predicted those changes with the coming of greater order and entropy within the whirling sea of chaos. Gone are many of the special elementals required to design special creatures like us.

'Thank utter badness, ours are the type with a strong mathematical co-linkage bonding, or else we would not have been here now having this conversation and the Javols might have overrun and eaten everything.

'But the Patriarch Masters may also be no more, and that possibility gives us a chance. With little opposition from inferiors we can rule the whole universe. Because, if those stupid and incompetent Javols have had such great successes, where does that leave us?

'Pity, we are not able to use them within any constructive or long term plans.

'Pity, it's in their nature to have no patience. Even incentives of real power are meaningless to them.

'It is now only a matter of time before we are visited from one of the other galaxies, when the first ill-informed and hungry Javols enter their realms. Because of their dormancy during the long intergalactic trip of over three thousand years, their bodies will be weakened and they will be easily captured and subdued before they begin to propagate their kind.

'Even so, the first invading Javols might still cause enough

damage for the others over there to want to exterminate them from the face of the universe. Then they will ask questions about the Javol's origins. When that happens, they will be traced back to our galaxy and their enemies will come looking for them over here, and complete the task of their destruction with the latest technologies. You know, any such visit could be disastrous for us as well.

'You know, those invading black ships were no-match for our more advanced equipment, but they had left Osmaron over three thousand years before, so their technologies would have advanced greatly since. Even so, our drive systems are now twenty times faster and can take us to Osmaron in under twelve collons (about 50 Earth years). But I do believe they could have been sent to deceive us into thinking they possessed a more primitive technology than is truly the case, which would make them even more advanced than we have estimated.

'How could they have known so quickly after the event, in order to have sent a fleet, even if some person or persons unknown had left this galaxy to warn others? I sometimes believe these moronic Javols have eaten every quatron of evidence, leaving us with so little data to go on, and the little we have remaining forms less than an incomplete jigsaw, with many components either missing or lost,' Lupher said.

'Do you then think that one of the Masters may still be around with a plan for domination? You know, the Plorans could have returned in the intervening period. They were always very hot on a tidier universe. Always hot on the preservation and ordering of primals in their own ridiculous fashion. They may have become bored like us and returned to rule virtually unhindered. But, Brother, if that is the case, it's not fair. The universe out there is large enough for all to play and we always chose small pickings by comparison.... only time will tell. But if they exist, so also might others...? If that's the case, it all makes for a more exciting future,' Dracma replied.

'I recently sensed a tremor... one of great magnitude and change, or perhaps more a transformation within the ninth. One that represents the birth of someone of enormous cosmic influence and importance.

'The significance of that great power could pose a threat to us

if it takes control of the fifth. It has chosen the main primal elementals for its foundations and I have no way of knowing of its capacities, cravings or intentions.

'Such a force could affect our communications media. Any intrusion here, could render us naked to interference and eavesdropping. Therefore, it is imperative that we find some other mode of intergalactic communication, if at all possible... in order to maintain order among our Javol subjects. Because, without such immediate control, they will once again begin to break away from our influence, to run amok, eating the remainder of whatever life there is left in this galaxy and beyond.

'I have already given that delicate task to MasterMind. Let's see what answers are forthcoming. But I am not convinced such technologies to be possible within this galaxy at this time. Perhaps it could have been several billion years ago, when the higher dimensional levels had greater significance,' Lupher replied.

'Brother, I sense a great storm coming. It's a storm that will shake the very core of our universe and we must be prepared for it,' Dracma said and Lupher agreed.

Lupher wiped his bloody mouth with his dark hands and took a Timit leg from the table. He stripped it to barest bones with his sharp teeth. Then began munching the bones rather noisily. Dracma joined him in a bone-chewing competition.

The two evil demonic brothers continued to confer on those topics of survival until they came to the conclusion that Andromeda was no longer a safe place to be. They also realized that many of Father Draco's caves could have remained in tact over the aeons. If only one of them could design a suitable ship to travel to their home galaxy Triangulum and locate such caves and a new civilization to coerce in their ways, then they would have a better chance to survive those dreaded challenges in the future.

CHAPTER 16

Little good witch

George had realized he could use his meditation room for Virtual Reality experiments and within that strange domain of the mind could design all types of devices. Since they were not real, but followed the same physics as the real world he could test his theories to a point of self-destruction without harming anyone. The real bonus was being able to perform such tests hundreds of times faster than in the real world. Once he was satisfied with his designs it was then the simple matter of converting them into the real world with special equipment linked to his Macron.

With the use of his brain implants, George was working on his own theories of dimensional physics when Cathy walked into his study to discuss her weekly schedule.

'Darling, I have arranged for our visit to Sol-Newtown in just two days and have ordered some novel gifts for your senior staff there. I have since learnt, from the list Venusa gave us, that there are several large portals in Sol-Newtown. With her assistance, the main one can be programmed to connect with our portal here and Sarah's manor in North Dakota. So I've arranged for them to be connected. Since the Terminal Disease is not a serious problem anymore, cleansing through our home portal will be enough for Eden and elsewhere. Slowly, our planet Earth is returning to normal?'

'That's nice to know. It will save us going to Sol-Newtown or Mars for cleansing every time we do interstellar travel without Micol,' George replied.

'Jerry and Miranda have been very busy organizing business at that end in preparation for our visit and the UN conference, and will be ready on time. I do believe, we should visit the outer federation worlds as soon as possible, but I would like you to select your own dates for that trip,' she said, with pencil, pad, and small computer in hand.

'Why don't we set aside three days for those visits and take along one of the big ships? Perhaps Martia's ship. Venusa's ship can continue with the building program on Mars. That way we can take almost everyone along with us - even Sarah and most of the Ancients. Please send an urgent message to Eden, notifying them of our intentions,' he replied.

'What do we do about Micol?' she asked.

'Yes. I see your point. He seems to have more experience in such matters than anyone else and doesn't like being left out of our adventures. Perhaps Ron might be able to assist us this time instead. Pity he is so large, makes it difficult for us to take him along on board, but he can always follow. Yes, he can follow in case we should need his assistance in an emergency. Anyway, Love, our visits in those systems are meant to be purely social. So I see little reason in taking him along this time. He can always be updated on our return and we can call him with H-Wave. Later, we can have special platforms erected on the sides of Venusa and Marcia for that purpose,' George replied.

'Is there anything else?' she asked.

'Yes. Just one more. I would like you to find me a suitable keyboard for Ron. You and little Clair must get used to using his facilities. Get one of the technicians to find a suitable interface,' he replied and she left. Then he pressed a few buttons on the new intercom that he had recently installed.

'Get me Andy, Please!' he commanded and not long afterwards Andy walked in, wearing combat fatigues.

'Sire! You asked for me?' he said, nervously saluting George in the process.

'At ease!'

'Please have a seat. I have observed your work-load for the next month or so and would like to give a little friendly advise. I think you will be very busy from now on with the intense training program that we've planned, both here and on Mars, and once the base there is completed it will be more or less a full time commitment for us. So I want you to settle down to some kind of routine, and get one of the young Andromedans to assist.'

'Yes, Sire! I was thinking along the same lines!'

'Can Joan organise your schedules and also manage Caefon Dome for you?'

'I'm sure she can!'

'In that case, if you have any problems in that department please let me know. You can always have more staff for computer assistance if you wish,' George advised.

'I don't see a major problem here, Sire, and what you have just mentioned is already on the cards. Joan is very good at that sort of thing and has been able to input a lot of data through her implants. She can work on it while she is asleep, or so she says. Something she calls Independent Parallel Processing, it was thought to her by Petra.'

'Nice to know!'

'I have another twenty recruits of mixed races and sexes to join us in a few days, so the program is now well on schedule,' Andy said.

'Are your Specials happy with the cramped conditions on grounds? They will have much more space on Mars, when the base there is completed,' George said.

Our new recruits can always spread a few more tents outside if necessary. Anyway, they are not meant to be on a picnic. Chad is also quite busy, and Warland is brimming with new recruits since his last Add. Those we have in training here are the best of the litter so far,' Andy replied, with a happy grin on his face.

'Seems, most of the young are joining in droves?' George said.

'My Sire, this is because many are worried for their futures and see our offer to be their only way out of an uncertain period in their lives. Many have also become concerned since the flooding of New York and Miami. Both cities with their tall buildings are presently beneath the waves, compliments of our latest hurricane. Sadly, not everyone escaped the waters this time,' Andy replied.

'Don't worry, Pal, one of these days the water levels of this planet will return to where it was a few hundred years ago. That will be after I get our Octan friends to station a Tetrion in space to reduce Solar radiation by about 20 percent for the poles to reform.'

'Tetrion, My Lord?'

'It's a large orbiting metallic net anchored in space to reduce Solar radiation for a period long enough for ice to reform in the northern and southern poles. It will reduce solar radiation and particles by about 43%,' George said.

'That should be an incredible feat of engineering!'

'I also want anti-meteor platforms and energetic magnatrons to divert dangerous radiation. When I am through, this will be one of the most perfect worlds within Osmaron!'

'Eat your heart out Eden!' Andy exclaimed.

'Anyway, changing the topic. I would like us to take along as many trained specials as we can on our next interstellar trip. I think we'll soon be visiting Eden, along with several distant federation worlds like Tarran, Polok and Lodor. Because of the nature of that trip, I only want your most responsible people along. Those that you think will be future leaders and you know the type I prefer. Keep me informed of any developments. That's all for now,' George said.

'Sounds great, Sire. I shall do my best,' he said, saluted as a soldier and left.

Little eight year old Clair was next to enter and knocked gently on the door three times.

'Can I speak with you, Uncle?' she asked, as she entered.

'Yes, my dear. Come here and sit down. Is everything all right with you?' he asked.

'Anne-Marie, Pamela, and Julie have gone shopping with Hercules and I am bored,' she replied.

'Why don't you do your lessons? That way you'll be able to write your own poems. You know, you've lost a lot of ground since your illness and I would like you to read and recite perfectly,' he said.

'But, Uncle, I can read perfectly already. Everyone tells me that I have to learn... to do something that I know I can do perfectly already,' she replied, in a defiant mood.

With that, he went towards the bookshelf and took out one of the religious books.

'Little Madam, begin reading from the top of page one hundred,' he said and handed her the book. She opened it at the page in question and began to read.

'And it came to pass, when Moses came down from mount Sinai with the two tablets of the testimony in Moses hand, when he came down from the mount,' she then closed the book but continued to read even with the book closed.

'That Moses knew not that the skin of his face shone by reason of his speaking with him...' she said, completing the paragraph.

'That is correct. When did you learn to read so perfectly?' he asked.

'I don't really know. I suppose it just happened. I just know I can do anything that I really want to do. Like a positive mental attitude. But it only happens with things like learning and information or finding out about new things,' she replied.

'That's incredible. In that case, could you tell me what's on page two hundred of this book without looking?' he asked.

'Yes, it's *'Earth ...'*

'Is that all?' she inquired. When he opened its pages to check, she was correct.

'You have the ability to know all things. I think you are a true psychic,' he said.

'Uncle, do you mean I am like a witch?' she asked, but he smiled.

'Not really. You are a special child of God and the Cosmos. Someone that will always guide mankind in times of trouble and those are not the qualities of a witch.'

'Yoo..pee! I am not a witch! I am not a witch!' She shouted, happily.

'Can you also tell good people from bad?' he asked.

'I get a feeling, but I do not like to probe. If I do, I feel guilty afterwards,' she replied.

'Yes, my dear. All you need to do is get a sense and if you detect evil, back away. Never follow danger around, or try and play with it. It always has a nasty sting in its tail,' he said.

'Do you enjoy living here with us?' he asked.

'Yes, Uncle. Here is much better than granddad's place, because he is seldom around to talk with me. But I always feel bored when they are out,' she replied.

'Well, whenever you feel like that you can always come and have a chat with me, if I am not too busy, that is. Why don't you visit Ron in the meditation room upstairs and ask him to run an adventure program on the virtual image projectors for you?' he said.

'Thank you very much, Uncle! Yoo..pee! ' she shouted with excitement and darted out of his office.

'I must get her a little pet or some interesting hobby to kill her boredom. She has such an active mind. Perhaps Ron might be good for her, with his vast knowledge of so many things. She can learn a lot from him, and he appears to have most of the answers,... that's assuming she doesn't already know those answers herself,' George said to himself, while continuing to enter data into his desk computer.

Cathy knocked on his door and entered.

'Darling, we have just received a 'YES' from Eden through Portalink. Sarah reckons they are well due for a visit to Tarran, Polok and Lodor, and Venusa can join Martia on her ship while Venusa's ship remains to complete the Martian program. Anytime during the next two weeks will be acceptable to them and I have made a list of possible dates for your perusal.'

'If you don't mind, I shall peruse after I am done with this new design,' he replied, while she observed the complex blueprint, but could not make heads or tails of it.

'Apparently, there is a problem near Polok with one of their stars. It's getting unstable, so they might need our assistance to evacuate some of their people with the big ships. Sarah thinks they might still have a few years before life there becomes too uncomfortable.'

'We can help! Next!'

'Venusa, has received knowledge of the landing of five giant federation ships on one of Lori III's moons. So I can only assume the surface preparations have begun for your special project... and lunch will be ready in fifteen minutes, Sir!' Cathy said, taking everything in her stride as usual.

'Come here!' he ordered.

'Make our visit for these three days, towards the end of next week and we can return via Eden.

'Contact Sarah. She can arrange it with Tarran, Polok and Lodor.'

'Will do!'

'Now, did you not worry for my safety in the Endohrian Cave?' he asked, pulling her towards him.

'I was a little worried, but had no sense of any immediate danger. These days I have tremendous faith and confidence in you. So please don't let me down,' she replied.

'You are definitely developing a sixth sense. Sometimes it's even stranger for me and most times even stranger than fiction. But I think after my final attack everything will fall into place and hopefully our lives should return to normal. I can't tell you in words how much I appreciate your dedication. You are my beautiful darling and I love you dearly,' he said, as he kissed her. But she tore herself away from his hold to continue her secretarial duties.

Later that week, George, Cathy, Andy and Joan, Hal and John visited Sol-Newtown. They were greeted by Jerry and Miranda who were spending time with Barry and Ann at their head office. They were to restructure Solarian Banking in line with George's plans and organise the forthcoming interplanetary Solarian trade fair.

Several mining franchises were being offered to many Fertilates who could now use screened Infilate labourers and operators. The almost dead robotic industry - made to run down by the lack of spare parts, specialist repairs and the servicing of equipment, was once again to be revived and many of those old avenues were being reopened. The wealthy Fertilates were taking the bate of almost total economic dependency on Solarian Banking. Such dependency would be a useful weapon in any future political struggle and George always liked to lay the traps early in the game.

On arrival within the massive Sol-Newtown dome, his subjects were overjoyed by his presence and virtually laid out the red carpet.

Sol-Newtown was the head office of Solarian Banking throughout the planet and although situated within the USA, was outside of its government's jurisdiction, with a signed charter and other agreements. Therefore, all their buildings were like foreign embassies and had virtually complete freedom from any type of interference by outside political systems.

He gave another one of his speeches and their psyche was once again fully charged, to carry on their labours with greater effort and enthusiasm.

CHAPTER 17

The Universal Healer

During his meditations George had an incredible idea that completely overwhelmed him. With excitement he immediately pressed the intercom button.

'Get Cathy and Andy to visit my study immediately!'

'Yes, Sire!'

'This is very urgent!' he barked and Parky communicated his urgent message to those concerned.

They nervously entered his study together, looking very apprehensive, and thinking he was on the verge of another of his unwelcomed attacks, but he was his lively self as usual.

'We are to return to Endoh's moon immediately. I would like to conduct a small experiment at that location to prove an important point and it cannot wait. Micol can take us back to the caves via Lori III. You will both be there in case I need you and there is no need for anyone else to join us,' he said and both gazed at him with astonishment.

'When do you want us to leave, Sire?' Cathy asked, strangely and politely.

'After I collect Ron... in ten minutes. We can have dinner on our return. It should only take a little while and both of you can come along in your present clothes. After all, we are not going on a picnic.'

'Ok!' Andy said, not quite knowing what the fuss was about.

'That's all for now, people!' he ordered, and they urgently left the room. Cathy had never seen George in such a strange mood before. He acted as a completely different person and his face shown powerful, with darker eyes and more marked outlines. His eyebrows and hair partly stood on end. Almost as if it had been highlighted by a make-up artist. He appeared to be possessed by a strange demon.

A little later they were in the ship Micol and awaiting transposition to the new place or places unknown.

'We are to visit Lori III's moon on-route, in order to assess progress there. Perhaps we can kill two birds with a single stone if my theories are correct,' he said.

Micol and his crew soon transposed to a position above Lori III's moon. Suddenly the large planet and several of its moons zoomed into focus with the relevant moon circled red on the large screen.

The Ship, Micol, transposed again and this time they were within the area scheduled for clearance and preparation.

The massive construction ships were still there, but the whole area was already cleared and its surface prepared. All of the giant earth diggers and movers had already returned to the transport ships and only a few thousand robots and androids remained outside, constructing a high security fence all around the large area. Even so, a security fence on such a remote outpost was not strictly required. Nevertheless it was part of their programming to complete the construction process.

'What a rate of production?' Andy exclaimed.

'How can they work at such an incredible speed, even weaving the thick metallic strands in the process as if it were wool?' he added.

George transmitted a thought to the master ship in question.

'My complements to you and your builders. You have completed a most satisfactory job. When will the fence be finished?' he asked.

'Within one hour, Master,' the construction ship replied.

George knew that the ship meant one hour in Lodorian time, which could have been somewhere within two point three hours, Earth time.

'Micol, can you give us a more precise estimate of completion?' he asked the ship.

'It will take them one-point-two hours, plus or minus 10 percent. I think we shall be on the safer side if we allow them one-point-five hours, Earth time,' he replied.

Once again George transmitted a thought to the leading ship.

'You are advised to lift off within the specified time of completion. You may however observe the moon's conversion from a safe distance in space. Can you comply?' he said.

'Yes, Master. I have already issued instructions to my teams to increase their effort by another 10 percent, but they are already working at full capacity,' the ship replied.

'In that case, I must leave you now,' he said.

It was almost noon at the area of the hunt on the mother planet below. Seeing that they had almost two hours of Earth time available to kill, Cathy asked if it was possible for them to visit the reptilian hunters and observe their progress. It was possible that Ooh-Kaa and his hunters had already arrived within the territories of the iguanas.

Micol began scanning the terrain for hunters and soon found a larger group moving in the same direction, but their markings were not of the same tribe and Cathy became worried.

'Do they have fights during these hunts and do they eat each other?' she inquired.

'It happens sometimes, out of jealousy, envy, greed and there are sometimes old tribal hatreds, natural enemies and scores to settle. Ah! Here they are... three miles towards the left, within the orange valley,' Micol said.

'What are they carrying?' Cathy asked.

'It appears to be their leader. Ooh-Kaa appears to be seriously wounded. He could have been mauled by one of the more ferocious iguanas that inhabit the lower plains,' Micol replied.

'Can we do anything to help?' she asked, but everyone remained silent as if anticipating the worst.

'No! He needs proper medical attention that can only be administered by a professional with a knowledge of his constituent parts. I am afraid, if he doesn't receive help soon, he will surely die. I also detect rhythms of impending failure within

his body,' Micol replied.

'Darling, can you please help?' Cathy asked, looking at George with those sympathetic and caring eyes as if begging for the life of one of her own children. She had seen him heal Miranda and then Clair and thought he could do the same in Ooh-Kaa's case. She pleaded until he just couldn't say no.'

'Ok...If we are to heal him, we are to do the job properly. So you should remain hidden here while I visit them in person,' he instructed in his powerful and changed voice.

He uttered a powerful thought to the strange casket and its cover slid open to reveal the cloak. He uttered another and the cloak flew through the air and fitted about his body as if by magic. Suddenly, his voice and features transformed into someone infinitely more powerful.

'I shall walk on air towards them, through the clouds,' he said.

Cathy and Andy were by now quite frightened and worried for his safety. Micol, not knowing George's true capabilities with that cloak, was already prepared, if necessary, to quickly capture his body in free fall through Lori III's dense atmosphere and higher gravitational pull.

Although still acquiring George's main features, Jull's complexion was slightly bluish. His lips and eyes were darker, with dense but shaped eyebrows, and he had become more massive and powerful.

Unhindered by anything in this universe, he walked through the thick wall of the ship and floated downwards towards the hunters. To Cathy and her companions, he appeared to be massless as he slowly descended like a light balloon, but in a controlled manner.

It was not long before the hunters observed the strange human figure, dressed in black but with no tail.

One of the hunters shouted. 'Dragons! Dragons!' in their language and they scattered, sacrificing poor wounded Ooh-Kaa to the so-called dragon god from hell. But his brave and caring younger son came forward to take his father's place.

'Please take me instead, for my father has suffered enough

already.' George understood every word he uttered. In his strange and powerful voice he began to speak in their tongue.

'Do not be fearful of me, little one. I have come to heal your father from his injuries in his moment of need,' Jull said.

With those words, the boy began to pray and the others observing him still alive in the presence of the dragon god gained courage and moved closer.

'Ooh-Kaa! I am Jull! You and your tribe have been chosen to fulfil many destinies on this world. For those reasons and others of love, I shall heal you and give your tribe greater powers in order to fulfil your ambitions and my wishes.
Your young son I shall bless for the future of your tribe,' he said.
Jull placed his gloved hand over the wound and closed his eyes. There was a strange glow and when he removed his hand the wound had vanished. It left behind the beautiful green and slightly scaled orange skin of the creature in that part of his body.

'Ooh-Kaa, arise!' he commanded, and to the amazement of all his hunters, he arose and shook his powerful tail as if in perfect health.

'Now little one. Come to me!' Jull commanded, and the little frightened creature went forward as a test of faith, placing his life in the hands of a powerful god.
'I shall call you Meradon. It is the name of a friendly world I saved in bygone times. I shall also give you the powers of vision in technology, so that one day your people may rule this world in the name of Jull.
'You and your people are never to visit the place you call the area of dragons that are beyond the Snake's Desert, for danger awaits you there. But all areas within this hemisphere is yours to take and rule with dignity, respect, and with the aid of the other tribes,' he said. Then he placed his hand over the little dinosaur's crinkled forehead and thought for a second. Then he withdrew his hand.

He moved away and with a single thought the place thundered and threads of energy leaped from his fingers towards the large facing rock-face overlooking the valley. The energies, like pens of fire melted and wrote into the rock-face the word *'Jull'* in Sunolingua, which although symbolic was unrecognisable to the reptiles. Then he descended upwards, into the clouds, and disappeared from their view and into the ship.

He issued another thought command and the cloak leaped from his body into the large trunk and the lid clipped into place. Cathy observing the whole episode of events was shocked and in tears when he arrived and the others could not believe their eyes.

'He has become a god!' Andy exclaimed and the others nodded in acknowledgement.

'What's all the weeping about?' he jested, while Cathy wiped her tearful eyes. Even the tough soldier, Andy, was severely disturbed by everything that had occurred. After that adventure, Micol had to update his memory banks on some of his more advanced concepts of dimensional physics. But after that adventure George had become his normal self again.

After normality had returned, Cathy could not help but kiss him. She had to show her gratitude for saving the life of one of her adopted life-forms and in such a spectacular manner. It was indeed Ooh-Kaa's lucky day, because what if George hadn't that mad urge to visit strange places that day.

'I don't know who I was worried for more, you or poor Ooh-Kaa. I thought you were possessed by one of those strange elemental demons when you left us,' she said, sympathetically.

'I am sorry, Love, but that cloak always brings out the worst in me. It transforms me into a dreadful warrior with the powers to destroy worlds and my body is transformed from flesh into some other cosmic substance that cannot be affected by anything in this universe. But it's all me, although I can't explain its modus operandi at this time.'

'Stranger and stranger?' Andy murmured.

'You know, it's like one of the dreams Clair had about that strange elevator. I felt a similar sensation of utter power when I walked on the clouds and floated down through the atmosphere.'

'Look, Darling, they are building an altar out of mud and are still praying. Now you have really started a new religion. Perhaps later we can teach them Senoism,' Cathy said, humorously.

'Yes, Love, and what better way to teach them moral values and ethics. Such moral concepts are necessary for all Solarians, young and old alike. Let's check the moon and carry out the remainder of our mission,' he said, as Micol transposed, leaving Ooh-Kaa and his hunters still dancing around one of their newly learnt lightening fires with spears in their hands and chanting: 'Jull! Jull! Jull!....'

CHAPTER 18

Stellar convergence

When they arrived back on Lori III's moon the large construction ships were getting ready to leave, so they waited until all ships were out of visual detection range before transposing to Endoh's Moon.

After arrival on Endoh's Moon he gave more specific instructions to Micol, The Ship, while the others prepared for any eventuality by wearing their special environmental suits.

'Please make me a list of all stars near the nucleus of this galaxy, with an equivalent mass and lifespan of our sun, and circle all those that are inhabited,' he said. Micol searched through his navigational charts and records. He displayed a list of stars on his large screen for the benefit of his crew. However, that same information was also relayed to their brain implants in an easily understood and digestible format.

That information was always available, because the whole galaxy had been charted by the Plorans and reviewed every millennium during their stock taking program. During that time certain worlds were reclassified, but other more sensitive items were constantly checked and updated. The ship, Micol, always had access to that data through The Greater Mind.

The Mind, sometimes called The Higher or Greater Mind, not to be confused with the Greater Cosmic Mind, was the Grand Lord's collective consciousness and a form of virtual space within another dimension, where all important knowledge was stored. Only his chosen few like the Shadites could access that knowledge and Micol was one. He was not just an inter-dimensional ship, but had been adapted by the Grand Lord millennia ago to assist his chosen few in the war against the Javols.

After leaving a small H-Wave focussing device George had previously collected from Endoh's cave. The conversion of that part of Lori III's moon was ready for a new installation.

'We must transpose within the cave if I am to use the suit,'

George said and Micol immediately transposed within Aron's cave. While wearing Aron's Cloak he communicated through the cave's master computer and transmitted a thought to the locator on Lori III's moon. Very soon he could see both areas transposed onto each other within his mind.

He sent another thought and there were more energy discharges as the base duplicated itself on the distant moon of Lori III. Even the creatures on the world below took to their caves and burrows in fright of impending disaster. But nothing of a catastrophic nature occurred and the brilliant glow of fire on the moon soon died away in the blackness of the night.

He then floated through the thick wall of the specially secured and screened cave, onto the surface of Endoh's moon. There he remained for a while, meditating on the dim neutron star, once their brightest jewel in the sky, but now a sphere of compressed blackness among its energetic neighbours. Within its sphere, a teaspoon of matter would have weighed many tons.

'I must make this theory of mine work... and send a thought to Micol... 'Be prepared to transpose my wife and others back to Lori III on the first sign of any danger. Now, please send me data of the closest and most healthiest star within the neighbourhood. It must be of a slightly higher mass, making allowances for any matter lost during the nova. It should not be supporting life,' he thought, and Micol sent all the data required, which Jull held within his implant.

'I must visualise both stars within the fifth,' he said loudly to himself in deep concentration, until both stars appeared to be in identical positions in space. Then he shouted with his hands outstretched in the rarefied atmosphere, as if challenging the whole universe.

'Transform to fifth and change positions! Transfer mass, rotation and inertias, and remain in your new positions!' He cried at the image now appearing within his universal mind. After a while there was a glow of light within the neutron star that expanded and exploded into incredible brilliance, showering the whole system with radiant energy within the electromagnetic spectrum. It was as if the whole system suddenly became alive. There was no explosion, just a transposition of stellar objects.

'**It works! It works! It works! Bloody hell, it works!**' he shouted with excitement.

'**So dimensional transference on a cosmic scale does work through the Cosmic Mind!**' he yelled. Even as the most fearful warrior Jull, he was very happy at having such incredible success and power.

Now at Endoh's moon close to the nucleus of Osmaron he went back to the cave to remove his cloak, still not quite believing his achievements. When he entered Micol his two companions were still there patiently awaiting his return.

'Did you have success with your experiments?' Andy asked, nervously. Whenever George experimented, Andy always expected a fearful outcome, but was now faced with an anticlimax by his quite normal entrance. That was because they knew nothing of the transformation of the neutron star. Their ship, Micol, was almost completely shielded from the outside by the effective screening of the walls of the cave, which had been designed by the ancient Patriarchs to prevent probing by external scanners.

'Success?' he cried, in response to Andy's question.

'I have just had one of the greatest successes of my entire life, barring my dear beloved, here.'

'Have you?' Cathy inquired, innocently.

'My Dear, my experiment was successful!'

'What was that, Darling?' she inquired.

'I believe this cave to be one of the safest places in the universe. In here, not even Micol can take a peep outside to observe the beauty of this system. Yet, something worries me, because I was able to communicate with him, even through these impervious walls. Perhaps I can now communicate to anyone or anything, through any media or substance and over any distance,' George replied.

When Micol transposed to the surface of the Endoh's moon, he displayed the bright new star with its previously dead system on his large screen. The dead world beneath - so many years held frozen in the coldness of spaced - boiled into life. Its lighter gasses began to melt and disperse within its previously thin atmosphere.

The incredible spectacle was unbelievable. They could clearly observe the damaged surface of that Endoh planet, once more given a new lease of life. Even Micol found difficulty in believing his sensors.

'Darling, how could you transform a complete star?' Cathy asked, but he nodded in an uncertain manner and declined to answer. Later, he tried to explain the process of stellar conversion as best he could.

'My Dear, the long and short of it is, that it takes zero energy to shift an object of equivalent mass and inertia from one inertial frame to another, or from one place to another through the fifth dimension.

'Energy is only required to overcome friction while moving on a surface or through mater. When overcoming inertia in a given mass, it is stored as a form of potential energy by virtue of its momentum. By removing both of these drawbacks, one can shift any object to anywhere in the universe once their masses and inertia levels are replicated.

'Portals on the other hand, work on a slightly different principle.

'When two identical objects - like an electron and a positron - come from the same parent mother particle and with the same causal history... their fifth dimensional vectors are identical, although opposite. So if one is... say... a mile away, undergoes some change in force vectorization, the other at a distance will be imprinted upon within the fifth, and can undergo a reversed order transformation to move oppositely.

'Therefore, any two empty and identical inertial frames are raw, historically, and to all intents and purpose are at the same points within the universe. That is, until matter or energy in some other form pays a visit, then one of those twin frames acquire historical significance, and from that moment on becomes a separate frame with a new historical component. Hence, one of the reasons for an expanding universe. However, every square centimetre of space within our universe has something, hence the notion of a space-time boundary. Anyway, that is what separate objects in space means.

'Portals only eliminate the space vector, in much the same way as identical twins can sometimes remotely feel each other's

pains. However, in a saturated universe like ours, matter cannot be created nor destroyed, if the universe is to maintain its own stable space-time boundaries. However, if I somehow could mislead the cosmic system into thinking that I was on Earth instead of here, in the centre of our galaxy, when I re-materialised I would be placed on Earth at no energy loss to the system.

'Does it make any sense to you?' he said.

'No! And I can't see a 5th dimension anywhere?' she replied.

'The 5th dimension encloses the forth, it's everywhere, but timeless.'

'So those stars must be almost identical for the process to work?' she inquired.

'Yes! That is why I asked Micol to make me a list of all Sol-type stars and their relevant data; because they live the longest and behave in a more stable manner over their relatively longer lifespan,' he added.

'I did not understand any of it and in all probability may never,' Joan said in all truthfulness.

'It's truly remarkable, even though like Joan I'm equally dumbfounded by it all,' Cathy exclaimed.

'And me!' Andy said.

By a miracle of miracles his incredible cosmic powers had created a new base in the Lori system by copying one of Endoh's moons. That system was close to Earth and just above OohKaa's world. Therefore, he intended to use that more local moon in future when transposing to Triangulum and later Andromeda.

They would be required in later years for the real wars against the Javols. With all that power at his disposal he could easily have taken a complete world apart by channelling hot plasma from anyone of Endoh's stars unto those worlds. But such powers would not be required immediately. Nevertheless he would have had to convert the other moons in Triangulum and Andromeda to use them for that purpose.

They were back home in time for a late supper. Andy and others of his gang could not understand or even interpret what they had seen into words, and the concept was almost too much for any normal human to contemplate.

'Anyone, that could alter a star like the biblical Joshua, could in no way be just human and must have some pretty good connections way up above, 'Andy thought.

With those new powers, George could help rebuild a dying universe by replacing waning stars in many threatened inhabited systems. He was now a cosmic saviour and also a saviour of the Cosmos.

Since his arrival, the universe had changed and that newer form of order was just another stage within cosmic evolution and his presence signified a new era had begun.

CHAPTER 19

The main Federation worlds

It was indeed a very labourious task, preparing Martia's ship for her visit to the three distant worlds. All provisions and equipment had to be transported from Earth to Mars via portals. Since the time was not yet right for any of the great ships to make an appearance on Earth they had to do it the hard way. Therefore, the first two days were spent preparing and transporting everything, from facial filters to refrigerated suits, to Admin dome before they could be loaded unto the ship by androids.

'You know, Cathy, there is no need to take all this foodstuff and equipment all the way to Mars in order to fumigate them before taking them on board Martia's ship. We can get much better stuff when we arrive on Eden and it's already bug free,' George said, but Cathy and the other women insisted they took along their own.

Although many of the items could have been produced within the great ships, Cathy and other gang members always preferred the equipment and resources to which they were accustomed. That was always the way they preferred their food, drinks, fashionable clothes and other items like cinematics and music. All steeped in Earth's traditions and the more local Solarian culture. Therefore all such items of importance were always kept close at hand.

After all, some things were beyond technology, or so they thought and gave very little leeway for technological change in those more culture-based directions. Nevertheless when they visited Eden to collect Sarah and others, even more items would be added to the ship's log for which they would be allowed a greater choice.

George thought of leaving the less important members of the mansion's staff behind. However, Parky, Hercules and the chief cook were to be included on the trip. They could be useful on board and learn from the unique experience of interplanetary travel. He also decided to take Madeline and most of her family along. There were also those friends from other parts of the planet.

Ulysses would remain behind to keep an eye on the mansion. Anyway, Hercules could always update Ulysses memory banks on his return. George wanted everyone to be together on this first real interstellar trip by ship, and invited little Clair and her uncle Donald Fraser, the President of the USA, along as his special guests. Hal and John was also invited and would join them later.

'I wonder if Donald will be able to tear himself away from his important duties at this time for just three days,' George thought, while completing his lengthy list of passengers.

He soon got on the Coms to Donald's office and when his receptionist heard the name George Peterson, she immediately buzzed his personal secretary and he was connected to Donald's hands-free monitor.

'Mister President, everyone in the mansion are going on a very long and exciting interstellar trip and wondered whether you could make it, since your wife and other members of your family will also be joining us. If you are interested, please visit urgently to confirm. It's very important to all concerned that you come along,' George said and Donald pressed a button to reply.'

'Ah! I knew it was you. Thanks for calling, George!'

'Is it very safe for my wife and kids?'

'It's safe as houses and there are no hurricanes and earthquakes in space, only fast moving objects and we are immune!' George replied.

'In that case, expect me on that trip. The White House and Congress is a little quiet at this time giving me a few windows,' he replied.

'It will be great having you along!'

'In that case I'll be free in the next two days, so expect my visit then, interstellar trip or no interstellar trip. My vice president Pamela can take over in my absence,' Donald replied. He assumed George was kidding him about the interstellar trip.

'When you arrive, Pal, you will see I am quite serious regarding the trip,' George replied and Donald was even more curious.

'Anyway, say hello to my wife and kids for me and see you soon,' Donald said and hung up.

As usual, they always refrained from giving too many details on the Coms, in case the line was tapped. George would explain the program to him in more detail after his arrival.

When Donald arrived the following day, George had a long chat with him about his parents and the tricks his father used to pull with his many disguises when he went to distant places. He also mentioned the use of lookalikes and android replicas that were designed to copy a human in every detail, and could deceive even the most critical and scrutinising of security systems. When he heard his parents were also on the list, the President was soon convinced that he had to take that trip.

'Sounds incredible!'

'It will be the greatest experience of your life!'

'Where on Earth are we going for this trip to be so important to you, George?' Donald asked.

'I have news for you, Pal. It's not on Earth, not even within our Solar System. Not even within the Solarian System. It's far, far away!'

'And you are not kidding?'

'Never! You remember once Meron gave a lecture, in which he mentioned the distant worlds, Polok and Lodor? Well, we are visiting those two along with Tarran and a few other very distant worlds that form the main members of The Solarian Federation. Most are about five thousand light years away.'

'I thought all that talk was to do with Meron trying to get rid of a few insistent reporters?' Donald replied.

'Just wait and see!'

'Anyway, how do we get to such places and how long will the trip take?' Donald asked, with an air of the ridiculous in his manner and worried frown incase George was right and he returned late for office.

'Not long! I have two federation ships the size of small cities parked on Mars. They can transpose through those distances in under fifteen minutes, despite their mass.'

'Transpose?'

'They travel mainly through the fifth dimension,' he said, leaving the president dumbfounded.

'Whatever you say, Pal, we'll try. But I don't want to get back for Christmas. Remember, I am still President of the USA and this is not the best of times for a lengthy escapade,' he replied.

'From what I heard, your vice president is quite capable!'

'Ok, I am won over! I'll talk to her, in case I'm later than planned!' Donald replied.

Later on that day Andy was called into his study.

'I want you to brief your guys on space regulations. We shall soon arrive on advanced worlds like Polok and Lodor and I want everyone that comes along to be receptive and collect some of that important space culture. I also want them to closely observe how the others live. So see what you can do with your company.'

'Will try!'

'You only have a couple of days to make them shipshape!' George insisted. He wanted no political problems on that trip.

'Yes, Sire. I shall make sure my team are as tame as bloody lambs!' Andy continued, saluted and was away.

'What a guy. He always takes his assignments so seriously and his wife Joan is just the same. Must be all that military training. Jerry and Miranda should be joining us shortly. I wonder when those two are getting married?' he spoke aloud to himself.

Wednesday morning couldn't have arrived soon enough. Many had sleepless nights in anticipation of the trip. Little Clair was most excited about their visit to planet Eden. That was when she learnt she was going on a special trip that included Eden as their first port of call.

George decided to leave Micol, the Andromedan ship, behind on call, including the cloak which he had left on board Micol. For security and other reasons of safety, Micol seemed to be the most suited place for that dangerous cloak of Aron. Anyway, Micol could be updated with their experiences on their return,

The mansion's portal could only take twenty-five passengers at a time, so several trips of sixteen were made.

The President and others, who had never seen a portal before, could not believe the time taken for their trip to Mars and even more unbelievable, were the massive ships. They were over five-hundred metres high and about two kilometres long.

The President suddenly realised that George was not kidding and he was dealing with a technology far beyond anything that he or any of his colleagues could ever visualize.

'Think of the future possibilities for Earth if one of those ships could travel from there to Mars in the blink of an eye,' Donald thought to himself.

On arrival, they used the local portal and were soon on board Martia's ship. Then they were guided to their living quarters, which were in the same area. Both ships had hundreds of levels, so each passenger was given a special ID card for getting about.

Soon George brought them together in one of the large conference rooms close to Martia's Mind Room.

'Friends, we are going on a long and exciting trip to some distant worlds within our galaxy, Osmaron, or should I say, a luxurious cruise to several systems within what we call The Federation of Worlds.

'Although some of you are not yet acquainted with certain facts regarding our new federation, Earth is also a member, although not active at this time. However, plans are now afoot to rectify that failing on our part.

'Let me show you what I mean on the main screen. This is Osmaron, our galaxy, as seen from Andromeda and here is our present position within what we call the Solarian Galactic Arm. As you see, that arm spirals a long distance from the nucleus within Osmaron and is a lot longer than the diameter of our galaxy. But it is only one of several arms.

'The one directly ahead of us we call the Polokan arm, loosely known as Polok and the one towards our rear we call Kryton, sometimes referred to as the Tarranian arm, which contains the system of Tarran. The Polokans call our galactic arm by the name of Beyond-Fille.

'If the small orange circle represents our present position, the blue circles correspond to the systems of Polok, Lodor and Tarran.

'Although members of the Federation, they do not lie within the Solarian arm. Solaria only relates to our own single galactic arm that includes Eden and local worlds like Lori III.

'Both remote systems are about five thousand light years away in opposite directions and we can complete the trip to Tarran in under fifteen minutes. However, we are to make Eden our first

port of call to collect some more passengers and supplies.

'Unlike the little Andromedan ship we call Micol, there is no need to return to bunks during the transposition process. However, it is always recommended to remain still during the process, because extremely quick movements can place one outside of the inertial frame of the ship, leaving one in deep space with disastrous consequences. However, such accidents are quite unlikely on a large ship like this one, even when technologies of the past did not prevent it, and it does. So take it from me, you are completely safe.

'The transposition sequence is made to oscillate in such a manner as to make the whole process almost invisible to us.

'Finally, I have a list of those to be transformed before the trip. While Andy calls your name, please move to one side and you can follow him to the place in question when the list is exhausted.

'Please enjoy your trip,' he said, and went over to Andy to hand him the list, then he rejoined Cathy, Jerry and Miranda.

Andy soon began to read the list in first names only, except where surnames were identical.

'Dr. Hal Seaton, Dr John Simmons, Pamela, Anne-Marie, Donald, Clair....Professor Jean-Claude Chairmowich, Jeremy...

'Captain Norton, Captain Jones, Captain Webster...' he continued until the list was completed, then he took them along to the transformation room. They followed like lambs to the slaughter, not knowing what to expect.

'I have orders from the boss to give each one of you the latest and most advanced in brain implants. The process is not painful. I've had one fitted to myself recently and it works a dream. It will increase your mental potentials by at least twenty times and gives you several doctors in the process,' Andy advised. Then he observed the worried looks on their faces. Those poor people couldn't refuse their leader George anything, including their lives. To them it was like a type of baptism.

They were each stripped naked, with all jewellery removed. Their bodies were then completely scanned for metallic and other non biological parts and implants. Then they were each placed into the first of two chambers.

Those casket-like chambers stood in pairs against a circular but sloping wall. Their tops were furthest away from the centre of the room. There was a large pulsating light in the middle of the ceiling and the floor had many different patterns and circles. Coming from behind the rear wall of the forty-eight pairs of caskets were numerous tubes.

The top of the circular wall was filled with many blinking blocks similar to those used for controlling Micro Robots.

It was like entering one of Count Dracula's lairs and the images made them shiver with fear, but they were brave and would never let their team down. Those caskets could have been some type of portal. But it was apparent that many different technologies were used in their construction. They had the ability to repair or even change a body to one of an alien type. Both life-forms would have to have been of an equivalent mass and their conversion was by some complex genetic equation. All carried out under computer control.

At least, in their case they were only going to be transformed to themselves, with slight age reduction and increased health, which was its simplest mode of operation. However they would be given the Life Saver Implants, which was a small device fitted inside the brain. Life-Savers were mainly used for re-creating their bodies in case of fatal accidents. The brain implants gave them the powers of linking minds together during communication or as a highly complex computer, that would increase their mental powers by at least a factor of twenty during military operations. It could also improve their training by placing them into Virtual Worlds where warfare could be enacted at great speed and to a high degree of realism without harm to the players. During that state of operation, movement and decisions could be speeded up hundreds of times.

And that was not all, the life-saver device could transmit a special signal to any transposer or available portal, through which their bodies could be re-created within a period of one-point-six days after accidental death. Hence, the name Life Saver. That way, accidental death or aging was almost impossible within Eden and now, for members of The Gang.

They had the option of transforming to a younger self every twenty years or so, but only bodies of an equivalent mass could be so transformed, although the computer could be flexible with height and build. For those not requiring the more extreme transformation via the Megotrons, there were also a serum and several kinds of age reducing capsules, to be taken daily over a period of time.

After they had received their implants, and were somewhat relaxed after their bath, George began to speak once again.

'My People, we have to fill some of our tanks with Hydrogen and a few other gases from one of the outer planets. This is payment to Polok II for previous supplies to Eden and was due since the evacuation of Caefon.

'If any of you wish to know more about stock control procedures within the Federation and elsewhere within Osmaron, there are several books and computer records in the main library on the subject. They were prepared and written by Sintra and Meron under the guidance of her majesty, Empress Sarah. Those two great people will be joining us from Eden onwards, so you may ask them questions during one such meeting, at which time we shall no doubt be further educated on that topic.

'I have arranged for the distribution of small personal computers to each of you. There are also Brain Implant trainers that are linked to Martia's ship and her main libraries, so please use them in conjunction with your implants to find your way around. Through them you may learn most of what you wish to know, including many exciting virtual games. Please collect them on your return and remember, they are a personal gift from my wife, Cathy, and myself.

'You may consider this day the first in your new lives. This is the day of your rebirth, may we always celebrate this day to perpetuity.

'Now, while we are all ready, we may depart to one of Jupiter's moons to fill our tanks before transposing to Eden,' he said.

Then there was a small flash of light, followed by a strange creeping sensation and on the screen was the large disc of Jupiter.

'We have landed on one of her moons. Perhaps Ganymede, but I am not sure?' asked Cathy.

'It is Ganymede!' Little Clair replied, in a most positive manner, while continuing to suck her straw, which could hardly locate any more dregs from the bottom of the small milk carton from which she was drinking. Milk was something that she had acquired a taste for since her illness.

'What a strange child!' Cathy said to herself. But Clair pretended she didn't hear her comments and continued sucking at her straw in as noisy a manner as possible, until there was absolutely nothing left to suck.

The ship filled her compressed tanks and soon transposed to Eden.

Once again George took the stand.

'People, this is a completely different world to Earth and is considered by myself and others to be the jewel in the crown. Here, there are no bees that sting, flies and mosquitos to carry disease, and absolutely no disease. As a matter of fact, it's the land of the gods and even more perfect than the Eden mentioned in the bible. So I want you to treat this and all other worlds we encounter with utmost respect.

'Although you may go sightseeing, I want no intimidation of their fairylike creatures or indeed any of their life-forms. They are to be respected as all intelligent life, with homes and families to care for. Decontamination is automatic on a ship like this during transposition, so don't worry about such matters.

'Eden's indigenous life are independent life-forms like you and I, and deserve their freedom and privacy. So just leave things as beautiful as they are.

'That's all I have to say for now on that topic,' George said and walked away looking more like a master of ceremonies than a Supreme Lord of Osmaron. Anyway, he knew all his people were lovers of the Earth and were very respective of all life. Yet, he was not quite sure of Andy's new recruits, even though they were well trained.

After their arrival on Eden, many were further tested for traces of certain types of bacteria and disinfected before disembarking to safe areas to stretch their legs while the ship waited for Sarah and her colleagues. Several androids were ported from Martia's ship to assist in the loading of supplies and in another hour they were once again on their way. This time to Tarran, the so-called planet of cats.

CHAPTER 20

Tarran - Planet of Cats

Tarran was known to many as the planet of cats and it lived up to its feline name in every respect. Nevertheless, to many of its visitors it was well respected as one of the most hostile worlds in Galaxy Osmaron. Not many of the most hardened human soldiers would survive for long within its plains and deserts. If they were not being preyed upon by bat-vultures or ferocious monsters the climate would soon get them. Its primary star was many times the size of sol, Earth's sun, and it was very unstable and erratic in its oppressive output. Its secondary star was slightly smaller than Sol, very young and stable, but more distant.

Survival on that world was wrought with many dangers and as a result its advanced life was extremely tough and vicious. Its cat people were probably the best survivors and hunters in the whole of Osmaron. Yet, they were built like humans, even though resembling and behaving more like cats than humans.

Over the years that particular species had evolved to fill many niches and as a result there were every imaginable type, including cat-horses, cat-dogs, cat-tigers and even cat-cats. With every animal a thousand fold more cunning and ferocious than any equivalent cat on Earth. That world was truly one of the harshest in the galaxy and to have evolved thus far in time had been a great evolutionary success for all those species.

Queen Bawaki of the Marawi Clan was now a fully fledged grade two Shadite and had taken the reigns from her mother after her retirement some forty Earth years before. Even so, being a Shadite and servant of the Grand Lord of our part of the Universe, including our local galaxies, meant she had to go on special missions to distant parts and local galaxies. During that time they would change their forms to match those of the inhabitants of their destination worlds.

She had in the past decades completed the major part of their new city, Ziona. That enormous task was undertaken with the aid of the Federation ships and that most fabulous city was built on the shows of the Sadana Sea. The city of Ziona was based on an Earth-type design and included air-conditioning and other refinements for comfort and work. She had learnt the ways of mankind since her days on Earth about half a century before. At that time she was in human form and a senior member of Sarah's household.

Ziona was soon to be considered the gem of Tarran and trade between her clan and others bloomed. Soon, even the rich northerners visited her tribe to sign trading agreements for the new technologies, and many used the city as their head offices of state.

There was at last peace and freedom amongst the clans. Even their warlike and tempestuous Zadi neighbours had formed part of that trading federation with open borders to all. The old disputes of the past were no more and Ziona was considered more like the capital city of all Tarranians. Bawaki had finally achieved her dreams and goals of bringing the tribes together for the common good.

At long last, waters were being pumped from the almost dead oceans, now lying well beneath the sun-baked sands. For sunbaked and storm-blown they were, within a system that was driven by two stars with the resultant hash radiation and erratic gravitational changes. The stellar binary so formed placed the younger star some distance away which moved like another giant planet in a highly elliptical orbit. Although relatively far away it still made significant changes to the system.

The combination of both created havoc on the planet's orbit and weather pattern. But that was not all. Their sun was also very old and dying, with a large yellowish disk, and orange hallo, multiple boiling sunspots and lots of turbulent heat. Luckily for its life-forms, the planet of Tarran was still young and with a hot molten metallic core and thick ozone layer, which gave rise to an intense magnetic field. The single factor of an intense magnetic field alone might have saved the planet's atmosphere from being literally blown away by the powerful star's continuous outpourings of dangerous radiation and CMEs.

At present the mulloks' hunters visited the desert in LPD ships to hunt crustaceans and other creatures at their leisure. However, many other industries, including mineral mining and farming had begun since the introduction of bio-engineered plants and other special equipment from Eden. Heavy industry was always banned from such federation worlds and even their limited mineral mining program would be transferred to other dead worlds when they had acquired the relevant technologies.

Gone were the days of the dangerous spring hunts and the celebration of the hunter's return. Nevertheless, many still trekked those dangerous places for fun, because that week in spring had since been made a public holiday. Even so, mass hunting of life-forms were now restricted and many endangered species were cared for by many.

The ship landed within the new space port at the outskirts of the city and after decontamination they were transferred from Martia's ship to Bawaki's palace through private portals.

Because of security reasons, secret portals were only installed within her palace. She didn't want her previously very primitive people to advance too quickly.

'To those of you who have not yet visited Tarran, this is known as the planet of cats. They are without doubt the most ferocious life-forms in the galaxy and would make our lions and tigers appear like little playful pussycats by comparison. They can tear and dismember a human body in seconds, so please respect its inhabitants. And captains, please keep a tight leash on your men,' George said.

After he had given his instructions in his usual manner, they were all to visit Bawaki's palace.

On arrival through portals, they waited patiently for Bawaki's presence before proceeding any further.

She and two of her much smaller male councillors soon appeared from a concealed entrance. The males were half the size of the females who were the most dominant sex.

Cat-women stood a little under two metres tall, and were covered completely from head to toe with fine furry hair. Their faces, almost like those of household cats, were full of character, with many markings of grey, brown and black. They also carried two thick and long whiskers which remained curled in a precisely maintained fashion. It was thought they could be extended for nocturnal hunting.

Their hands and legs were also similar to humans, although slightly webbed, with sharp claws and their feet were more human, although hairy. Those lower toe claws were trimmed to allow the use of thick leather sandals and sleeves that protected those areas from scaly desert snakes and other smaller but poisonous predators. They were bipeds in the truest form, but the males tended to use all-fours more frequently than the females.

Cat people had no tails and held a similar form and upright posture to Earth's humans, although capable of using all-fours for high speed retreat to escape an enemy.

The males being just half the size of the females were considered the most docile and inferior members. But presently they were treated with much more respect since becoming highly technological. It was said that the females on Tarran had enough aggression for both sexes.

Despite their ferocity and fierceness, they could be considered human, with similar emotions, feelings, aspirations and desires. However, they never killed wantonly.

Because Tarran was one of the harshest of inhabited worlds within the galaxy, with deserts of sand where oceans once lay. The whole planet was infested with giant scaly monsters, giant sand spiders, scaly sand vipers, bat-vultures and numerous other types of predators. Those also included its most common desert crustaceans, each preying on the other for mutual survival and here, only the toughest survived.

Since Tarran became a member of the Federation, many of its industrious males had been sent to Eden. While there they were thought the latest technologies and on their return began putting some of their ideas into practice. Since then they had constructed new irrigation systems and started building new machines and equipment which their tribe could sell to others.

As her people became wealthier, their living standards increased significantly. Yet, they had a very long way to go by Earth's standards. Queen Bawaki had observed the similarities between both species and in so doing had preferred Earth's and its not too advanced technologies for her people.

Despite all those changes, Tarran was not the place where Earth's humans could go on casual walkabouts. Its noon temperature was sometimes as high as fifty-six degrees centigrade and many humans would soon faint under those conditions, even in the shade.

Bawaki had quite a reception prepared for her guests and the whole palace was pleasantly lit and air-conditioned. One had the impression she felt uncomfortable with the lower temperatures in her present cat-form, because she constantly wore the thick leather jacket she brought from Earth decades ago. That was when she lived with Sarah at the manor, but at that time she had transformed through the Mind into a beautiful human female.

Presently, she was back in her original cat form and wearing her beautiful jewelled headband. It was a present given to her by the Grand Lord. Around her waist was a tightly fitting Lodorian translating belt, for communicating to those without brain implants. She also had the usual implants and could communicate telepathically to those similarly transformed without the need for translation. That feature was already built into her implants.

'Lady Sarah!' she cried with excitement through the communicator and then rushed up to embrace her in a most gentle manner.

'You look beautiful as ever and so does your husband. I sometimes wish I was back in Solaria, but I had to take care of my people here during this time of change. Where is your younger son, George... the one I am hearing so much about these days?' she inquired. Sarah then pointed to him and he came forward to shake her paw.

'A very handsome male and you are his wife?' she asked, turning to Cathy.

'Yes! And I am very pleased to meet you, Lady Bawaki,' Cathy replied, with a slight curtsy. They always addressed each other in such a manner and on equal terms during such visits.

'I am looking forward to spending a little time with you and your people,' he replied through his implant with sincerity and she suddenly realised he could understand her every thought directly.

They introduced the others and followed her into a spacious

sitting room. Earth drinks and snacks were served while she caught up with news and gossip.

'A supply ship visits us once a month from Solaria, so we can put our paws on most products from Earth and Eden, including Whisky, Vodka and other alcoholic beverages,' she said.

George carefully observed the decor and materials used and couldn't tell any difference between them and any posh hotel on Earth. Everything in that room, including the chandelier, was designed from some Earthly pattern.

'George! Do you like my palace?'

'Very much! It's almost like my home on Earth,' he replied.

' Most of the materials you observe are manufactured here by our males, but to Earth's designs.'

'I love it so much! I have brought you a large painting for that wall over there,' he replied.

'You have?'

'Yes! It's one of my favourites. I think you will love it as much as I have!' he said.

'Thank you very much. I will be very appreciative!' She replied.

'When I lived on Earth, at Madam Sarah's place, I spent lots of time collecting information on such designs.'

'You have?'

'Yes, I now have a library of such designs. Although I love Eden and its very advanced technologies, I find Earth's designs more suited to our requirements,' she said.

'I understand and like the idea very much. Perhaps we should create a direct link between libraries. Perhaps a main Federation Library where all such designs can be shared. I shall see to it!' he replied.

'You will? This is a fantastic idea!' Bawaki could not be more pleased.

'There is another matter that concerns me about your world, however. Perhaps you could visit me and my wife in private later today to discuss it,' he said.

'If it's as important as you think, I shall visit you after supper,' she replied and continued talking to Sarah.

Later that day she visited George and Cathy in their plush suite.

'Here I am!' Bawaki said, and he sat her down to explain his ideas.

'Queen Bawaki, how would you like to exist on a Tarran with large oceans and a beautiful stable sun?' he said.

'That would be my greatest dream, if it was at all possible,' she replied, but Cathy interrupted.

'He changed a neutron star at Endoh's moon-base into a normal star like Earth's. We and The Ship, now called Micol, witnessed the entire miracle. Do not underestimate his powers, Bawaki, for he is Jull the Supreme Patriarch,' she said and Bawaki was astonished by that knowledge.

'Would such an incredible transformation cause inconvenience and discomfort to our other life-forms within their varying habitats?' she asked, with concern.

'Only a little and they will readily adapt in a reasonable time. The temperature will gradually drop to around forty-five degrees centigrade and the atmosphere will begin to shed most of its accumulated moisture in the form of rain. However, you will retain your binary system, with its lesser turbulence, although tenfold more stable and pleasant from your point of view than it is today. After many millennia your world will slowly return to paradise, giving all its indigenous life-forms enough time to adapt. Anyway, most life-forms undergo extreme cold at night. After those changes the climate will be less turbulent and extreme.'

'I am all for paradise, even if we have some inconvenience for a while,' she replied.

'Your main star is highly erratic with a relatively short lifetime remaining. After my transformation it will be removed and will not be in this part of the galaxy. So when it becomes a nova no lasting or serious damage will ever be done to Tarran from any of its future positions in space,' he added.

'Will this process of transformation take a long time to complete?' she asked.

'No!' he replied. 'Only about a few minutes and I can increase the rotational rate of your planet at the same time, so that a day on Tarran will be equivalent to twenty-four hours, as on Earth, if you like?' he asked.

'I never thought anything so incredible could be done and here you are discussing the remodelling of a complete world as if you were God carving a live statue from the heavenly stars,' she replied, as if in a daydream.

'If you can and there is no great risk involved to my world? You have my full permission to do it, even without the other tribes consent,' she replied.

'Great! I shall send for Micol. He will love the intrigue. We can complete that task at sunset. That way you can admire a brand new sun at dawn tomorrow,' he said. She remained thunderstruck. Hardly believing in any of his last words uttered. They left to join the others.

Micol, the ship, received his message and suddenly appeared on a local lawn, thus creating an uproar among the female palace guards. When nothing of a threatening nature ensued, they stopped their screeching and settled down.

By now everyone was gazing at the large object in question that was parked on the lawn in front of the palace. There the small ship stood on its three massive legs, almost like a large tank-like alien. Meron, Lumak and the others realised how strange he must have appeared to the cat people.

George suddenly got up and turning to Bawaki he communicated through his implant.

'I have a list of suitable stars within Osmaron that I can use for this purpose. But I might just swap both of your suns over, since the small one is almost the size of Sol. However, I shall have to adjust the orbits of the planets to compensate,' he said. Then he asked Micol for all relevant data on both stars and planets within the system. He soon found that the dynamics of the system gave him great flexibility, even when the smaller star was just within his minimum limits to give enough system tolerance. However, once initiated, the planets would settle into new and more stable orbits within a period of several years.

He made his usual calculations through implants and having visualised every minutest variation, changed their present topic of conversation.

'I can accomplish the changes with your present stars, but with a slight adjustment to the planets,' he said to Bawaki and they continued with their friendly chatter. Finally he decided to transpose their main star away from the system and use a more stable smaller secondary star. That way, the world would still retain its two stars.

CHAPTER 21

A stellar miracle

Andy and his men found the whole scene, with the inclusion of strange catlike females, very incredible to say the least. Here, the large human-like cat, Bawaki, was with her two leopard-like near bipeds, communicating in a most educated manner. Could this be an Alice-in-wonderland dream, they thought? Her two smaller male cats were also drinking the wine and weak liquor, and what would happen if the other larger female cats got drunk and became violent. That would be something else worth watching from afar and could not even be imagined, with one considerable mess to clear up afterwards.

Bawaki had never freely introduced alcohol to any of her people, fearing their ferocity, should their mental faculties be in any way compromised.

Since her conversion, Pamela was now a beautiful 25 year old and looked the same age as her daughter Cathy. She was presently conversing with Bawaki, Sintra and George about the Great Book, the Anachromagnon. They were giving their different views on perspectives when Bawaki left to join George and Cathy.

'I would like to assist you on Earth, if you need an extra hand. My councillors here can always run things in my absence and I can keep an eye on them with an occasional portal visit. I also have many here that can be trained to help fight the Javols. So please let me know how I can assist before you leave.'

'No problem! Send me their measurements so I can get them special protective suits. I shall soon have words with Hal about the possibilities of using the Satan's Bug on this world,' George said.

'Satan's Bug?'

'It's a virus that only targets Javols. It infects their metabolism so that they get hot and explode,' George said.

'Nice one!' Bawaki shrilled and laughed.

'We think so, but we must make sure it's safe to use on your world,' George advised.

'You know, I do miss the old days on Earth. Here I feel more caged in this palace, with so very little to do these days,' she said.

'I can give you my answer right now. You can come with us and visit Polok, Lodor, Nervia World, then Eden, before we finally return to Earth. You also have the choice to transform into a human if you so wish,' he said.

'Can I really?' she replied, with utter excitement. She was overjoyed by the invitation and immediately called one of her councillors, had quick communication and he was on his way to make the necessary arrangements.

'Perhaps your mother can assist while you are away?' he asked.

'No! She can't! She is ill and I think she is dying?' Bawaki replied, suddenly saddened by that thought.

'Please take me to her immediately!' George commanded. Then turning to Sarah and some of the other Ancients that her mother knew, she whispered.

'Why don't we go and see Mother now?'

They followed her to the first floor, into a darkened room with curtains drawn and dimly lit.

'Mother, I brought you some visitors,' she said and her aged mother turned around to greet them. She was not the same person Sarah met several decades before. The poor cat-woman was aged and crinkled.

'I saw the little ship arrive. With all the commotion, how could I miss it. I wondered who it was. 'Ah.... Lady Sarah! How are you?' she said, showing much physical weakness.

'What is her illness?' George whispered to Bawaki.

'It's something inherent in our genes. When we get to a certain age, our bodies quickly wind down. The process is both psychological and physiological. We have tried every conceivable medicine, but a cure has not been forthcoming,' Bawaki said with sadness.

George did not wish to understand the strange natural pros and cons of that world, but instead went up to her and placed his hand upon her forehead as if checking her temperature and she began to shiver. Then he removed his hand.

'You are now completely whole once more, to do as you wish!

How would you like to be queen again for a while during the absence of your beloved daughter?' he asked.

Ignoring him completely, she jumped out of bed and opened the curtains, thus showering the whole room with bright light. Then Bawaki realized she had miraculously changed to the person she was when she was a young queen.

'Yes, My Lord. I would like that very much,' she replied trance-like while gazing through the curtains. But even she couldn't quite take in what had happened.

'Mother, is that really you? Oh my god! She is healed! Completely healed! And now even much younger than her age!' shouted Bawaki, but to them a thank-you would never have been enough, so they remained silent as if in prayer.

'Come on, People! Let's return to the party!' he insisted and they followed George, later to be joined by her mother.

Later that evening, when the sun appeared on the horizon amidst the orange and reddish images of sunset, George left the group and made his way to the ship Micol, passing several palace guards on-route. No one did anything to prevent his progress from whatever he was about to do.

As he got closer he transmitted a thought and while they looked, its side melted into a shimmering staircase and entrance. Then he walked on board, gave another thought and the cloak was already on his body. Then he walked out of the ship.

He concentrated deeply unto the two stars and very soon saw them merging, he transferred inertia and other essentials, then he shouted to the winds and the skies.

'Be replaced!' he cried, as if waking the dead. The vibrations of Jull's voice shook the buildings in his vicinity. Suddenly the whole world became completely darkened, but soon there was a bluish speck of light at the distant horizon where that old sun stood only a few seconds before. He floated into the air and became enmeshed in thick threads of energy that circled everywhere. They spiralled away in every direction and filled the planet's atmosphere with energy, to such an extent that there was severe lightening discharges everywhere. Discharges even flew from buildings and walls like spaghetti lightning.

All the denizens of Tarran, from its highest mountains and

plateaus to its deepest chasms, became fearful of disaster and took shelter wherever they could. But soon, large black clouds were forming within its misty sky and as the thunder and lightening continued, so did the rain begin to shower continuously.

When the strange threads of energy ceased, he floated down towards Micol. By that time all the brave guards had disappeared within the palace for cover, fearing the worst for everyone and everything on that world.

After he had altered the planet's rotation, he gave the usual thought instructions and the suit was back within its casket. He had not swapped the stars in that system. However the older main star was swapped with another the size of Sol. The smaller one still orbiting more or less as before.

'Micol, please follow on with Martia's ship,' he said, and sauntered off casually to his group of friends.

'The job has been done. Now it will be just eleven hours to sunrise,' he said, while they gazed at him in amazement but still fearful of his powers.

As the torrential rains poured many went out to take advantage. They had always considered water to be the most precious commodity on their world and presently it poured in bucket fulls from the sky. It was probably the first time that anyone on the surface of that world had a proper bath with rain water.

The female guards soon considered him to be their god, but so also did most of his own group.

When the sun rose the following morning, there were shouts everywhere. The large orange sun with the halo had shrunk into a stable yellow star with a much more pleasant output and the second star looked even smaller, while the original sun was nowhere to be seen.

Although the rains had caused some unexpected flooding, it was a welcomed blessing on a dry planet that was mainly desert and it did not cause severe destruction to habitats.

In a few days large clouds could once again be seen forming naturally within its atmosphere and its rains would be frequent and torrential enough to reduce its deserts and increase its seas and oceans. The climatic and other dynamic cycles would shift significantly due to the change in moisture levels within the lower atmosphere. However, it would not drastically alter the desert's life for thousands of years, giving the creatures enough time to readjust and migrate to more suitable habitats. Nevertheless the new world of Tarran would become a lot more fertile as a result giving life a better chance of survival.

That day, George and his gang, now also including queen Bawaki, visited many of the male laboratories and universities within Ziona City. They were showered with every type of gift and many went for strolls within its streets, Earth-type shops and cafe's. There was great celebrations throughout that world when they realized their heavens had changed for the better.

When it was almost time to leave, George went to their local television station which was another one of the technologies introduced from Earth. He thanked them for all their fine presents, blessed them and told them he would be back to spend more time when it was convenient.

CHAPTER 22

A visit to Polok II

Back on Polok II Captain Malik linked into the master Lodorian computer to access new data on the super active star in question. When he had compared the latest data, he turned to his assistant.

'The star has increased its output by another ten degrees on average, with a twenty percent expansion. Magnetic turbulence have almost doubled. I just hope she holds out for another six months. By that time she should have move out of her present erratic cycle of activity.'

'It seems to be the case, Sire, from our latest computer models!' Sontral interjected.

'However, if she takes the disastrous course and decides to expand, we shall not have enough time to evacuate twelve-point-five million people from that system. Even if we used the giant ships we would be unable to find a place large enough to put all those evacuees in time,' he said, with a strained look and a deep frown on his forehead.

'Sire! We are expecting your special visitors tomorrow. Shall we postpone their visit for now?' his assistant Patri asked.

'No Patri, let me communicate with them when I am ready. But keep me up to date on any important data,' he said and walked out of the office.

'Sontral, please take control in my absence!' he shouted on his way.

Commander Malik took a portal to his palace and on arrival was immediately greeted by his wife, Mira.

'You look very tired, my dear. Come and listen to one of your favourite Earth symphonies while I make you a cool drink and we can have a quiet chat afterwards,' she said, full of compassion for her husband. She was looking forward to Empress Sarah's visit, with the great ship, Martia.

'At least Tonal's star has stabilised, but predicted values indicate some more expansion. If she moves within the critical zone, I am afraid she will blow and when that happens we'll also get a bit of it here in about five years,' he said.

'I know the Lodorians haven't the technology to assist us, but what about the Grand Lord and his God people. Why can't they help? After all, isn't that the main duty of Shadites... to help in situations like this,' she said.

'There are already two Shadites on the scene, but they are just organising the people in preparation for a mass evacuation. They don't seem to think the star will blow this time....!'

'How can I take the chance and risk over twelve million of my own people?' he replied.

'What about Sarah and her people. Can't they help?' she enquired. With that sentence, he went to a special communicator and passed a thought into it.

'Dearest, thank you for reminding me. I have to tell them to cancel their visit. They can go directly to Lodor III. Perhaps they can visit us another time,' he said. But she suddenly leapt towards the com-unit to override his command.

'I shall not allow you to take my friends away from me! Star or no star! We need them here at this time. As if you did not remember their first visit - when we won that war against Lodor - and other things besides. If anyone can help, I am sure they will!' she shouted at him and usually he followed her wishes.

'Ok, Dear! You win! What shall I tell them?' he asked.

'Tell them the truth and also tell them we can do with a little help at this time,' she said. Then he reconnected with Martia's ship.

Martia's Ship was still at her docking bay on Tarran when the message was received.

'From Malik and family.

We look forward to the pleasure of your visit and have many things to catch up on, so don't be long in coming.

Sorry friends, but we have a potential disaster on our hands here. Trouble with one of our stars. That one has decided to go erratic during one of her sunspot cycles.

We have over twelve million people within that system, on Toral III.

Can you advise?

End of message,' it read.

'Send a message back to Malik and state as follows: Do not

attempt rescue before our arrival, which will be within the hour. We can definitely assist you with that problem. End of message. That's all!' George said, while sending the thought pattern through Martia's ship.

'Lord Malik must be very worried at this time. So many souls remain in that system. Where will he place them all in an emergency?' George said, while sitting next to Sarah with Cathy's hand on his. Sarah was finally close to her son, observing how well he had grown, even without her direct motherly intervention.

Since she learnt George was her stolen son, Sarah had the overwhelming desire to set things right. But after all those years of neglect, she felt guilty, and had to first get those feelings in the open before she could become his real mother.

'I would like a private word with you and Cathy, please, if you don't mind. Your father can remain here with Meron for now. It doesn't concern him anyway,' she said.

'Well, this is as good a time as any. Why don't we visit our suite?' George said, and all three got up and went towards the nearest portal. On their arrival she went towards the drinks cabinet and thought the door open.

'Cathy, you should have realised by now that I am George's real mother and Doctor Longhurst his father,' she said, while pouring the drinks.

Cathy stared at her in utter surprise and disbelief, with those beautiful, yet probing eyes and decided to listen to what she had to say. She then took the glasses over to them and handed them their drinks.

'I know all this is very embarrassing for all of us, but I must speak my mind. I had no choice in the matter. It came from the Grand Lord himself. From the moment of your birth on Earth, you were taken from me. I thought you were stolen by one of those gangs, until my husband, your father, told me otherwise twenty years later... something to do with causal contamination.... It relates to some ancient prophecy, which indicated that you would be born at a certain precise time on Earth and should grow up as a natural Earth child, and so on.'

'I always saw a close resemblance!' Cathy interjected.

'We on Eden and elsewhere could in no way affect your future development. Any such influence could have affected your natural causal history and would have created many problems, including the possibility of your premature death or a profound change in your personality and attitude towards cosmic life.' Sarah added.

'The Cosmos has its unique ways!' George replied.

'The prophecy also indicated that if you came to see us by your own will we could assist. That way, we would be players in your game and not the other way around. And even then, we couldn't impose our will upon you. So everything was arranged, even without my knowledge, through my father who you called Uncle Bengi at the time. But even he was not allowed to influence you, so he stayed away most of the time as well. And now, it doesn't matter anymore, because it's all your will anyway and we are all small players in that greater game,' she continued. Suddenly there was a change in her expression.

'If at all possible, I would like your forgiveness for having been such a rotten mother to you for all those years. Since the day you were taken from me, at the manor on Earth, I have never felt like a whole person,' she said and with those words she broke into tears.

'Can you ever forgive me, my son, for having been such a neglectful mother?' she sobbed and both went over to embrace her.

'Mother,' he said. 'It would have been a great thing if you were around when I needed you as a child, but that was not to be and we cannot reverse the past. What I feel at this moment, is the accumulative effects of all those past experiences without you, and they haven't done me any harm. So why don't we let bygones be bygones and begin again from scratch. I am still a young man and we have the whole of eternity in front of us,' he said. By this time Cathy was also sobbing.

'I only realised the connection when Bawaki mentioned it. I saw a resemblance and certain signs of affection which made me a little suspicious. But even then I never realised the truth and now I have a new mother,' Cathy said, full of emotion.

After they were finished with their reconciliation, they finished their drinks and three of the happiest people in existence ported back to the main group.

When they arrived within the Polokan system, Polok II was already on the large screen with many massive stations about the planet. That world had transformed significantly since the wars and its virtual destruction by the Lodorians many decades past. Presently it had been restored to another most beautiful world in Osmaron. As always, most of the federation worlds followed Eden as their perfect planetary model. However, their main city of Miran looked more like New York, with many skyscrapers.

Martia's ship transposed again into the main space port. Malik immediately ported on board Martia's ship to greet his visitors with his wife Mira and two councillor sons.

'It is so pleasant to see your beautiful faces at this time,' he said, then he went to shake their hands, eventually stopping with Lumak.

'Please meet my youngest son, George!' Lumak said and George firmly shook his hand. Malik had also received information from one of his ships during the construction project on one of Lori's moons and he was curious as to the purpose of that strange installation.

'The Lodorians have analysed a strange message from one of their construction ships, on one of Lori's moons and are presently quite interested in you, George. Volt, their chief technical advisor, didn't realise the possibilities of transposing a complete city from distances unknown.'

'Really?' George smiled.

'You obviously have some new technology that the Lodorians have little knowledge of and they will do everything in their powers to get hold of it, you know. Presently, they are completely confused by the whole affair. Anyway, we can discuss those and other matters at our leisure, when we return to the palace,' Malik said to George, who smiled again.

Then Malik went over to Jon and his group, to catch up on old times. Mira remained with Sarah, and George with Malik's two sons, also with Lumak and company.

Suddenly Malik clapped his hands to gain their attention.

'I have arranged some celebrations at my palace, so please follow!'

Lord Malik appeared to be the same extrovert that he was some fifty years before, although somewhat stressed with worry at this moment in time. Nevertheless, his damaged body had been reformed and he looked twenty years younger, even younger than his own children.

They arrived at his beautiful palace which was on a small plateau overlooking the city of Miran. That new city was named after his wife and meant "belonging to Mira". The city was named immediately after its construction, about four decades ago, during one of their special ceremonies. It was built freely for them by the Lodorians as reparations for war damage.

Miran had become a most prosperous city, with many Solarian-type venues. They included many imports from Earth through Solarian Banking and other members of the federation. His proud people were finally very happy, having regained their freedom since the great war with the Lodorians.

Many Lodorians could be observed in human-like android forms. Their real octopus-like bodies, just a fraction of a metre long, were contained in small electronic tanks within those human-like vehicles. They were one of the oldest and most advanced races in Osmaron and decided to assist Malik in the rebuilding program since the end of the war. Being very inquisitive, they were also patiently awaiting George's visit on Lodor III and neither did he wish to disappoint them, because that was his next port of call.

The whole purpose of the interstellar trip was so that George could spend more time with Cathy, Sarah, Lumak (Doctor Jeffery Longhurst his father), and the other members of his gang from Earth. Those few he considered his real family. Others like Anne-Marie, Donald, Clair, Bawaki, Venusa, Martia, Hal, John, etc., were slowly becoming part of his trusted gang, although not yet fully committed.

Jon and his Andromedan group had only recently arrived to join

The Gang and were just feeling their way around. The older Ancients hadn't yet committed themselves to his cause, being fully involved in maintaining life on Eden and elsewhere. Yet, he was certain, when asked they would all say a resounding 'YES'. They were obviously keeping their distance for fear of corrupting his future. Perhaps his father could tell them the dangers had passed after his 21st birthday and so he thought.

George shouted above their happy voices. At that time everyone was chatting and laughing in the large palace reception room on Polok II.

'I would like to say a few words if I may. I realize we have chosen an inopportune time to visit your beautiful world and system. Even so, we are all federation members and should go out of our way to assist fellow members in times of need. Even though, the treaties and charters relate mainly to trading and does not insist on any of its co-members cooperating in matters of state, I intend to override those rules when safety and life is threatened by natural catastrophes.'

'Agreed!' shouted Malik.

'In any event I do believe it's time we made the usual amendments to those old agreements, to cover the whole of Osmaron. With those important thoughts in mind I think we should nominate a suitable race of engineers and scientists for that purpose. Perhaps you on Polok and those on Lodor should be nominated to manage all stellar systems on a truly galactic scale. By what I intend to propose, our stellar engineers of the future will have little need for chemical resources and they will gain even more importance by those they assist within our galaxy. Such efforts would include the building of large machines to remodel and replenish old dying stars and their old planets, or those ravaged by war. By so doing, the problems we suffer now may become inconsequential within a relatively short period of time. I have therefore taken the liberty to rewrite the contracts with the addition of those changes and propose that they be signed on Lodor III by its three main members.' They remained silent.

'With that out of the way.... may I thank Lord Malik, his

beautiful wife, Lady Mira, and senior members of his esteemed council, for accepting us at this most difficult time. I am sure we shall enjoy every moment of your world's hospitality. Once again, I thank you!' he said, briefly glancing at Malik and his wife. Then he rejoined his mother Sarah, while Cathy and Malik followed.

'Do you seriously think such a gigantic project can work? I mean, taking on the whole of Osmaron as one complete federation or Empire?' Malik asked, still somewhat confused by his speech.

'With the correct technology I am sure we can manage the whole of Osmaron in much the same way as we have done on Eden. Obviously, we shall require the most suited people for the job. We already have a large federation Navy which travels the extent of Osmaron and elsewhere. Our only real problem is a lack of resources in building such ginormous ships and machines. Have you or the Lodorians ever lost out on such operations in the past?' George said.

'You are quite correct. We have always gained by those advances and whenever we have worked together for the common-good we have always learned to enjoy our lives. Anyway, what does it matter how long such projects will take, since we live forever. I also think a new challenge will make a refreshing change. The Lodorians are getting restless for new information, even a brand of new science to challenge their minds. Can you really help us in that regard?' Malik asked, but instead George drifted away from the topic.

'Perhaps?' he smiled, deviously.

'You have a most beautiful system, but your planet's atmosphere can be revitalized. Did you know, its atmosphere is still severely contaminated from the fallout of the long war. Presently, it contains extremely low levels of ozone with several radiation gaps that are spreading. Lodorian technology can only accomplish so much within a normal human lifetime. I can give your world a new lease of life by optimising its gasses, ozone, carbon-dioxide levels, and so on. What if we had powerful machines to do the same without inconveniencing its inhabitants. Like a complete world having a timely make-over,' he said and

Malik looked as if not fully understanding his implications, but realising that he didn't move his lips and was communicating directly through his implants although somewhat different to his type.

'Yes, George. I understand our requirements. But such a gigantic project would absorb energy and scarce resources on a gigantic scale.... Resources that we have such little of at this moment in time. Remember, we are rebuilding most of our damaged world,' he replied.

'My methods take zero resources and energy. But you will know more about such projects after our visit to Lodor,' George replied. Then they took another glass of almost non-alcoholic whisky from the waiter and went over to Lumak.

'How is your eldest son, David, and his wife?' Malik asked.

'He is away on business for the Grand Lord, but I sense he'll be back with us soon. His wife Moran is back on Eden, taking care of the palace and children in our absence,' Lumak replied.

Cathy soon came over to join George, with little Clair tagging behind.

'Darling, they also have those giant leaf plants here. I wonder if they will grow on Earth?' she asked, out of curiosity.

'They seem to grow in most places, but Lord Meron is the one to ask about such things. He is in charge of all such programs within Solaria,' George replied.

'I know where it's from and I also know whether it will grow on Earth,' Clair insisted, and their attention turned to the little girl.

'It's from Kanaefon, uncle Lumak's home-world. It needs little nutrients from the soil and creates its own water within its leaf, and it will grow on Earth,' Clair said.

'I brought the first ones from Kanaefon two decades ago. When my wife insisted that we took some bulbs back with us. Now they are growing everywhere and can create their own moisture within their single folded leaf.'

'They can? They look so incredible!' Miranda exclaimed.

'You may have as many as you wish after we build your golden palaces on Earth as on Eden,' George said and the women were ecstatic.

'They can sometimes unfold their single giant leaf in the deserts to capture more moisture when there is heavy dew about, then they fold to prevent evaporation. Their single leaf stem can collect nutrients from the soil by acidic digestion and absorption through a process akin to osmosis.' Clair added, as if reading from a book.

'This is incredible. Clair is correct in every detail,' Lumak said, staring at the strange little eight-year old girl.

'She is a very special person,' George said and little Clair listened patiently to her uncle's complements with glaring eyes. Because of her previous recovery from cancer and near bald head, everyone tended to dismiss her as the strange little girl, except her uncle George, of course.

'Another one like you?' Lumak asked, but he changed the topic.

'Dad, when did you last visit your home-world?' he asked, suddenly realising he had another family somewhere else in Osmaron.

'As I said, I visited my people about twenty years ago, when I took your mother to see my family?' Lumak replied.

'How far away is it?' George inquired.

'It's within one of our largest globular clusters. The one we call Kalboron. Would you like to pay a visit sometime?' he replied.

'Yes, Dad, I am sure Cathy would also like to see some relatives from your side of the family,' George replied.

'It's a very strange but beautiful world and you might have to transform in order to fit within its culture. Leave it with me for now and I shall arrange a visit,' he said. But even George had little idea that his father Lumak, now in human form, was really a beautiful Semonite, bee-like creature on his own world. Even more incredible, was that he used to be a sexless worker within one of those large hives, with a single queen and many drones and workers. Each individual in that society followed a set plan that was initiated from the moment the egg was laid within the large hexagonal cells. Nevertheless, they had a very advanced culture and were another highly intelligent species. Lumak had assumed the human form and sex after his transposition to Earth. That was when he was sent to Earth as a Shadite to complete an important mission for the Grand Lord several decades before.

'When are you to pay us a visit within Solaria? We have so

much to discuss,' George asked Malik and Mira.

'If it's convenient for you, after we have dealt with some of our own problems here. You know, we might have to evacuate over twelve million from the Toralian system and only God knows where we are to put them. We are not used to displacing that many people in an emergency,' he replied.

Despite the pleasurable party, Malik appeared to be very tense. Still worrying for the welfare of his people within the threatened system, just over three light years away.

'Do not worry unduly, my friend. I have the machinery to transform Toral III's dying star into an almost brand new one. Do you think I am able to just transpose small city areas on moons? Ask my father and he will tell you of Tarran,' George said, trying to relieve Malik's worries.

'What does he mean?' Malik asked Lumak, and George walked away, again smiling.

'My son has many great powers. One of those is the ability to transpose complete stellar systems by the use of dimensional transposition on a massive scale. He swapped over Tarran's main star before we left and increased the planet's rotational period to that of Earth's, modifying its atmosphere in the process. All this he completed within a few minutes. So, my friend, I do not think you have a great problem here now,' Lumak replied.

'Is he another Grand Lord, then?' Malik asked.

'My son could be a lot more, but every Grand Lord have their own specialities. He was prophesied to take control of the universe in later times, but to be assisted by our present Grand Lord and us in the battle against the Javols. He takes his powers from the Cosmos and The Greater Purpose, if you wish. Most of the tasks he performs use zero energy. Just pure thought,' Lumak replied with greatest pride.

'You appear to be serious, so I am not going to question your words. But I find it difficult for any single individual to contain such incredible powers. This whole thing is truly incredible!' Malik replied. Mira was presently holding a separate conversation with George and Cathy to one side.

'The universe with its many forms of matter and energy is just another type of order and all types of order can be circumvented by powerful minds, and he is one of the most powerful,' Lumak replied, proudly.

'I still find all that very had to believe,' Malik said.

'Then we shall have to wait and see,' Lumak replied with confidence.

'Great God of my father. If what you say is correct, the Lodorians will make him their king. They enjoy all that stuff,' Malik replied, and George and the others rejoined them.

'I am just a normal guy like you, Lord Malik, with a normal wife and one day soon, even with normal children. When I change cloaks, I become a great patriarch Supreme Being called Jull and the Cosmos becomes my playing fields, to do with as I wish. What you may call ultimate power. But I can construct machines to do the same jobs and perhaps someday construct a stellar factory at the very centre of our galaxy. We may even build large Dyson Spheres to save energy. That way, many life-forms now driven to extinction by aging and dying stars may be saved from extinction.'

'If you can weald such changes, it will be the greatest miracles of all!' Malik was utterly intrigued, and realized his future would be undergoing greater changes while building more incredible machines.

'However, with all such powers must go certain responsibilities to all primal life and caring for those that depend upon us,' George said and Malik was suddenly a much happier man, realizing he spoke in saintly terms like his since departed father, king Olav.

Malik left them immediately to communicate with Tarran and when he received confirmation that their complete stellar system had been transformed and Tarran into a new Earth type world, he went back to join his friends in an excited frame of mind.

'Would anyone like to dance?' Malik asked.

'Well, please follow me into the main hall. We haven't been able to arrange an orchestra, but I have a very powerful speaker system, with several classical discs that I have collected from Earth and Eden over the years. So let's have some fun,' Malik insisted.

After the party was over, presents were handed out to Malik and his family before they retired for the night.

CHAPTER 23

A brand new dawn

Later that night, while George and Cathy got ready for bed, he became restless.

'Darling, I have a little job to do before I join you,' he said.

'You want to go and fix that star?' she asked, intuitively.

'Yes, Love. We have a tight schedule ahead of us and I must do it tonight if we are to leave by noon tomorrow and visit Lodor's city in the afternoon,' he replied.

'In that case, I am also coming along and don't you try to stop me. We can always tell the guards we are going for a walk and hope no one follows us towards Micol,' she said.

'In that case, please put on your special suit and let's leave right away,' he insisted.

They gingerly walked unto the palace grounds where Micol was parked. On arrival, he sent a thought to Micol and he melted into the stairway and entrance. Another thought and the ship was ready and on its way to Toral's star. George soon received up-to-date stellar maps of the area from Micol and after scanning through the data, found a suitable donor star. They soon arrived at Toral's star and were amazed by the sight of the stellar fury they beheld.

'What a massive star compared to our sun. It's as if she is boiling over,' Cathy exclaimed.

'The beginnings of full helium combustion will commence shortly after this phase. She has used up most of her hydrogen and is now trying to compensate. But if she doesn't break out of her present erratic cycle, she'll begin to contract as gravity takes over and continue to contract until she triggers helium combustion. Once that happens she'll begin to expand again because her gravitation is not able to compensate enough for the higher energies generated. That is the time when she will go nova, depending on her present mass and other dynamics. My calculations tell me that she'll go nova at her next cycle which is in another twenty-one years. Luckily for this system, she is not the type to go supernova.'

'Supernova?'

'It's a much larger explosion that might destroy our present world as well. Supernovae are created by stars that are much larger. In this case, she will just become a white dwarf in yet another dead system,' he said.

'Can white dwarfs be brought back to life and be used again?' she asked.

'If they haven't used up too much of their original mass during their lifetime. You know, the majority of stars loose on average millions of tons of energy each second of their useful lives. But if two dwarfs could be brought together, we might be able to transform their heavier elements back into hydrogen which could be channelled to a new position in space and left to reform into a new star. The whole process can be speeded up by technology within such stellar nurseries. Another method could be seeding the star with a hydrogen type nuclear virus. Such a virus would infect the heavier atoms and split them back into hydrogen atoms. Giving the old star a new beginning. But planets could not evolve quickly around such stars. They will be just stars made to order, to replace those that are dying within present systems,' he replied.

'Can it be done?' she asked.

'Let me give the process some thought,' he said, while communicating with the casket. The cloak suddenly appeared on his person. Then he walked through the wall of the ship into deep space and gazed at the boiling star in the distance. There he remained for a while in meditation. Then he stood up and began gesturing at the star.

Suddenly there was a much smaller blueish point of light, which appeared to be superimposed upon the larger boiling disc. Then the larger disc simply faded into the smaller, more brighter disc, now perfectly stable. By that time Cathy had become very excited by the transformation and began to make a few gestures of her own. Shouting at the large screen in sympathy with her husband.

'Hooray! Hooray! Hooray! You did it! You did it!' she yelled again and again.

George was soon back inside Micol. The cloak was within its

casket while he stood next to a fearless Cathy.

'A good evening's work, my Darling. I am sure they must now be rejoicing on Toral III,' she said.

'Either that, or they are scared out of their wits, but either way, I would like some shut eye,' he replied.

When they arrived back at the palace, they quietly walked back to their room, with just one guard noticing them on-route. Yet, Malik and the others were none-the-wiser of the great stellar miracle that had occurred.

Later that night a small Lodorian craft appeared at the palace and several important android officers, including Volt, got out. Malik was instantly awakened to meet his important guests. He wondered why they used a ship when they could easily have visited through long-range portal.

'What urgent matter brings you here at this hour?' Malik inquired.

'A very urgent matter. It was inconvenient to visit through portal as we had a non portal stop to make on-route,' Volt replied.

'Please follow me into the library, we can have more privacy there,' Malik said. Then Volt gave orders to his officers to remain in the ship and followed Malik.

Malik was now thinking of a worst case scenario regarding the star. Why should such an important person visit so urgently if there wasn't some kind of a disaster? Yet, there were two Shadites on that world and none had yet communicated with him, so the disaster could not have occurred yet, or so he thought.

'The greatest miracle have occurred! I cannot find another human word to describe the enormous thing that has happened. Toral's star has been transformed from its present type to a normal young star. Our probes, of which there are many in that area, relayed the information to us before I left Lodor to observe the aberration myself. We cannot understand the reasons why such a thing could happen, because such an occurrence defeats the very laws of physics and contravenes the very nature of science,' Volt said.

'I think a little God might be at work here... and I might just know his name. Are you absolutely sure that your sensors are not at fault due to the extreme radiation in that area?' Malik asked, sarcastically.

'No! Lord Malik, our systems were designed to cope with a hundredfold increase and I went there myself to observe, via my ship's sensors. We were positioned well away from the star. It was a different star, even when we communicated with Shadite Peter on Toral III. We have since received Peter on Lodor. He is to assist us in discovering the reasons why,' Volt said.

'Are you in a great hurry to get back?' Malik asked.

'Not great, but I have to prepare an urgent report on this situation for Chancellor Bailor at the earliest,' Volt replied.

'Please remain here for a while, there is someone I would like you to meet. I am sure he will be able to give you answers to your searching questions on stellar transposition,' Malik said, as he buzzed George's room. George, knowing of the arrival of the Lodorian ship, decided to go and meet Volt, but Cathy could not sleep either, so they both got dressed and went down to Malik's library.

'Darling, I can't take you anyway these days. Always creating a rumpus. This time you have them peeing their pants,' she said and he grinned.

'You know me, Dearest. I'll do anything for an exciting life,' he replied.

'Councillor Volt, please meet Lord George and his wife Lady Cathy. He is Empress Sarah and Lord Lumak's last son and Shadite Peter's younger brother. He is the one with the knowledge and powers to transform stars. No star is safe whenever he is in the vicinity, but he only replaces bad with good and thank goodness, never the other way around,' Malik said, leaving Volt completely confused and nervously twitching his right cheek. Then Malik went up to George to embrace and thank him for the great miracle.

'Thank you, my son, or should I say, My Lord,' he said in earnest and with overwhelming gratitude.

'My family and your family's paths are always crossing. First your father saved my father's life and now you have saved so many of my poor subjects from imminent disaster. From now on, my world and my home are yours and also your family's to use as you wish,' Malik said, full of emotion. With that, George and Cathy went over to Volt and shook his hand, but he just stood there with his face still twitching in utter astonishment.

'I am pleased to meet you, Lord Volt,' George said.

'The complement is mutual, my greatest Lord,' Volt replied.

Later that evening, he called the selected twelve into Malik's library.

'You are on my list for our visit to Lodor today. We leave at noon in order to get to their world during their morning and we take only twelve along with Micol, The Ship. The others may remain here in the mean time and take advantage of the facilities on this beautiful world. I will join you later,' George said.

CHAPTER 24

Lodorians in preparation

The City of Lodor, called by the same name as the world, had changed significantly since the ship Micol's first visit with Jerry and others many decades before. That was over thirty years ago and just after the great war between Polok and Lodor. Since that time, which included their incognito visit to Earth, Bailor their chief councillor, had decided to introduce much of the Solarian culture throughout their world.

Soon after, the Lodorians had special sensors fitted throughout their androids and could appreciate almost any new forms of alien culture. Previously, even music was considered of little value to anyone, until they began to appreciate sounds in a more conceptual manner, more as a whole, instead of individual wave parts. That was because they had not developed those sensations as a species. Nevertheless, when it came to new concepts, they caught on very quickly.

Those new dynamic additions significantly enriched their culture and reduced the boredom threshold of their people, giving them many new toys to play with. That process had opened up a brand new panoramic universe for them to study and experience and they were constantly searching for more.

After that new renaissance of culture, many of their dormant people were removed from their underworld watery tanks and given android forms for a more complete and happy existence on the surface. Further, they were now a lot freer to travel within the federation on many missions in the name of the Greater Purpose.

Councillor Bailor was presently their chief of command, but Lodorians were democratic and he was more like their supreme chancellor.

Lord Bailor had heard of the many strange occurrences, which tended to follow the little ship, Micol, wherever it went. Soon after, they worked out a common denominator; namely George and Cathy Peterson who were always close during those occurrences. George tended to be the most predominant figure. So what special devices did that human person have created? What new technologies had he discovered, albeit by accident, to have caused changes of such magnitude on one of Lori's moons?

They had checked their data numerous numbers of times, but there it was. He George asked for its surface to be prepared in anticipation of some new design. Then thirty square kilometres of complex installations of an unknown, even alien design, were suddenly transformed to that very area and within precise dimensional limits. An installation equivalent to a small city. We might have much to learn from George, so we must make him and his friends as welcomed as possible.

If only we knew of one of his important relatives? Someone that we could construct a replica android of in his honour. Yet, perhaps we could get him a beautiful present. Something even a human will remember us by and so Bailor and his other councillors thought.

Soon, news came of changes in Toral's dying star and that new transformation was just as sudden, like cosmic magic. Yet, there was George, his wife Cathy and that Andromedan ship again, hardly four light years from the scene and they could easily have visited the system in question with that little ship.

Were there any similar changes in a previous system they had visited? Bailor got Volt to check data down the line. He was suddenly informed of the changes to Tarran's star and the planets of that system. They double checked all data through the master federation computer, to be backed by personal witnesses of the events. Fast ships were sent and data confirmed.

'Some new energy convertor beam? One that can be fitted to a small craft? Bailor queried.

'Not correct, my Siend,' Volt interjected.

'Stars were swapped over and changed at Tarran. They were literally shifted from one place to another, as if by the hands of God. Then the larger one was swapped by another,' Volt added. Then Bailor, seeing the complexity of the situation gave up any further theorising. For even Volt, who had better understanding of such matters, could shed no light on the subject and didn't like to pontificate on what may or may not have been. Bailor was again communicating to both Volt and Stradon, simultaneously.

'You have both received the preliminary report, of which I consider the implications to be conclusive. It suggests that the human sibling, George, has some new device that can alter the structure of causal frames and energy transformation on a cosmic scale.'

'If it exists. It will be the ultimate weapon against the nasty Javols!' Stradon said.

'The other alternative is that he possesses certain innate powers within his being. This latter alternative I consider too frightening to even contemplate. Yet, I want you Volt to pay an immediate visit to Toral's system and observe the spectacle for yourself.'

'Already on my way, my lord!'

'You might also consider getting an important observer from that system to visit us urgently, in order to discuss those matters. Then you are to visit Polok, under the pretence of a carrier of important information. They might not have yet received information of the miracle. However, all hyper-wave communication from Toral III is now being monitored, so you will be informed of any changes in status if and when they occur.'

'Will do!'

'Further, you are to observe the human sibling, George, and stick to him like glue, until his visit to our world,' Bailor said, then terminated the communication and Volt was already selecting a suitable fast ship for the task ahead.

Bailor, as Senior Councillor, was always trying to score extra points with his council and the more benefits he made for his people, the more they respected him as their leader. To him, an exciting existence was far better than any existence and he was just playing harmless politics. Unlike most of his predecessors who were now resigned to the underworld tanks for past failures. He was a very active leader and would have gone to great lengths to gain more perquisites for his people.

Like a clever detective, he would always try to be ahead of the game and his competition. For after the complex puzzle was unravelled he would always be the most likely to get a larger slice of the cake. Those that were unsolvable stimulated his ego even more and his people had always gained and learnt from those adventures in the past.

The red carpets were laid wherever necessary and the whole city was signposted in anticipation of a grand event. There were many of George's android lookalikes walking the streets of Lodor and the people were happy in expectation of a great event.

Despite their own physical limitations, Lodorians were a very practical and hospitable race. Gone were the strange boxlike vehicles on traction that were used fifty years before. Now, there were portals of every description. Earth type entertainment media could be accessed even within their large watery tanks. Here, many still remained like large octopus-like slugs in their underworld tanks until they were reassigned to a suitably constructed android that would be almost unidentifiable from a normal human body. Nevertheless, they had brain implants and the most advanced computers that could place them in any Virtual World of their choosing. Thus they could become anyone they chose to be for as long as they wanted.

Despite their advanced minds, they had always paid little attention to primitive cultures and their associated inclinations and ceremonies. But that was before Bailor began to adopt, senseless and illogical habits like music, cinematics and others, including taste appreciation.

After their introduction to those more primitive cultures, his people suddenly became less bored and a lot more enthusiastic, even with the extra computers needed to unravel those sensual perceptions.

Suddenly, they had found new forms of creative art and a new type of communication had been stimulated once one had a knowledge of the cultural rules. The knowledge of which came from the humans on Earth and on Eden.

CHAPTER 25

A visit to Lodor

George decided to take the small ship, Micol, to Lodor III. The trip was only to include those he considered essential for the visit. After all, Lodor was not a human world and any large company would have had to remain on board Martia's ship. Anyway, the others could remain at Malik's palace and relax during their absence.

He decided to take the following along: Cathy, Sarah, Lumak, Jerry and his grandfather also Jerry, the previous President of the USA. There was also Miranda, Malik, Bawaki, Jon, Hal and Meron. Just twelve important Solarian passengers including himself. That was the maximum number of humans with bunks that Micol could transpose safely. However, he also carried Ron, his small computer, on such important missions for advise. Ron also gained hands-on experience by so doing.

'Malik, please send a message to Lodor. Tell them we are to visit their city in the morning and add that, they are to expect twelve with the famous little Andromedan ship. They will know what I mean. We can take a long range portal from here, but it's not the same, is it?' he said.

While they walked down Micol's shiny stairway, Sarah and Lumak were the first in queue to be greeted by Bailor, then Stradon, with Volt and Peter, standing to one side.

Peter, the Shadite, was George's elder brother. He couldn't help wondering what his mother, father and others, including the young unknowns, were doing with them on Lodor III during that minor stellar crisis.

When George descended the stairway, he was wearing a most spectacular cloak which drew tumultuous cheers from the large reception and crowds, and Peter wondered who the very popular and handsome stranger was. By that time he had become very curious, because the young man so much resembled himself, despite his younger appearance.

George and Cathy were last to follow down the shimmering stairway amidst shouts of, 'we love you' and others, and many of those in the crowds looked exactly like him, but wearing an assortment of different clothes. There were numerous lookalike couples representing Cathy and George, some even holding hands as a gesture of love and happiness. He wondered how strange the occasion was, but appreciated their affection and consideration for someone they had never met before.

George was dressed in a very lively, white satin like cloak. It had a high collar that fanned upwards from behind his neck. The shoulders had circular creased bands and the whole outfit was a spectacular dream.

Although slightly resembling the Cloak of Aron, it was one of the first to be designed by Venusa's ship. It was engineered to his specifications for protection against the harshest environments, including attacks from Javols. It was indeed a technological breakthrough and constructed from the most advanced microids.

It included numerous hidden fields with powerful generators, long range communication and computer equipment, all invisible to the naked eye and using the latest Class 7 engineering techniques.

After they were introduced, Bailor led them to the large council building dead ahead. That one had been designed more like an amphitheatre for holding political debates in public, but they were never shy or private within their androids while outside of their underworld tanks.

They boarded one of the moving walkways, similar to the ones on Eden, but at ground level, and soon were in the centre of the great stadium. They entered the official reception area and were greeted by many councillors.

Bailor, took the rostrum and began to speak.

'My beloved people, it gives me the greatest pleasure to greet our honoured guests from Solaria. Many questions now concern us about the future of our esteemed federation and of other incredible deeds observed within Solaria and elsewhere, answers to which we await with greatest enthusiasm and anticipation.

'Shall we first listen to Lord George Peterson and perhaps we can take a recess for lunch afterwards?' he said, bowing to George in the process. Then George got up and walked towards the rostrum.

'Before I mention a single word on any of the topics indicated, I must offer sincerest thanks on behalf of my people, to all my friends here on Lodor. I must also thank you for such a grand reception and my heartfelt gratitude now extends to all throughout your fantastic world.

'Lodor has always been respected and appreciated as a senior member of the Federation of Worlds. But henceforth, her position will become even greater in the scheme of things, if she seriously considers my proposals.

'We are now able to harness incredible powers to create a brand new galaxy and very soon we shall begin the revitalization program of all habitable worlds within Osmaron. Then we can move towards the greater universe. It has always been the true destiny of The Greater Purpose to make life easier for Primal life within the Natural Order. Those particular changes will begin with us.

'I propose the design of many machines. Machines capable of transposing complete stellar systems anywhere in Osmaron, with inbuilt inertial compensation. There will also be machines that will change the elements into types more suitable as energy resources. No more shall we need to mine for rear chemical and fossil fuel. With this new technology we shall also be able to create Dyson Spheres to extract all forms of energy and heavy elements from stellar masses. Since they are the source of almost all energy in the universe.

'If you decide to accept my proposal, the design and manufacturing of such machines shall be placed in the competent hands of both Lodor and Polok. While we in Solarla and elsewhere shall concentrate on maintaining order and life in all its habitats. That means defending our realms from the evil Javols.

This position exempts you from direct involvement in wars against the Javols, although you will be free to offer your services if you so wish... and also build weapons for us if you so wish.

'From henceforth, we are to take on the role of protectors of Osmaron. While you become the builders of Osmaron. However, we still abide by those original codes of conscience and non-intervention or involvement in other specie's internal affairs. That is, unless they are threatened by an external crisis of magnitude serious enough to warrant our involvement or they affect our own existence in a detrimental way. Like Toral's star, for instant, then for the greater good all such matters of privacy will be automatically overruled for the survival of its species. Life must always take precedence.

'We had to find a way to protect our fragile primal bodies from our enemies, the Javols, and the rigours of space, by designing a special cloak.

'The one I wear utilises the latest portal and advanced microid technologies. It will enable its wearer to travel anywhere undetected and be invisible and virtually indestructible. It can take its wearer out of this plenum into his own universe and well away from the destructive forces of this one.

'These cloaks, I shall present to certain worthy Osmaronites in the future. Those worthy of becoming emperors of their worlds, by virtue of their determination to do what is right for their people and our galaxy.' When he uttered those words, a bright ring of light began from the bottom of the cloak and started to ripple upwards, until it reached the top of his head and there it hovered like a saintly ring of light.

On observing the strange transformation, the audience was stunned into total silence. The cloak attained the colour of a deep violet. His apparently darker figure began to float in mid air above the rostrum, as if completely massless. Yet, he was anchored to the new position he had chosen by his own will.

'Friends, my present form is indestructible to anything within this universe. Like this, I could enter the densest neutron star, the hottest plasmic inferno or the worst place anyone could imagine.' Then he floated down and sank through the solid floor, with half of his body still visible. He floated back to his original position and transformed back to his previous form.

'This is a brand new age. This is the beginnings of the new patriarchs of the universe. Although this program begins with Osmaron. My intentions are to eventually clean the whole universe of predator species like the Javols and others. All of those who pose a threat to the natural order of life within the Cosmos. We represent the Greater Purpose in all this and this is the time for the beginning of that greatest of all programs.

'All antisocial species with a desire to wantonly destroy others for their own selfish reasons will be banish to a special galaxy I have chosen for that purpose. Within its domain they are to live and survive as they wish. A twilight Galaxy from which there will be no return.' With those words, George pointed his index finger to a spot. A large almost spherical, but translucent object appeared in mid air with numerous bands of galaxies.

'This is our universe and here at this remote area is the Penal Galaxy of Zilorium I. Like Osmaron, this galaxy is rich in many resources but scarce in advanced life. It can also give freedom to criminals and elemental demons. Their loss will be a small price to pay for a cleaner universe. Within that galaxy they may prey upon each other to their hearts contents. Only those serious criminals that cannot be rehabilitated will be dispatched to that penal galaxy through one-way portal.

'The Federation of worlds has been extended to cover all of our galaxy of Osmaron, so our responsibilities will henceforth be also increased in magnitude.

'Finally, a few words on resources within our galaxy.

'I have recently come to understand that there is a lack of resources in certain civilized systems within Osmaron. In particular regarding certain rear elements and carbon-based chemicals. Well, because of new technologies, such chemicals can now be directly extracted from old and dying stars. Therefore may I propose the mining of such stellar bodies for those rear resources...since we now have the necessary technologies to complete the task quickly and efficiently,' George then made a gesture and the large almost spherically shaped tree of the universe disappeared, to be replaced by a small disk.

'Perhaps I can answer a few questions before lunch,' he said.

'How did you transform Toral's star, how long did the process take and by what means?' an astonished Volt asked.

'It took me just a few seconds. I can transform stellar bodies directly through my mind. The process is one of superimposition through the fifth dimension,' he replied. The senior councillors including Volt were numbed by that reply. They had considered such a feat impossible and had been proven wrong.

'Are you to be our God, to assist us when we are in trouble as a race? I mean our personal God?' Bailor asked, full of excitement. He reasoned that anyone with such incredible powers was better on his side than against.

'From now on, I am to be responsible for Osmaron and most of all, its senior members, whom I also consider to be family. So in answer to your question, my reply is yes. But I do not wish to be worshipped as such. Just think of me as your caring leader or perhaps a senior brother, if you wish. Yet, I shall respond to anyone in trouble and hope that my spiritual powers will transcend all of Osmaron, to heal those in pain and assist those in desperation.' With those final words he handed the special disc to Bailor, who thanked him and handed it in turn to Volt for analysis. Bailor then went to the rostrum.

'Friends, I think this is as good a time as any to end this meeting. Any additional information may be acquired through the normal channels,' he said. Then he eagerly led them out to a portal that would take them to a more human environment that was prepared specifically for his guests.

On arrival, they went into a private room where the new treaties and other documents were signed and stamped, then they walked towards the large dining room that was prepared for the occasion.

During lunch, they were entertained by a large Lodorian orchestra. It was playing one of their own symphonies and a ballet with many beautiful ballerinas and male dancers that followed the complex rhythm in a professional and precise manner.

The performance was quite pleasant to watch and soothing to the mind.

The Lodorian levels of android technology were probably the

most advanced in the galaxy, and each android form, like a complex work of art, could be constructed to almost any level of complexity and form.

Those precisely engineered bodies, when linked to the Lodorian being, could be considered in much the same way as a human brain within a human body. The brain being the Lodorian octopus-like being and the human body, their precisely engineered android form, with all its computers, sensors and field interfaces required to supply the necessary signals to their minds in the correct manner.

Despite their inadequate basic forms, they had even greater freedom than humans from the viewpoint of mobility and flexibility. Being able to change bodies in much the same way that humans were able to change clothes and they also benefited from that last freedom as well.

Bailor and his senior officers were overjoyed with their present company. Although still apprehensive of George with his incredible powers. Yet, they relished the company of Jerry and Meron, who they had seen several times in the past and also enjoyed the social interaction and small talk. In the past Jon's wife Lira was the one mainly responsible for changing their general way of life and fashions. Therefore, they always appreciated and loved her.

'Why don't you all visit us at Malik's palace later today and meet the others at the party?' George advised, with Malik's full approval.

'We would appreciate that pleasure very much, if it's not too much trouble, your highness,' Bailor replied, humbly. But George insisted he called him by his name and left out the highness bit.

The Lodorians now had information they could use for the good of all Osmaron. They were now able to harvest the raw materials from dead and dying stars that could be supplied at a profit to depleted worlds. Then there was the reforming and remodelling of many dead and dying worlds, by terra-forming and giving them new atmospheres. Therefore, they had much to gain by this new venture.

Malik was also part of that venture and could replenish his

systems with those resources. Such systems like Toral's, with all the necessary mining and processing facilities could be used for the storage and fabrication of those products. They soon realized the source of such wealth was inexhaustible.

After a long lunch and many discussions, another thank-you speech was made by George. Then Bailor presented George and Cathy with a most beautiful tapestry of their system, with all its life, cultures and industries. George thought how grand it would look when hung on one of the mansion's walls. However, he also realized that all the mansion's walls were already filled with paintings from all over the world.

They journeyed back to the ship via a closer portal, and walked the remainder of the distance to Micol while being cheered by the many bystanders.

George followed along the railing to say a personal hello to the people and shook their hands. Finally, he shook Bailor, Stradon and Volt's hands before going onboard, leaving Peter, Bailor and his company to find their own way to Malik's palace.

It was already evening when they arrived back on Polok II and they immediately went to freshen up and change into more comfortable and casual evening wear before joining the others in the main palace reception area.

Peter appeared soon afterwards with the Lodorians, Bailor, Stradon and Volt.

'I have received a communication from my people on Toral III. They would like to thank you in person for saving their world and they insist that you must visit.' Malik said.

'If they insist, then I must visit!' George replied.

'I thought we might take one of the big ships and have some more celebrations there tomorrow. If you don't mind?' Malik asked George.

'Yes, my friend. Why don't we take Martia's ship? Set a time for tomorrow and let them know as soon as possible,' George replied.

George was speaking with Cathy and Sarah when Peter joined them, still wearing his Shadite's cloak.

'Peter, please get out of that dreadful outfit! Anyway, the emergency is now over.' Sarah admonished her eldest son.

'I have some appropriate clothes, so please follow me to our suite,' George insisted. For some reason he couldn't take the colour black at a time of celebration, and Peter followed.

He put on one of George's lighter suits which fitted him perfectly.

'Are you a close relative of mine, on my mother's side, perhaps?' Peter asked.

'No! I am a lot closer than that!'

'Even closer than that?'

'I am your long lost brother,' George replied.

'I never knew I had another brother?' he said, utterly surprised by the knowledge.

'I was taken away when I was very little and could not have returned until now. It's a long story and couldn't be helped by anyone.'

'This is truly incredible!' Peter couldn't believe that sad tale.

'Mother will explain the whole story to you when we return to Eden,' George replied.

'Do you really have the powers to move stellar bodies?' Peter asked in amazement.

'Yes, and a lot more besides. But it doesn't prevent me from being your younger brother and a good husband to my wife, in much the same way that you are a great Shadite,' George replied.

'Yes, my... brother, I understand,' Peter said and embraced his long lost brother before returning to rejoin their friends.

Malik decided to visit Toral III the following evening, which corresponded to early morning at their main city.

That once uninhabited world was quite old and strewn with many mining colonies. There was also many sealed domed cities that isolated their living quarters and shopping centres from the more dusty planet.

Although most of the raw minerals had been mined to almost nonexistent levels over the years that world was used mainly for processing the raw materials from other worlds in that stellar system.

George realised what Malik meant when he said 'reduced resources'. Many of the worlds within Malik's empire had been mined for centuries and very little resources remained. Yet, they also supplied a large proportion to Lodor which were now almost completely dependant on Polok. So it was a good thing George had a new plan to save both very important systems of the Federation. They could now update most of their machinery and equipment for refining the new residue materials from the energy and matter convertors.

When they arrived at the mining planet of Toral III, Malik introduced George, Cathy and others to the governor and his officers. They denoted a beautiful replica in miniature of their system, made in platinum, which was still a very rear and expensive metal. Those miniature worlds and moons rotated in much the same way as the real worlds they represented, although at a faster rate. It was a beautiful memento and George assured them he would always cherish it in their memory.

After much celebration they left several hours later and arrived back at the city of Miran on Polok II, to spend a little longer with Malik and his family before saying farewell, with open invitations either way.

Soon they were on their way to Nervia World.

CHAPTER 26

Nervia World

Nervia World had been visited by Lumak several times since his first about a century before. That was during another one of his special assignments to resolve yet another interplanetary conflict.

Although within Osmaron proper, it was situated just beyond the Sheol Nebula, which was several hundred light years distant from the Polokan systems.

Lumak had on that occasion visited the Trinus-Aradnii federation, which comprised three systems: Suk-Prime, Py-Renus and Tuil-Tre. The predominant life-forms on each of the three systems were varied. They included the giant intelligent reptiles on Tuil-Tre, to the little furry but clever Moksai on Py-Renus. However, the empire was sited at Suk-Prime which was mainly populated by near humans. Their system being situated about one hundred light years from Nervia World.

At that time their systems were invaded by Zahkan and his many large ships, after they had completed a long and difficult space voyage of several thousand years.

That harsh survival journey had been made by several massive space arks which had been designed and built for an extensive existence in the vacuum of space until they found a suitable world on which to settle. Their survival journey into the blackness of space had begun shortly before the nova of their local sun. During that catastrophe their world and all their remaining people perished. Yet they had planned for the disaster, by sending an exodus of some of their young people towards a more populated region of the galaxy. Only the very educated and trained youth were allowed to make the trip and they took with them the remnants of their past civilizations. They had been told to find the promise land and had traversed great depths of space in search of that promised world.

When they arrived within Trinus-Aradnii several thousand years later, they had lost over 50 percent of their ships and people.

They were short of resources, with many ships needing urgent repairs. Zahkan, now their proud and independent leader, decided to take what they needed by force. Any way, they were unable to communicate with those local systems and were fearful for the sake of their bedraggled families. They were in despair, although still with very advanced technologies and weapons.

Soon, many of those worlds were under siege by Zahkan and his very competent warriors. It was during that time that Cran Sulman V, the emperor of Suk-Prime, transmitted an H-wave message, asking advanced civilizations for urgent military assistance.

King Olav of Polok II, Malik's father, received that message and took some of his best warriors along to assist the distant system in distress. It was during that visit and under strange circumstances that he came to meet the Shadite, Lumak, who subsequently saved his life in a damaged space fighter. Nevertheless, Lumak also made friends with Zahkan and his family. He subsequently stopped the war and led Zahkan and his people to the beautiful paradise world called Nervia, on which they finally settled. In the intervening years they had begun trading with the Trinus-Aradnii systems and all worlds were now at peace and formed their own federation. However, they were not yet part of the more advanced Solarian Federation ran by Sarah.

Presently all the more advanced Solarian Federation worlds within Osmaron utilized large interstellar portals for transferring people, produce and equipment under strict security and Lumak saw great advantages for those aspiring worlds with such technologies.

After his last visit several years before, Lumak had promised Zahkan that he would be back some day in the near future and finally he was to keep that promise. He argued that if Zahkan and his system became members of the Solarian Federation the other local systems would soon follow. With those ideas in mind he called George away from his elder brother, Peter.

'Son, might I have a private word,' he said and they both discussed the matter through their implants.

'There is another world I think we should visit before our return to Eden. It forms part of a much larger system.... I knew their leader well and I think they are now ready to join our federation,' Lumak explained.

'This is incredible news, Dad. Perhaps we should visit them first and explain things to them before our ships arrive. After all, we don't want to scare them out of their wits,' George replied. He subsequently transmitted a thought to Martia's ship and their plans were already in motion.

George was dressed in his special white Cloak and his father, Lumak, in his blacker than black Shadite's Cloak. They were both to take Micol, The Ship, to Nervia World ahead of Martia's ship. Soon, Micol transposed into the dense autumn clouds of Nervia World. There they remained, directly above the main city they called Nervia City.

Nervia City presently boasted a population of four and a half million humans, with several hundred thousands of Moksai, who had since assisted Zahkan's people and decided to settle there permanently.

'Son, I once told Zahkan that he would one day be visited by a Lord of the universe. Now I think that prophesy is to be fulfilled,' Lumak said, while both men walked through the walls of the ship and floated downwards, through the dense clouds. They descended like Gods towards Nervia City.

The moment they were observed, several crowds began to gather within the large square close to their central pyramid and many were kneeling in prayer.

Zahkan and his son, Chaun, received communication of the strange aberration. They soon arrived on the scene to observe the human figures, one in black and the other in glistening white, slowly and gracefully descending towards their position through the clouds. As they approached, Zahkan could just recognise Lumak and from that moment he was overwhelmed with joy and began to wave madly at the two figures.

'My God, it's Lumak the messenger... and he has senior company. Do you think he could be a god... as well?' he said to his son, who was also dismayed by the strange ordeal. When they landed, Lumak embraced Zahkan and then introduced George to them both.

'This is my son, George. He is also a great one and is now in charge of most of our affairs within Osmaron, our galaxy, and beyond,' Lumak said. With that, both men bowed to the figure dressed in white, but he pulled them back unto their feet.

'I am very pleased to be here and look forward to our future associations,' George said. He then stood back from them, gazed towards the heavens and waved his hands above his head as if commanding the heavens. Energies spiralled away from his fingers and went towards the clouds. Soon the firmament was divided into two separate halves. As he gestured, so did the clouds recede from that part of the planet, leaving Nervia City and the surrounding areas in bright sunlight. The crowds fell on their knees in prayer, but as they chanted Lumak began to speak.

'Friends, I once said I would one day be back. This time I have brought along a great one that we must all respect. Not only for his incredible powers, but also his unending sense of humanity. May we always love each other and remain in peace and harmony with our neighbours and The Greater Purpose?

'There is also a very important matter that we are to discuss with you all and be prepared for a passing visit from one of our giant federation ships,' he said.

'Perhaps you can call an assembly of your most senior members, so that we can discuss something of danger that concerns us all,' George said and Zahkan guided them to a large auditorium within the pyramid. He communicated with all concerned then took the strangers in a small room for refreshments.

After that, many senior members began to arrive. Then Lumak removed the block from his cloak and showed them the images of the Javols consuming the population of Caefon in Andromeda. Finally, he showed them images of Solaria, its technologies and wealth, and they all wanted to partake. After Lumak was finished, the ship landed.

Martia ship's crew had found themselves on an Earth type world, with green grass and many similar animals and vegetation, although a lot younger by comparison.

That day, Zahkan, now a very old leader, and his family entered the Megotron chamber and were given implants and eternal life. They also wanted to visit Eden in the immediate future for a vacation and the signing of some important documents.

'Master, I've received communication from Suk-Prime. They are ready for a visit from the great ones,' the Moksai said.

'That's fantastic news, we can all visit them tomorrow in the great ship and sign a lasting agreement to our mutual good,' George replied.

Once again, another recruit had been added to the Greater Purpose, to aid in the battle against the Javols.

CHAPTER 27

Beautiful Orban

After visiting Suk-Prime and the other worlds in that system, George decided they had one final stop to make.
Therefore he call his people together on board Martia for briefing.

'We shall now visit a part of Osmaron that is closest to the Andromedan galaxy. That part is under collision by a dwarf galaxy by the name of Balion. The dwarf galaxy was once the home of the Plorans like Lord Vektron.

'This is close to where the first Javols will arrive, so I must ensure that part is well secured against their invasion. We are therefore to assess this part of our galaxy for future defensive screening. While I'm here I shall make a few changes of my own.

'Within this region are many beautiful worlds, but the jewel in the crown is the one called Orban.'

'Do you mean the world of the Octans and of our ancient profits, as in our holy books? ' Lord Meron inquired.

'Yes, it is the same. Lord Seno and his people have much to do and I must protect them from our mutual enemies. However, you may treat this journey as another pilgrimage, to your holy city.' George replied and Meron and the other Ancients were the most happiest of all Andromedans. They were all Senots which was an ancient religion followed by most of the people on Eden. The revered profit, Lord Seno of Mond, respected all life and was the founder of that most noble of all religions more than five thousand years ago.

He and those great Ancients had also drank from the well of eternal life and even after all those years remained as young as the others. Seno had always remained by the side of king Melor and the great Micol. He was also the one that had advised Micol in the building of the first city of Cantor on Caefon in Andromeda. They were later taken to that world in ancient times by the Octans and given incredible powers.

The Octans were not human, but had evolved in the oceans of their worlds as a form similar to a large octopus. However, after discovering the necessary technologies they also dwelt on land. Presently they were so advanced that virtually nothing was difficult for them to create. They were the ones who constructed the Great Maulars in the past for Vektron and presently had the technology to transpose complete worlds to other parts of the universe. Some say they were the first to create Portal Technology.

'They are not part of our Federation and come under different jurisdiction. The Ploran, Lord Faemon, runs this part of the galaxy and is also responsible for the inhabitants of Balion. Therefore, we must be on our best behaviour in all things,' he said.

Soon a star appeared on the screen and a small dot marked the spot where a planet was supposed to have been, but there was no planet. Then numerous red dots appeared throughout the local systems.

'These red spots mark defensive bases within this area of Osmaron. They can phase in and out of this universe when needed. At present they are phased out so that they have noo effect on our universe. That way matter can pass straight through them unaffected,' George added and they continued to observe the large screen.

'We have now arrived,' he said, but there was no world in view. That was until a large docking platform appeared in the sky and the great ship landed.

'I suppose everyone of us would like to visit the invisible world below,' George inquired and they all remained silent.

While George spoke, they were engulfed by rays where they stood and suddenly appeared on the planet's surface below. They couldn't believe their eyes for the sky was blue and there were beautiful buildings and vegetation everywhere. They were put down near the great monument of the Ancients. It was built by Lord Seno and others in ancient times as appreciation to the Octans for saving them and their world Caefon from certain disaster.

The Octans appeared semi transparent against the green background and could change their colours at will for more natural communication. It was akin to humans communicating by mouth. However, they were too advanced to use such outmoded forms of communications for reasons other then ceremonies and social activities. They floated about in the air silently, as if they were weightless, but were most likely aided by the most advanced technologies.

The Edenians, including Sarah, Lumak, Meron and others went towards the monument to say a prayer of peace and lay a wreath for the ancient and others in Andromeda that had died at the hands of the Evil Javols.

It was indeed a most solemn moment, which brought back sad memories to Meron and others of his older group who had witnessed the massacre on that world.

They were able to communicate to the Octans via their implants as if they were humans, for such devices made them at one with all other races in the galaxy that used Sunolingua, a common language of the Ancients.

Soon they were taken to another area. This time it was a large dome with a human city that was filled with Ancients of every description. They had sea-blue eyes and six fingers like Meron's people. Like him, they were the descendants of Micol and Sefran. They were taken through the massive structure an showed the different venues. It's environment was very much like their Caefon of old. Even the buildings were exact replicas of their ancient city of Cantor before its destruction by the Javols.

'I had no idea. Our ancient city of Cantor has been rebuilt and constructed stone by stone on this most beautiful world, which also closely resembles the world of my ancestors in ancient times. It is true what our Grand Lord said of our settlement in Osmaron during the last days. Now I know our enemies will be defeated for sure,' Meron said and knelt to say another prayer.

Finally they visited a beautiful palace. That one was used for administration by their superiors. In that place was a golden throne with many more Octans.

CHAPTER 28

The ancient Ancients

This time they were greeted by a band of ancient warriors with shields and swords dangling in scabbards by their sides. George and the others were curious who they were, but the Octan, Plynimias, came forward to introduce them.

'Friends please meet, Prince Seno of Mond, King Melor of Nim, Lord Micol, Lady Sefran and their family. The group went forward to meet those people of old who had worn those garments to remind them of their ancient history. But as they watched, even before their eyes they changed into white braided gowns similar to the ones worn by Meron and others on Eden.

'Sons and daughters of Osmaron, our enactment of the past shows us the changing patterns of life. We were once the poorest and now we are the richest because of our endeavours to do good for the sake of all life and the future of our children,' Lord Seno said.

Then suddenly the Shadite Siit appeared from nowhere, wearing his blacker then black Cloak.

'Lord Faemon will soon be with you,' Siit said in Sunolingua. Suddenly a greenish glow appeared about the throne and a black globe appeared with the usual insignia. Some say he was the brother of Lord Vektron. He then floated towards the group and went towards George. Then he began to speak to them in his strange way.

'This is truly an auspicious moment in the history of our galaxy, for in front of me this day is a Grand Lord of our universe. One that will tear asunder the plans of the evil Javols and save us from the jaws of death and destruction at their hands,' he said and George realized his true purpose in that part of Osmaron. He needed a third moon like Endoh one close to the centre of that galaxy and by so doing could protect those worlds. However, he also had a plan for creating the greatest spectacle of all.

'My Lord, Faemon of Balion, and the forward parts of Osmaron, this is indeed an auspicious moment in the history of our galaxy and one to be marked by my presence. I know we are under a different jurisdiction to you, but nothing is wrong by visiting us on occasion. To this end, may I suggest the placement of secured portals that will link your world directly to Eden, which is currently the main world of our federation. That way our many friends on this world may visit us whenever they choose to share council. By so doing we stand a better chance of fighting our mutual enemies.' George replied.

Later that night George was restless again.
'Not another of those stellar transpositions?' Cathy inquired.
'Not just one, my love. I just had the most incredible idea and it will prevent a few stellar collisions in the distant future,' he replied.
Then while everyone was asleep they tiptoed towards Micol and was soon onboard.
'Micol, please find me a list of the systems at risk from collision by the motion of both galaxies and also find me a moon similar to Endoh's,' he said.
Once again a message was sent to Lodor and several giant ships was sent to clear an area on the dead moon. When the task was completed he transferred another of Jull's installations to that moon, which now formed a protective triangle to include many systems.

'Master, there are just eight systems at risk from collision within this part. The first will collide several million years hence,' Micol said.
'It doesn't mean I shouldn't act now. All those systems are inhabited and I am sure their occupants will prefer to exist with greater peace of mind from impending collision,' George said.
Finally he began transposing complete stellar systems to a local volume of space that was free of stars. The eight systems now formed an octagonal pattern of eight stars, with a massive black hole at the centre of that engineered constellation. All the stars now orbited that ginormous black hole in the centre of that stable system.

Soon Octans were in uproar. They called Lord Faemon to observe the stellar miracle, for there in their night sky was eight stars forming a perfect octagon to remind them of their past and even more, would be there for all time for all their future generations to observe.

George and Cathy returned to their sleeping quarters as if nothing had occurred, but were soon awakened by the commotion.

Soon they were taken to the palace again and were placed in front of Lord Faemon.

'Thank you my gracious Lord for moving those systems at risks to a safer place. Now I feel a lot happier because of their permanence and it is also a good thing they form such a magnificent spectacle in the night sky, and particularly for the great people of this world. They will serve a constant reminder of our existence in this part of Osmaron,' he said.

They spent another day on that beautiful world and were soon on their way home to Eden and then Mars.

CHAPTER 29

The fourth malady

After their return to Eden, George, Jerry, Andy and their wives visited the area of their three palaces. They were soon to be constructed by super-efficient robots and androids within their protectorate. Their lands bordered those of Mallory and his Special's and many palaces were within viewing range. Although now vacant, Mallory's were maintained for whenever he and his people returned from Polion II. That area was about the size of France and there was space for many more palaces.

When they returned to Sarah's palace, Ron began to speak to George in private.

'Master! Just a reminder. Your next experience is due in one day's time. I think you might prefer to be at the mansion and on Earth during that attack,' Ron said.

'Then we must make plans to leave at the earliest, because I also have some scientific work to complete before then,' George replied.

Cathy kept a note in her little personal computer and also whispered a few words in his ears later that evening. But he may have known even before Ron reminded him. He just didn't like to think about that particular topic.

When he told his mother, Sarah, that he had to leave on urgent business, she insisted that he remained until late that evening. That was because she intended to arrange another one of those temporary farewell parties, during which time all important guests would be invited.

When Martia's ship arrived on Mars, the complete area had been significantly changed from when they had left. Now there were black hexagonal sections as far as the eye could see. They stood together like one massive dark grey honeycomb against the Martian sky and numerous robots were still at work constructing even more buildings. They were like bees in a hive, carrying and positioning those large brick-like sections in precise position with little effort and quite oblivious to the harshness of the Martian environment.

The train station in Caefon Dome was almost completed, from an operational standpoint, and the LPD train was presently under construction within the Admin Dome, with its new access tunnel to the main one.

'You've done some incredible work here during our absence. Is everything going to schedule? George inquired.

'My Lord, presently I think we are ahead of schedule. Building in this environment is a lot easier then on Eden and I made my estimates on our previous work on Eden,' Venusa's ship said.

'That's good, it means we will finish ahead of schedule. It's a pity you couldn't also come along this time, but save your energies for later. Soon we will have a war to fight. Anyway, Martia and Venusa are back. They can update you on our fantastic experiences,' he said and left.

It was estimated that the program would take another fortnight before all installations were completed, then the interior utilities, furnishings and decoration would be next in line to be fitted.

George was very pleased with progress and made those feelings clear to Venusa's ship.

Martia's ship was parked in her usual position, next to Venusa's ship and could also assist with the program. Both twin ships tended to work a lot more efficiently together.

As usual, their human duals in the form of Councillors Venusa and Martia always visited their ship's mind-rooms after such trips. Their visits were meant to update the ships memories with their experiences and this time it was Venusa's turn. Although they could have completed the process through implants, it was not the same as while in person.

The group was soon back on Earth via portal and were tired enough to retire almost immediately on arrival.

In the morning the mansion could well have been the liveliest place in the states and even Ulysses showed signs of welcoming emotions. Parky and the chief chef were changed people since their visit to the stars and all realized that George was a powerful being with cosmic powers. However, some still contemplated their incredible experiences as some type of dream. Yet, there were the presents and mementos, so those experiences must have been real enough.

Cathy and George brought presents back for everyone, including those on the trip and decided to share them after breakfast. Therefore, that day was more like Christmas at the mansion.

The few recruits left behind were soon to be joined by others during their absence and even those were given duties about the mansion.

That time was filled with excitement and everyone including the recruits were invited to partake under Andy and his captains' supervision, but only champagne and cocktail were served. George insisted everyone had the day off to celebrate their first encounter with other intelligence outside of Earth. It was also his first time and the time of his reunion with his parents and Shadite brother, Peter.

'We had a most exciting trip and have met many friends across Osmaron. You can now appreciate how well we are respected and loved by all. During our visits we enjoyed ourselves, but also did significant work which we shall build on in future years. Although some of you may think you just came along for the ride, you played an important part in the process and I love you all for your efforts. We are going to have many such visits in the future, if not just to assist our friends in trouble. So let's drink a toast to our friends and families within Osmaron,' George said and they lifted their glasses and shouted, 'To Osmaron, family and friends!' Then turning to Bawaki, he again spoke.

'It's nice to have you on board, Bawaki,' he said. She had transformed back to her adopted human form and was now a most beautiful woman.

'It's a fantastic place you have here and I thank you for including me in your gang,' she replied.

'By the way, we now have a direct portal to my mother's manor, so why don't you, Bawaki and some of the other ladies pay granddad a visit. Perhaps you might also be able to assist them in organising their wedding, which I think is to be in just seven days time. Please talk to Cathy, she has all the information. I shall be away for the remainder of today, so if you need me for anything, please say your piece now or wait until tomorrow. Now people, if there are no more questions, I must depart your presence for now,' George said and left the room.

'Pal, it's so nice to be back home!' he said to Ron, his little computer.

'Master, I fully agree with that observation,' Ron replied.

They both went directly to the meditation room and George decided to run one of those soothing meditation scenes. It was similar to the one at Sarah's palace and in Virtual Reality. He spent sometime relaxing and then began to concentrate on specific areas of the varying scene.

He could hold on to certain relevant areas of the scene by wanting them to remain, while others he consciously allowed to fade away. That way he could adjust the dynamic scene more to his mood. Soon the whole seen was relevant to what he felt and it became in unison with his thoughts at that moment.

The master computer which generated those Virtual Images was mainly controlled by his implants, although one was never sure whether he was able to interfere with its programming directly without their use.

This time the scene changed into his first two visions, which tended to move much quicker than on previous occasions, as if realizing he had been through them before while trying to get to a more important part that was relevant to the present. The flitting images slowed and he found himself in a beautiful forest moving towards a rock-face. The overhanging rock was covered by many centuries of moss and vine creepers.

He walked into a side entrance that led into a dry, but cleaner ancient cave. It had a large mound of pebbles, each curved and well worn from the constant beating by waves on an ancient beach in times past.

He was able to observe subtle differences between each pebble and went towards the pile to collect a very symmetrical one that was close to the apex of the pile. That one was very elliptical in shape and could have been an odd-man-out, although similar in size to the others.

George observed its curvature, by placing it in his right hand and realised it was not really a pebble at all, but a kind of ancient machine that was still operational.

When he squeezed it in his right palm, his whole body lifted into the air and began moving through the forest as if it was not there. He could visit anywhere by simply having an image of the place and if he didn't, he could travel until he found where he wished to go by trial and error.

George could travel in any direction and at any speed by just wanting it. By so doing nothing in the universe could have hindered his progress. He simply went through the trees and rocks without any damage to them or himself.

He awoke from the strange dream with a slight sweat and could hear Cathy's voice outside the door, so he asked her to enter.

'It has happened again. Clair has recited another one of her poems. It's even stranger than the others, and here it is,' she said.

> *It was on a very hot summer's day,*
> *Within an overhanging rock display,*
> *A shady cover, a shelter cool,*
> *Temptations offered. I was a fool.*
>
> *As I entered an opening appeared,*
> *A little cave or so, I feared,*
> *I wandered into an airy silence,*
> *Of black and damp, of cobwebs dense.*
>
> *The route I followed guided straight,*
> *To some small area and seal my faith.*
> *While I bravely stood on a surface firm,*
> *I felt a strange and piercing hum.*
>
> *The door I entered would suddenly close,*
> *An impervious wall or something, my senses froze.*
> *The surface on which I stood soon moved,*
> *Ever downwards it descended, I disproved.*

*It stopped one hundred metres down,
And I was ushered towards a strangely mound.
A place inhuman and in a strange light.
A ghostly pyramid ahead, just within my sight.*

*Of dismal grace,
A cold embrace,
Of ghosts I dread,
This place, be feared.
In danger lurks,
A black that sucks,
A hell's desire,
Thank God! No Fire?*

*Instead a chill,
To make me still,
No roaring Lion,
No dreamy Skeleton,
For now I see,
A landscape, free,
And way beyond, a shiny sea.*

*I shouted: 'Please be revealed!'
But no one answered; my faith was sealed.
And echoes most resoundingly,
Reverberated chillingly.*

*Alone, I decided to explore,
Perhaps towards the sea and more.
On second thoughts, my tracks not lost,
Towards the surface fast, at little cost.*

*For reasons hard to understand,
Towards the mound I moved, on land.
Within its dome, the elevators lights dimmed,
While awaiting someone to the surface, it seemed.*

I entered thus and with one gust,

The outer door slammed shut as if no rust.
A humming sound again declared,
My movement to the surface shared.

Several hundred metres passed,
By then the humming sound had ceased.
The outer door most suddenly and furiously opened,
while bright sunlight once again beckoned.

I ran along the narrow cave,
My life, dear Lord, I must now save.
A few more steps will see me through,
The overhang, a little more, and life's anew ...?'

Cathy recited the poem, but stopped at the point where Clair recovered from her trance.

'It sounds more like a nightmare than a poem. Perhaps she is giving vent to her pent up feelings. I shall discuss it with Ron tomorrow. But I don't think it's important,' George replied.

The following day, George went up to discuss the dream with Ron.

'Can you explain my strange dream and Clair's poem to me?' he asked.

'Clair's poem, when taken as a whole, does relate to certain concepts. A route was taken and completed. Yet, nothing of a material nature was gained other than the knowledge of your experiences, which although nightmarish in your mind, was quite a safe adventure.

'Despite the webs, there was no giant spiders, no skeletons or hell fire with demons. It was just an empty place, yet functional and with much information if you wished to explore.

'Therefore, I think it's to do with two aspects, one of which is fear. The other I think is knowledge and both fear and knowledge tends to go side by side. That dream is saying that you should conquer fear if you are to conquer knowledge and then wisdom will come with experience in the use of such

knowledge.

'This fourth malady, which relates to the seventh dimension, is to do with knowledge and control of fear in the pursuance of such knowledge.

'As for your own dream, here again we are on a similar theme, but a lot more positive. It seems to me that Clair's psyche reflects a more negative, weaker and more darker side of your own being, perhaps as a reminder... the other darker key to that locked pandora's box.

'Both visions indicate two sides of the same story. Clair's poem stress negatives and yours, that you have already conquered those fears and feel free to journey through the forest of existence with all its dangers and setbacks.

'You were able to select the correct pebble from a pile of thousands. Then to travel through the trees and move freely anywhere. If you didn't know the route to where you were going, you could find it by trial and error. That simply meant that you could always find the answer when you search for truth. Knowledge is one thing, but true knowledge is yet another.

'Therefore, you should always strive for truth in all things. In both dreams, knowledge, wisdom and fear seems to be predominant, so I would like to think of the fourth malady as the one to do with knowledge,' Ron said.

'It does make sense when you interpret them in that way. But, are there hidden dangers in the future?' George asked.

'No, Master. Not if you take the warnings of Clair's poems,' Ron replied.

Then he left to rejoin Cathy.

CHAPTER 30

Home sweet home

Professor Khan's marriage ceremony and reception was held at Sarah's country manor. He had enthusiastically decorated both houses for the occasion. With all the Infilate problems on Earth, he had found little time during the past decades to even consider such a close partnership. But alas, the Infilate problems of the pass decades had dissipated, as the antidote distribution abruptly came to an end, giving him time to consider a better future with someone he loved. He had met his future bride in Iraq, during one of his infrequent visits and had become very close to her since. Nevertheless, he wanted that marriage to be his second and last.

After the death of his first wife, Alexandra, who was Sarah's mother, he thought he would remain single for the remainder of his life. But after all those years his views had changed. He had met someone that he really loved and realized it didn't change the love he had for his first wife nor his memories. Presently, his only problem was Sarah's acceptance. Although she had given him her blessings, it would be a permanent change in both their lives and Sarah never liked such changes.

Both buildings of the manor were crammed full with guests from Eden and elsewhere, and the portal between the primary manor and the mansion was constantly in use, like another door to an adjacent house by Solarians.

George was best-man and usually handled such occasions well.

After the ceremony was over he offered his grandfather the job of his personal ambassador, to which he accepted joyfully.

He could now visit many countries, places and businesses that George could not have attended due to his ever growing list of appointments and their demands.

His much younger bride appeared to be very happy, despite their age difference, chronologically. Nevertheless, Professor Khan (Ben) looked a little older than his bride at close to thirty years physically, despite his well over 100 years, chronologically.

Dr. HAL SEATON & Dr. JOHN SIMMONS

Those two doctors now considered George their leader and were constantly improving anti-Javols weapons. They were also involved in designing some of Georges own weapons with the assistance of the two great ships, Venusa and Marcia.

JERRY JUNIOR, MIRANDA & OTHERS

Sarah's country home brought back many pleasant memories to Bawaki, Jon and his group, and Ancients like Meron. They began once again to enjoy its tranquillity and simplicity in Earth's rugged ways.

Plato was also present from another one of his Shadite missions and had a lot to catch up on by way of gossip, including knowledge of Sarah's long lost son, namely George Peterson.

Ben didn't realise he had so many friends and was overjoyed with the enormous turn out, which also included Mallory and Roseanne.

After the celebrations were over, George and Cathy returned to their Hurst Mansion, accompanied by Jerry and Miranda. They were each given a glass of champaign and were sitting comfortably for a friendly chat.

'How are you handling your new jobs as president and vice present of Solarian Banking?' George inquired.

'I enjoy it very much. It's so dignified. I feel like a little queen running a small empire of my own... and yet, it's the largest organization in the Solar System. But most of all I like the people, everyone in Sol-Newtown is so polite, androids and humans alike. Well, I can hardly tell the difference, anyway. But I also like the hard work,' Miranda replied.

'And you, Jerry?'

'Miranda said it all. It's nice to be one's own boss. I still can't believe we have gone so far in such a short time. And by the way, I have proposed to Miranda and she has accepted. So I think we are going to have another wedding in the gang very soon. If you don't mind the inconvenience, that is, you being best man again?' Jerry said with a broad smile.

'That's fantastic news!' Cathy Yelled.

'This calls for a mega party. Thanks for considering me for this greatest of all duties!' George replied.

'Have you set a date yet?' she asked.

'We are thinking of sometime next month, perhaps towards the end, but we'll let you know in a few days,' Miranda replied.

'Looking back, it's so strange how events happen in our gang. You know, since Cathy and I met, I thought you would be the first to get hitched that way, but better late than never, and it makes me very proud of you both for taking that important step.'

'Yea! And now, we being head of Solarian Banking. Who would ever have guessed!' Jerry said.

'Yea, but I always thought Miranda to be one of the most responsible, hard-working and caring persons, except of course my beloved wife, so you couldn't have made a better choice.' George said.

'By the way, I have accepted an area on Eden on your behalf and all our palaces are being built to the most spectacular specifications in a similar area, so it might be ready for your honeymoon. Your grandfather is a brilliant architect and I saw the drawings. If it's not ready by then, you can always stay with me,' George said to Jerry.

'That's fantastic news. I would love another break on that incredible world, particularly for my honeymoon,' Jerry replied.

'Hopefully, your beautiful palace should be ready by then!' George said.

GEORGE'S NEW DESIGNS

George decided to spend the next few days within the mansion. He expected three more attacks within the week and wanted to prepare himself for their occurrences.

So far, they had not affected him physically or psychologically. Every attack just added something invisible to his being. Like a type of invisible force akin to gravity that was not felt when matter was vectored, yet when solid, could be felt and was attracted by other objects.

He would spend the time at home and complete the new projects that he designed with the aid of Ron and his Macron. The meditation room, which was also a form of Cyberspace, was subsequently used to construct and simulate their operations in Virtual Testbeds. The simulations were as real as matter. With the exception that any part could easily be dreamt-up, dissolved or made to fail under extreme temperatures and stresses. Then they could be altered at quick notice to such an extent that there was no difference between the end-product and its simulacrum.

ACTIVE LODORIANS

The work on Mars was continuing to completion and Satellite Gimbal was begging for another visit from George.

The Lodorians were in the process of completing more long range portals from Mars to Lodor. Then to Tarran, Polok, Nervia World and others within the federation. They were also to construct a large installation within the northern regions of Lori III, with a smaller link to one of its moon installations. There would now be direct portal links between Mars and all important federation worlds within the galaxy. However, security had been increased and Javols could not use such methods for travelling through our Osmaron galaxy. Anyway, the portal Macrons were quite intelligent and could scan both passenger and cards during transit by genetic codes and other more subtler methods. That way it was virtually impossible for any imposter to travel the system.

There was also constant communication between George and Volt regarding their new stellar projects. The Lodorians had found their new god in the form of George Peterson and would do anything for him. They were presently fully fledged members of the Federation and quite wealthy because of it. Gone were the days when most of them remained in underworld tanks. Presently, they were all playing an active role in the greater Osmaron Empire and enjoyed the new freedom with all its variations and new discoveries. The security of our galaxy, Osmaron, was increasing in leaps and bounds. The next phase were the massive stellar destroyers designed by George. It was hoped such powerful weapons would be used to vaporize large swarms of Javols in a single burst.

PROTECTIVE SUITS & JAVOLS

With the assistance of Hal and John, Venusa's ship had completed the special suits and many new weapons, including the first prototypes of the Anti-Javol's improved Mind Probes. They were of a microid design and specifically made to take the place of Javols and mislead their companions into thinking they were genuine Javols through odour and subliminal signals. Also constructed from microids, they could sense Javols and supply them with erroneous data including destructive Subliminals. That could be done after receiving their opponent's identification codes. Then they would simply take their place, after the genuine Javol had self-destructed due to contradictions within its transformation bonds and circuits. However, Javols could only self-destruct during the transformation process, which could only be initiated by them when the necessity arose for their survival. The survival instinct in Javols were too strong for them to be suicidal, so they would always transform to avoid any hazzards imposed upon them.

Subliminals caused a type of human hallucination that made them see bright lights, enjoyable humans and other enticing forms, the temptation of which was too great for any Javol to resist.

The LPD-driven Mind Probes could also blank out communications, by jamming transmissions within preselected areas of space. Thus, preventing Javols from communicating to local bases and their MasterMind.

It was intended to install many such devices around Caefon in Andromeda and within deep space. They could warn of impending invasions from the centre of that galaxy to any new human colonies on that world. However, such visits by Javols were thought highly unlikely, since their animal food resources were now quite rear in that part of the Andromedan galaxy and they had already been and gone.

There were not many Javol renegades about since their MasterMind had taken control of almost everyone in that galaxy. Nevertheless, there could have been many storage installations and farms that were installed locally in the intervening years. Those would cultivate all kinds of food for Javols consumption. The larger animals would be fattened by the slaves for their own biological needs. Then their masters, the Javols, would feast on their near-human Timit slaves. Caefon could well have been one of those chosen planets, with its forests and grazing fields still in tact.

Such stations would report almost daily to their MasterMind. Therefore, those installations were also to be neutralized before they were taken over by duplicate Javols, if they were to alleviate any suspicions from the Javols' MasterMind.

UN CONFERENCE & TRADE FAIRE

Many diplomats and foreign people had begun to arrive for the UN Conference, which was made to coincide with the main trade faire and other exhibitions that were organised by Solarian Banking.

George decided to display information on the more advanced class-seven technologies, which also included inter-dimensional drives. There was also other information on life in general within Osmaron, which gave the participants an idea of life outside of the confines of Earth. There were many devices unknown to human technology and here again, they were introduced so that many would become interested and ask questions. Since the whole of Osmaron and Andromeda would be opened to mankind in the future, it was in their interest to partake at all levels within the Master Plan as George called it.

Solarian Banking had hired the complete trade centre over the duration. That great feat was achieved with the influence and backing of Donald, the President of the USA. George had decided to open the trade fare two days before the UN Conference.

The massive federation ships, Venusa and Martia were to be stationed in the sky just above those buildings and were also to be made accessible to those delegates with an interest in space travel, commerce and resettlement. People could freely visit both ships from two temporary portals that were fitted within the Conference and Trade Centres, respectively. Temporary portals for that purpose were also fitted to Gimbal and Caefon Dome on Mars. That way people could visit those places and ships freely. For security reasons the Eta Satellite remained a no-go area.

George decided to stir the planet in a positive direction during that all important conference. Therefore Earth's smaller population were a lot more active than usual in anticipation of something positive about to happen and many also thought it was due time for change in an insecure environment.

INFILATES vs FERTILATES

Despite George's negative attitude towards Infilates in the past, they respected him for his honest and direct approach and felt they could trust his words. Therefore, many of the few remaining wanted to know where they fitted into his plans and whether they would still be considered the scum of the Earth as in the past. That attitude had been fostered by most Fertilates since their separation, amidst all the inter-city violence of that period several decades before. His only real problems were the rebel Fertilates who for one reason or another had felt left out during previous years and were still fighting for their cause.

The more violent periods of the past, with its many child-kidnapping, had driven the Fertilates away from the main cities. However, the populations of those major cities that was not under the rising oceans had reduced by a mere fraction and most of the dangerous criminals and Infilates had since died from disease or old age. The vicious gangs that were controlled by the young Fertilate dropouts had been hunted to virtual extinction by Mallory's Specials. Thus leaving behind just the few young criminal "Fertilates" who had sided with the elderly only to get their hands on their wealth.

Since Jerry's kidnapping, many Infilates had become sympathetic and respective of George. Many had realised that they were mainly to blame for Earth's problems of overpopulation and the extinction of so many animal species. The list of which was truly enormous and included life-forms like the Elephant, Giraffe, Rhinoceros, Hippopotamus, Lions, Tigers and many species of birds, fish, insects and plants. The lists of extinctions were almost endless.

They were willing to accept most of the blame for the negligence of their forefathers and themselves for their monetarist ideology and utter selfishness. All of the problems facing Earth were as a direct result of their insatiable desires, to practise business purely for the sake of greed symbolized by capitalism, globalism and self-indulgence. To them, it had always been more than just a way of survival, more like an addiction, but they also knew that they were unjustly blamed for all of Earth's ills.

They were like children, constantly being scolded for bad behaviour which made them rebel even more and sometimes in a worst manner than before. If not just to prove to themselves that they were still alive even though neglected by the authorities.

Nevertheless, it was also to score an extra point or to gain just rewards for their constant persecution and neglect. They gained personal satisfaction and relief in the process. Their culture was unlike the Fertilates, who were strictly controlled by Solarian Banking and were specially chosen genetically. They had everything, including a code of ethics handed down by Ben and Solarian Banking to follow. Those had been learnt through leaflets and other methods of assistance, including the Anti-Drug propaganda and other information on healthy living. Further, in the past they depended for their antidote from Solarians who could always have withdrawn those supplies. They had also been given generous incentives and had become the most wealthiest people on the planet.

With all the global problems of the time, the political systems could see no benefit in assisting Infilate survival. Between global climatic and other changes, there were high costs involved in ensuring just basic survival, from increased sea levels, tornadoes, hurricanes and frequent floods. Insurance premiums had become so high that no one but the very rich could pay. As a result, many such companies went bankrupt. Therefore the governments had to hand out large subsidies from their disaster funds which had in many cases become greater than 50 percent of their GNP.

Luckily for Earth, many of the now nonexistent species had been bred within special forests and domes on Tyrrel 2 and Eden in anticipation of a better Earth. Those would be reintroduced into their original habitats after the population had reduced below five-hundred million. At that time, the population of Africa could have reduced to just twenty million African human Fertilates. Then there would be a suitably trained organization to assist in the reintroduction program.

Unfortunately, over the intervening period, almost half of Africa had become The Greater Sahara, and many of its predictable weather patterns along with its rivers had disappeared in the process, causing havoc with its ecosystems. South America had followed a similar faith while the Amazon forest was decimated by slash and burn.

Therefore, major remodelling of the planet would be necessary to support the complexity of life in all its habitats, food chains and niches. However, because of mutual dependency in such complex ecosystems, even after the introduction of key species in those environments, it would have taken several millennia for any return to a semblance of normality.

EARTH'S NEW HUMANS

George had many plans for taking Earth away from the path of overpopulation and abuse, to one of paradise, but he would never do it by his type of spiritual magic. Whatever he did in earnest could never be reversed and he always preferred to involve the people concerned in an adventure. Something they would be proud of, once having taken part in its creation.

Such memories of great adventures and deeds gave them a

talking point by which they could relate and communicate with their children and friends. By so doing they also leant more about themselves, their capabilities and limits.

He also realised that every individual needed to flex their muscles. In so doing, they would gain exciting memories of adventures as part of their causal history or else, day-to-day living to many would become boring and meaningless.

He realised that Earth's humans would always be self-indulgent children and could never be allowed to take the reigns of their planet again without the necessary controls and limits. They had a tendency to bear offspring for its own sake without due consideration of the greater environment and its habitats.

He thought that freedom was not a birthright, in much the same way as it was not possible for Earth humans to exist without their police forces. Therefore, in future it should be earned through respect for life. By first respecting oneself, their families, friends, other life-forms, Earth and Osmaron. In that order.

Earth's humans would always require android policing because of their inability to always do what was correct in hindsight, barring small mistakes.

Many didn't care what the results of their actions would have led to within an hour, never mind what happened as a result in a day or week. But he also thought that as its people became more conscious and aware of the Cosmos, those responsibilities would come naturally, despite their peculiar mental makeup.

Many of Earth's children would be given the appropriate military training and sent out to patrol and maintain order within Osmaron. Many would become scientists, engineers, explorers, soldiers, entertainers, artists, musicians and others. The lists were endless. Everyone, then living up to the higher standards and ideals of the Solarian Empire.

However, first of all, there was that war to be fought against the Javols. He wanted that one to be an excuse to take mankind outside of the limitations of their world in order to show them a different way of life. One more galactic in scope. The experience gained by those adventures would benefit mankind in a myriad of ways, as he began to spread his wings throughout the local galaxies and beyond.

Therefore, recruiting of soldiers, enhanced by a new type of discipline were an essential part of his plan.

THE NEW TERMINUS CITY ON MARS

The original Martian domes were to be cleared and used for growing vegetables. Caefon Dome would be transformed into a park with forest, a small lake and animals. Meteoric defensive weapons and screens would be positioned locally to safeguard that area of the planet from falling projectiles.

The present Caefon Dome population would be rehabilitated and given well-paid jobs within the new Martian city that he decided to call Terminus. That was because that area of Mars presently housed the main terminals for all long-range portals to the main federation worlds and Earth.

Terminus City was composed of ten-kilometres diameter of hexagonal buildings which appeared like a complex honeycomb on many levels. Each building was one hundred metres across any two parallel faces and included at least one hundred floors. That corresponded to a thirty square kilometre area of the city on just one floor, and over three thousand square kilometres when the total area was considered. With facilities and room enough to contain over five million people in relative luxury.

Smaller portals led to every hex unit which was numbered and included moving walkways, stairways and elevators. They were all security coded and those used by special people could only be operated with brain implants.

Each hex unit could be sealed from its neighbours in times of emergencies by airtight doors and could rapidly inhibit decompression caused by falling meteorites or explosions. The defensive system would be constantly searching the skies for any unidentified intruders, with the domes and main city area as their targets.

The nuclear generators were placed several kilometres away, deep within the surface of the planet.

Just two kilometres from Terminus' perimeter was the training centre, which was composed of seven large hexagons and sealed environmental domes for training. They covered an area of under one square kilometre with all the necessary training facilities. It also contained its own moving LPD underground train, but portals also existed for those with implants.

Both environments could be extended ad infinitum, until the training centre found itself within greater Terminus if need be.

It was truly an incredible feat of engineering, as all raw materials like silicates and metals were mined from the Martian surface by the miners from Caefon Dome, and Venusa ship's robots.

It was then their intention to fit large portals to the dead outer planets and satellites like Ganymede. Those would be for the transfer of hydrogen, oxygen and other essential life sustaining gasses that were to be later purified and modified by special processes. George also realized that any future atmosphere on Mars had to be held in place by strong magnetic fields. This was essential to prevent the degrading effects of the Solar Wind. That was because the almost solid Martian core was no longer strong enough, magnetically.

Those powerful orbiting machines or Magnatrons, were based on a technology using powerful super-conductive coils that deflected the Solar Wind towards the artificially created polar regions of Mars.

CHAPTER 31

The fifth malady

George was now forced to remain close to the mansion because of his forthcoming more regular attacks. He had decided to assist Jerry and Miranda by organizing many aspects of the Trade Fare. When not organizing and planning, he was selecting and manufacturing a few special items for the main display. That left the couple (Jerry and Miranda) more time to plan their wedding. However, his main effort was in ordering the more specialist samples from within the Solarian federation and to ensure they arrived on time for the main opening. Those few additions were essential for their special displays if the fare was to start with an impressive bang. That grand display of all advanced sciences and technologies were to be held at the International Trade Centre and within other chosen cities on Earth.

All exhibitions were organised and timed to coincide with the UN Conference, although to begin two days earlier.

Jerry had selected an army of agents from within Solarian Banking. They would organise and assist in every aspect of the project. During this period, their Publicity and Exhibition Departments were stretched to their limits, due to the short timescale in which they had to arrange it all.

Several androids were imported from Eden to assist in the more manual placement and testing of the exhibits. While the heavy systems like powerful Solarian generators were made available for special equipment that used their own types of power.

The Ancients, with Lord Meron in charge, also decided to organise their own stalls with the latest Virtual Image Projectors, Drives, Medical and Terra-Forming Equipment and others.

Lumak would become one Doctor Mansell, just for the exhibition. He had decided not to use his original Doctor Jeffery Longhurst for obvious reasons. Some old people on Earth may have recognised him as such with possible undesired consequences. There he would display his latest efforts in

Microid Technology, Macron Computers and LPD Drives, now over one hundred times more powerful and faster than anything on Earth. But Inter-dimensional Drives and Headrons were not shown. That technology was classified as type seven and above, and only type five and under could be allowed on Earth for trading purposes, with the usual inbuilt viral self destruct which was either installed with a timer or triggered by data entry using special code. Class 7 technology could only be viewed but not demonstrated or used.

All of The Gang members were now able to communicate directly through implants, but such communication was limited to a maximum range of just two hundred metres within buildings.

With the special Coms Transceivers, that range could be extended throughout the planet and as far as Gimbal. Then with special boosting, to Mars and beyond, but with the usual delay problems as they were limited by light-speed.

When basic H-wave was used, with its necessary local transceivers, communication could traverse the whole galaxy almost instantly.

A most comprehensive worldwide publicity and advertising campaign was planned over the mass media throughout many countries. Many news journals and bulletin boards carried articles on Solarian Banking and George during that period, backed by many added incentives from Solarian Banking.

Their own printing presses were in constant motion and those departments were very busy despatching millions of synthetic brochures, leaflets and invitations. Those were sent to embassies, companies and were also distributed through newsagents in many countries. Particularly those that preferred the written word.

Very soon, most people on Earth were well informed on matters relating to the Trade Fair, the UN Conference and of local exhibitions in their own countries.

From the feedback they had received, many delegates, VIP's and business people were to be expected and many hotels, partly or fully owned by Solarian Banking, were literally taken over for the event. Yet, no one disapproved; for it was a time for them to have a full house in a period of mild recession. Further, all visitors would be rewarded and all such endeavours were refundable at a substantial profit to all concerned.

George was probably the only member of The Gang that was left at the mansion during that period. However, the others commuted through hidden portals several times daily from the Trade Centre to keep him informed on progress.

George was slightly nervous of his fifth attack which corresponded to the fifth dimension. That one was to take place in the afternoon of the following day.

On that morning, he got as much work done as it was possible, gave a tight hug to his wife Cathy and she in turn returned those feelings with apprehension. He did not know what strange new powers he would acquire that day.

'Darling, why are you so nervous today. It's like someone had walked over your grave,' she said in jest.

'As you well know, it's another one of those days and I can never get used to them, not knowing what to expect,' he replied.

'I know, Darling, but Ron reckons it's nothing to worry about and I think he is right. So far you've had four and I can't see any physical changes other than when you put on that Cloak of Aron. So don't you worry,' she said and his nervousness dissipated.

Having completed most of his important duties, he retired to Ron's room and immediately went into meditation with one of those tranquil scenes, which was preferable to the other violent ones with Javols.

He had stopped giving Ron direct commands verbally, but found that if he asked him in a gentle manner and with the word 'please,' his powers never affected Ron's psyche in a detrimental manner. That way, he seldom needed to use the special keyboard.

By now, Cathy, Clair and others of The Gang could also communicate with Ron via their implants.

George realised the incredible potentials of his powers, but given a choice, he would always prefer to be a normal human being, although with the capacity of eternal life.

He never used those powers in vain or to boast to his friends, and only took that course when life was threatened or when he wished to make a universal point of supreme importance.

When he had completed most of his important duties of that day, he peacefully walked up to Ron's room. As he entered, little Clair was also there relieving her boredom by using Ron to give her answers to many things that she had observed, including certain parts of her daily schoolwork. Most of that information she could have found out by her methods of searching, but she preferred that process of learning with the little Macron computer. George decided she could stay if she remained quiet and allowed him the use of the meditation program on the projector, to which she agreed.

He sat in his usual position on the soft thick foam rubber floor and Clair copied his position, as she had already decided to do her own meditation.

Once again, he had a mild concussion, during which time his previous dreams tended to flit by until they came to an abrupt end. Then the new dream would begin.

This time his vision was even stranger than before and Clair also recited another one of her bizarre poems, but he could not see or here anything during those brief moments other than the contents of his vision.

After little Clair had left, he remained to discuss the fifth vision and poem with Ron.

'I beheld a large bird sitting upon a nest and the nest was made of what appeared to be of coal and twigs, the coal may have been from the smouldering of the twigs.

'When the bird moved away from the centre of the nest, I could see a small flame there burning. Whenever the fire got too hot the bird felt uncomfortable and shifted its position away from the flame and it would dim, but when it was smouldering and on the brink of going out, the bird would return upon the dying fire to increase or rekindle it. This process appeared to continue to eternity.

'However, when I arrived on the scene, I saw the flame reduced to such a level that I thought it was not possible for the bird to rekindle the fire by sitting upon it. I then chased the bird away in order to assist by way of relighting the flame with my modern lighter. But the bird, realising that I had taken over its job, flew

off into the bushes to a freer existence. Then I took the lighter out of my pocket and lit the flame even brighter than it had ever been, even when the bird had laid upon it. However, because of its new brilliance, very soon all the twigs were consumed and I constantly had to go searching for more twigs to put upon the bright flame.

'It soon came to a point where I would have given anything for the original bird to have returned upon it. For its method was obviously the most efficient from the amount of twigs used and the times needed to replenish the flame. However, the bird could not now be found to release me from that all important task that had also become my eternal prison,' George said.

'The flame represents continuity of purpose throughout the Cosmos embodied in the Natural Order. The large bird represents the old order that could depend upon your future actions.

'This dream is a simple warning, which tells you to refrain from making changes to the natural order. Such changes may permanently affect a certain balance within the system that may not be reversible, thus placing you within a prison of your own making.

'Grand projects are good to watch on the drawing-board, but always have negative after effects on the natural order. Such effects can also be accumulative, so beware, for you must look and see before you can leap.

Clair's poem is as follows:

It was in a distant land of time,
Perhaps of Roman for a crime.
A narrow cell so dimly lit,
A passing guard, as if to flit.

In passing words, he pointed to me,
And in a foreign tongue he stressed: 'be free!'
A senior figure appeared, with little fuss,

And mentioned sternly: 'Mari di bracus!'

Could this have been my timely past,
In some other life, an experience cast?
A replay of a moment had,
Within a past, so strangely bad?

I nodded my head as to agree,
Perhaps now chained unto a galley.
For freedom in an age like this,
Could only be attained through bliss?

And yet, I wonder of its significance,
Perhaps a vision for future reference.
For thus in past, the future seem,
Repeating, for life's but a recurring dream.

'Here again, we have a poem of warnings and 'Mari di bracus' could represent the sea of events throughout the Cosmos. It appears that you were a prisoner about to be released, but we are all prisoners in one way or another.

'The simple guard in passing warns you to 'be free' before his captain arrives. He obviously thinks you need the warning as his captain may be up to some deceit in tricking you into an even worst task or prison than before. Yet, here again although you did not know what was expected of you, you agreed with possible disastrous consequences.

'As always, this poem is a worst case scenario. It's a warning that you should look and see before you leap or else there may be even a worst prison ahead waiting for you. In this case, Mari di Bracus. This could mean the Sea of Salt in some ancient dialect.

'I have now come to the conclusion that the fifth order relates to the power of seeing and insight which relates to understanding. At least this is how it shows itself within our third dimension,' Ron said.

CHAPTER 32

The last maladies

After the Gang's return from the Trade Centre the following evening, Cathy immediately went into George's study.

'I heard someone say today that the planets were moving to form a straight line with an arrow pointing to Earth. When the alignment is complete, Earth will be the only planet left on the other side of the sun. The sun becomes the head of the arrow and Pluto its tail. They also expect a lunar eclipse the day after their alignment. And guess what? The alignment of the planets is expected in three days time, which is also the day of your sixth attack. I know it must be something to do with you, Darling,' she said.

'I expect any changes to be more material this time. After all, the third is my physical home dimension, hence, effects will be greater here than within the others,' he replied.

'Many people are frightened because of their rapid alignment, that were not expected by astronomers, who are themselves baffled by the strange occurrence,' she replied.

'Yes, Dearest, it must signify a new cosmic era with Earth as its focus. For never before has such a quick transformation occurred, but it should have little effect on us physically and I shall not make any changes to improve the situation,' he replied.

'I shall be a very happy woman when it's all over,' she said.

'Don't worry, Love, it will be all right and just the last two to go. Then we'll be free like birds in the tree,' he said, but she realized he was just as nervous as the last time.

After another three days he went up to Ron's room once again and there awaited the sixth attack which represented the third dimension. The planets had adopted the perfectly straight line from Pluto to Earth and all were now placed in a near perfect elliptical plane around the sun.

This time, he had no convulsions or dreams, just a sensation of supreme power and he felt that nothing could contain him.

Little Clair did not recite a poem and she was also there with him doing her own meditation. Ron thought it was because the third and first were within the material domains. Then he should not have the higher order convulsions and dreams which seemed to be the only way their powers could be felt by him, within the third dimension. He also thought that the third would be manifested by a physical event like the planetary alignment, and the forthcoming eclipse during the afternoon, the day after, corresponded to the first dimension or whatever it represented.

Yet, George didn't even wish to know what would happen if there was a zero, which also corresponded to something on that cosmic wheel that showed thirteen, unlike the horoscope that showed twelve. Hence, he prepared himself as best he could for the worst and always made sure that Clair was always there, in the meditation room by his side, just in case he needed her, since she appeared to be the main key.

During all this time Cathy kept well away from the mansion, being fully occupied at the Trade Centre. But she was probably the most worried of them all and didn't wish to hear or mention a word on the topic from anyone.

When the seventh malady, which corresponded to the first dimension occurred, he felt himself sinking into complete blackness, with an absolute negation of all his powers. As he descended, Clair appeared as if from nowhere in his dream and lent him her guiding hand.

'Please follow me. I have something to show you?' she said. She guided him towards a little light in an odd and unexpected direction. As they approached the light, it increased in size until he found himself back within the meditation room and awoke from his ordeal.

'How can that be?' George asked Ron.

'You are a three-dimensional being, therefore, all dimensions above give you greater powers. But it is also apparent that the first dimension takes those powers away from you. As always, there is an inbuilt safety feature in the design and Clair has the key to that part of your being.

'If for some reason you were not capable to continue in the

correct manner, that prison could be invoked and her refusal to use the key would condemn you to its domain for eternity. However, you may never in the whole of eternity ever need to visit the first, which is a complete negation of all things. But if you did, you would have to take Clair along with you in order to find your way out again.

'In that case, she is almost as powerful as you, for she can invoke that situation and also controls that form... which is the opposite of your powers,' Ron said. But he didn't know what the first truly represented.

'Is there a zero?' George asked.

'Since most of the dimensions so far are odd and zero is even, I doubt there is one. Even so, I am not 100 percent sure. The zero is also the point on the wheel just beyond the thirteenth; for the wheel is continuous like the face of a clock. If it exists beyond the first, it will enable you to acquire infinite powers. Clair may also use it to increase her senses of perception to infinity. For here, zero also means infinity on the continuous wheel, if it exists.

'To you, it will mean infinity in power and to Clair, infinity in perception. But those are my conclusions from what I have analysed so far,' Ron said.

The following day, and when the zero was expected, nothing of any significance occurred, although both felt perfect within themselves and for the first time little Clair had a tranquil and happy disposition. Yet, he was not sure whether he had retained his original powers beyond the fifth and he didn't want to test them without a proper purpose.

Even so, he was overjoyed that all those attacks were at last over and he could now get on with his normal life without the planning and preparations required for those special days.

Cathy was also very pleased when everything, including the eclipse, had passed without a hitch and arrangements were soon made for him to visit the Trade Fair before its official opening. He was very pleased and impressed with what he saw on that day.

'You know, this effort of ours is going to shake this world of ours and move it well into the 22nd century,' he said and they agreed.

The following morning he visited Ron for another discussion on the strange topic and Ron soon began to sum it all up to him.

'This is my brief summary on the manifestations of these dimensions and on the way they appear to affect us and our dimension.

Zero is also Infinity on the perpetual wheel, but since it's missing is not significant.

The First is the Negative Key to all things.

The Third is to Be before you can See.

The Fifth is to See before you can Know.

The Seventh is to Know before you can Become.

The Ninth is to Become before you can Control.

The Eleventh is the ability to Control before you can truly use the Positive Key.

The Thirteenth is the Positive Key itself, which is on one side of zero and the First the Negative Key which is on the other side of zero. It forms the complete order of all things, even mathematics and thought, in perfect symmetry and harmony,' Ron said.

'So there is really a Cosmic Mind that controls everything in multiple dimensions? This is all so symmetrical, perfect, orderly and complete. No wonder I feel so complete within my being. And I sense no side effects from the ordeal. I must therefore take warning and only use my powers when they are necessary for assisting universal life,' he said.

'I shall always be by your side to counsel you, so always ask for my advise when you are not sure.' The little computer Ron replied and he nodded his approval.

Later on that day he had a private chat with little Clair.

'How would you like to visit the Trade fair with me today and see aunty Cathy, Anne-Marie and the others at work? After we help them a little, we can have some lunch together and you can choose whatever you wish from the menu. Then we can have a good look around the other stands, my little sister,' he said.

'Am I really your little sister?' Clair asked.

'Yes, and you must get used to that little fact, because it's our destiny and it's my duty and aunty Cathy's, to take care of you from now on. When you get older you can then make your own decisions, but until then you are our responsibility. Because of that fact, I have already opened a personal bank account for you, which will grow on a weekly basis until then. So, you have nothing to worry about that aspect in the future.'

'Thank you, Big Brother!' she exclaimed.

'In the mean time, this mansion is to become your permanent home, to use as anyone else. So go and get ready my little sister for we leave in half an hour,' he said. But she turned to him with great affection in her sympathetic light brown eyes and grabbed him about his waist, as far as an eight-year-old could reach and he bent down and kissed her on the forehead. As she left, she turned around.

'Ron was correct my big brother. Now you are even more powerful than you had ever been before,' she replied, knowing that it was the only thing he didn't know about himself at that moment, unless he tried his powers which she also knew he would not have done for that purpose.

He then realised how powerful she really was, for just knowing the fact of having eternal powers could well have been more important than the powers themselves at that moment.

Later that day he called his friends together.

'My Dearest, It's time we had another party to celebrate my coming across. Make it a prologue to Jerry's wedding. This time we must truly shake the mansion,' he said and Cathy agreed.

CHAPTER 33

A grand display

At the morning of the Trade Faire, two massive spaceships appeared on Earth. They cast their enormous shadows over a large area of the city of New York. That was the last part of the submerged city that remained above water. Their size were frightening to most of its remaining inhabitants. Oblivious to the city's remaining population, there Venusa and Martia's ships remained firmly anchored in space, seemingly untouchable by anyone or anything.

Although the city was partly submerged by the rising waters of the Atlantic Ocean, much work had been done over the years to ensure certain buildings were elevated and isolated and the trade centre and UN buildings were included on that list. However, their replacements were currently being built elsewhere, outside of New York on well chosen higher ground. Presently, underground tunnels led to that isolated part of the city, with water pumps going day and night to remove any seepage. However, there were more than enough facilities for landing LPD craft, helicopters and such like in the area of the Trade Faire.

The President's limousine followed in front of George's and was accompanied by special guards on LPD motorcycles without wheels. Those single seater craft could travel above the surface and in the air at high speed while maintaining a precise distance above ground. They were ridden by Specials with Plasma guns who were the most formidable of warriors.

That day George took along Ulysses to guard other important members of The Gang like Jerry, while Hercules remained at the mansion to secure that area.

On arrival at the Trade Fair, they waited outside the building while greeting many in the crowd. They posed for a while in front of the photographers and others of the press before entering the building.

'Lord Peterson, will this mark a change in the affairs of

mankind on this poor world of ours,' a reporter shouted from the rear of the crowd to George.

'Yes, it does! So my good people, you must have faith in me and the future. I swear to you all, that very soon this damaged world of ours will once again become one of the most beautiful planets in our galaxy. We now have the technologies to reform planets like Earth and bring them back to normality. So you must have faith,' he said.

The exhibition was on several floors, and they decided to begin at the lower level and gradually work their way upwards to the more advanced levels.

George, Cathy, Jerry and Miranda took Donald, Anne-Marie and his senators around, introducing them to staff and explaining the products in as much detail as was possible. But most of the show was for the benefit of the USA senators and other foreign delegates which formed the main bulk of that moving crowd.

All members of the Solarian Banking staff wore grey suits, with the winged Solarian crests pinned to their left lapels. Donald was very proud with his son's effort, knowing that Jerry was mainly responsible for its planning and implementation.

Reporters were everywhere within the large building, taking photos and videos for the media and press.

The first floor displayed items from Earth, and many rooms carried themes on conservation, deforestation and endangered species, with relevant technologies for their maintenance and future survival.

The second floor was partly shared by Gimbal, Eta, Moon, Mars and other planets of the Solar System.

It displayed their chemical constituents, geography and mining products, and there were many models depicting what could be done in future to transform them into more habitable worlds. That floor was mainly represented by the hardened patriarch miners from Mars.

The third floor displayed items and technologies from Eden, including the latest in virtual image projection, medical equipment, microid robotics and androids, macron computers, protective suits, brain implants the size of a pinhead that could increase brain power by over 20 times, genetic engineering and many more. Those rooms were truly incredible to view and displayed images as real as life that could change to the mood of the individual. The equipment could sense their body temperature and other vital signs. Those images also extended to subliminal advertising, medical therapy and others.

There was a medical device with a synthetic nose many times more sensitive than a dog. It could sniff out any type of illness and recommend a cure. They would simple point the nozzle of the device to a patient and it would read out every metabolic deficiency, blood pressure, infections and such like. The unit could be operated at a distance and well away from the infected patient.

There were also many rooms dealing with astronomy and astrophysics. Advanced robots and androids were also on display performing very intricate tasks. Such tasks were impossible for humans, even with the best tools. They were so fast that their operations could only be observed in slow motion playback.

The fourth floor contained products of the other federation worlds, including Polok, Lodor, Tyrrel and Tarran. Here, many alien life-forms were displayed with their planets, technologies and resources. There was also a small section on Javols and how to destroy them with special weapons that were also on display.

The fifth floor contained information on the two ships, Venusa and Martia. That information included their inter-dimensional drives, weapons that could be fitted, their special minds and other onboard technologies.

Special trips were to be arranged from the centre to those ships via portals after the commencement of the UN Conference.

The sixth floor related to the universe and George's more advanced technologies of Stellar Transposition, Planetary Remodelling, Dyson Spheres and other major projects, including the Anti-Javol's Cloak, Mind-Probes, Nano-Warriors and weapons both small and large. But detailed information was not given on those special weapons as they were considered to be Class 7 and above, which was higher than Class 5. At that time Earth was limited to Class 5 technological advancement. A Class 5 technological level represented an advancement 10^5 or 100000 times more advanced than Earth at that time. There was a brief display on a variety of Titans. Under the heading of Titan Warriors.

George tried as best to explain those major projects to many of Earth's scientists that were present, but he soon realised that those concepts were well beyond their notions of reality and they assumed many were from the realms of science-fiction. No one could easily believe in a technology that created stars, swapped stars and remodelled complete worlds without first evacuating its occupants.

Then there was the weapons' room, which displayed Plasma Beams. They were guns that accelerated super hot matter close to the velocity of light within an intense magnetic field. Such energetic matter were given a spin within a strong magnetic field. Then the outer shield was released through a magnetic window tangential to its rotation. Such beams could create large craters on the moon just seconds after leaving Earth and with the most explosive effect. However they were better used outside of dense atmospheres.

There was also the intense Gravity Beam or Gravitron as it was called. The intensity of its beam could be adjusted by focussing. Therefore, it could become a tractor beam, to capture asteroids and ships. It could also be intensified to suck matter from a star. Such hot matter could then be focussed unto another local body in space. The larger versions of that weapon could be used to slice through the crust of a planet with disastrous consequences to its inhabitants.

There were many torpedo carrying probes, satellites, communication systems and weapons. Then there were the safe weapons that were designed to target a particular life-form like the Javols while being almost completely safe to animals and plants.

There was also a brief mention of H-wave and portal technology which was used extensively by the Federation worlds.

Just before lunch, Donald left with Anne-Marie and George, while Jerry and their partners remained to continue the trek through the upper floors. By that time the building was almost full to bursting with visitors. Then trained androids took control, to take the visitors around and answer their questions in any relevant Earth language or dialect. Those androids were linked to a Macron, which was programmed with every possible eventuality relating to the fair.

'I never realized Solaria was so advanced. How can any machine manufacture stars, cut planets in thin wafers and place such an orbiting ring of continents and oceans about a star to form a Dyson Sphere?' Donald exclaimed while wiping the sweat from his brow.

'Well, a ring of such wafers will contain infinitely more space than the surface area of any one planet. However, we'll not change the natural evolution of such bodies, Only uninhabited worlds will be used for that purpose.' George replied.

CHAPTER 34

New Vogon

George was in his study contemplating new strategies when to his surprise there was a strange noise then a thud at the back of the mansion.

'I know that noise. It sounds so familiar,' he muttered. Then he ran out the front door and towards the rear.

'My God! It's a new Vogon! Why did no one tell me you found her replacement?' He shouted, aghast by it all.

'It was meant to be a surprise! She is not as decorated as your original, but I think she will do!' Shouted a young Professor Chairmowich on his way down the shiny metallic ladder.

'John? For Heaven's sake, is that really you?'

'It's me alright!' Jean-Claude (Normally called John by his friends) replied in one of his funnier moods.

To George's further surprise John was followed by Karen, Marion, Timothy and others from the Turkish gang. As they came forward from the ship to greet him, just behind George stood Cathy, Miranda and others of the gang. They couldn't believe the sight they beheld. There they remained stunned by the radiant ship.

'She looks almost identical!' Miranda shouted.

'I think she was originally from the same batch. This one was found all the way in Punjab, India. It was used by an Indian Prince, but developed a problem, so we got her for a song. She needed a new set of LPDs,' John replied.

'Nice one! So you got her some new ones?' Cathy inquired.

'Not really!'

'What do you mean?' Miranda inquired.

'We sent her to Eden for a refit. She was loaded unto Martia's ship on Mars.
She is now a fighting ship of the realm,' Jean-Claude said.

While he spoke the Solarian Crest suddenly melted into her undercarriage and she began to glisten like non other.

Miranda was curious enough to mount the ladder and enter into the bowels of the new ship.

Please go in and see for yourself! I hope you are not disappointed!' Jean-Claude shouted.

However, instead of a beautifully decorated interior was what appeared to be an alien environment with strange black and grey striped formations.

'My God, It's all black and grey in here. I can't see a thing! It's like being in another universe!' Miranda shouted.

'She has been remodelled on Eden to a new spec.'

'Remodelled?'

'Focus through your implants and she will become what you wish. Think of what you will like her to be!'

As Miranda focussed so did the interior of the ship change into that new design.

My God! Another nano-bot ship, but so beautiful!' She exclaimed.

'There was a slight glow ahead of her and the hologram of a most beautiful female figure appeared. Miranda was taken back by her sudden appearance.

'I am sorry for my abrupt appearance. My name is Daisy. I may be your captain, trainer or adviser. My presence is mainly for those without implants,' she said.

'You are not the real Daisy I heard so much about?'

'The same!' she replied and curtsied

'I am very pleased to meet you,' Miranda replied and bowed a little.

'My ship can be changed through implants to any interior. However there are standard formats that may be selected. You must be outside to change its basic shape, but that process is automatic while in flight,' Daisy said.

Daisy soon disappeared as Miranda decided to leave. Miranda soon mounted down the stairs, but as she left the ship melted into a stairway very much like Micol.

'Dai...sy! Dai... sy! Is on board!' she exclaimed, trying to catch her breath in the midst of the unbelievable occurrence.

'She says Daisy is on board!' Cathy shouted. They all mounted the glistening stairway to observe the interior and Daisy.

'She is beautiful, isn't she?' Jean-Claude said.

'She appears to be a lot more than beautiful?' George queried.

'Much, much more, I'm afraid!'

'How much more?'

'Well, among other things, she has a new type of inter-dimensional drive and is also a long-range portal. So you may take her anywhere and be sure you can port from that location. There is a similar conversion for Micol, but he is already inter-dimensional,' Jean-Claude replied.

'And she can change back into our original Vogon?'

'That too!'

'John, you are the greatest! Thanks for everything! Now you can assist me with some new designs for Lodor. Jeremy can carry on with his new Megotron and Psyrotron designs for now. All one happy family, Eh!' George said as they walked towards the front door of the Mansion.

CHAPTER 35

Home within Terminus City

Under George's orders they were obliged to take time off the Trade Fair. Since that operation was presently under the capable hands of intelligent androids it was time they focussed their attention elsewhere. That was just before the start of the UN Conference and George had an extensive program to complete. Therefore they left all such operations on Earth in the capable hands of their competent deputies, who would hold the forth in their absence.

During the previous busy preparatory period, the mansion had been unduly neglected and even with the hired help their homely duties were piling higher by the day. There was also several other important matters that required their attention. Finally, there were the Martian construction projects to inspect and implement.

During the early morning of that day George called The Gang together, less Andy. He was away on one of his training missions to Warland and was expected back later that evening.

'Friends, It's nice that we have received our new Vogon. A Vogon of the most latest technologies from Osmaron. She will be very useful during our assault on Javols. However, I think we should change her name from Vogon to Daisy.'

'Great idea!' Miranda shouted.

'Any more votes?' he yelled. All hands went up.

'So Daisy it is! Changing the topic, the new city of Terminus is almost completed and is to be another of our homes in this system from now on. I have therefore selected the first three layers of innermost hexagons for ourselves. Each hex contains one hundred levels of over ten thousand square metres each. The most central nineteen hexes belong to us. They have the potential of over one thousand five hundred beautiful apartment palaces.'

'Palaces on Mars?' Cathy exclaimed.

'Why not? Each palace has its own portal, stairs, elevators and each hex, its own recreation, gymnasium and swimming pools, which are filtered for domestic consumption within that same area.

'Sounds cool!' Tim shouted and the others laughed at that dig.

'Seriously though, the hexes are completely sealed environmentally and have been manufactured from one metre thick thermally insulating material, hence, there are no windows. But, the computers have been able to project virtual images for windows, passageways and entrances. They may be programmed to create interactive scenes of the environment outside of our mansion here, for instance. Anyway, you will be able to see it for yourselves when we arrive there after lunch. Because I want us to have a good look around before we make our choices,' George said.

'When do we make the move?' Cathy asked.

'After the UN Conference. During this time Ulysses can remain here with a few members of staff. Jerry and Miranda will come with us today and can choose their palace apartment, but they can remain at Sol-Newtown as long as they wish, for now. Anyway, portal links exists in all our houses and apartments, so commuting is not a problem.'

'Is everyone included?' Cathy inquired.

'Yes, and there is space for much more. Anne-Marie also has a palace for herself and Donald, when he is ready to leave Earth. But visits are now much easier from Earth via many portals, so we haven't a commuting problem and there will be lots of help about when the local population of miners in Caefon Dome are evacuated to Terminus.

'Wow! A large city on Mars. I never thought it possible!' Miranda commented.

'Anything is possible with this gang!' Tim replied and they giggled.

'This change is necessary during our preparation and training. It is also essential during the rehabilitation of Earth and the training of our Specials for the fight against the Javols. Many Infilates will also be transferred to Caefon in Andromeda through the Omegron Portal for settlement purposes. So we have lots to do on Mars during this period. Furthermore, Earth will become highly turbulent during this period of readjustment, so it will be better for all concerned if we went away for a while. At this time, Hal and John are in charge of Earth. They are currently creating several space-observation-platforms around Earth with screens and weapons. Those will defend Earth in future against invading Javols. Gimbal and Eta will also be updated and armed.

'Many recruiting centres will be opened in every country on Earth and also within Infilate cities. Such centres will carry the hexagram symbol and all recruitment will be carried out under the aegis of The Osmaron Empire. That way, Solarian Banking will not be targeted as in the past.

'I have ordered several thousand android recruiting officers from Polok and Lodor for that purpose. They will be updated by our Warland Macron. Therefore, our work on Earth is now at an end until the time is right for us to return,' he said.

'Will we have to be trained again?' Pamela asked.

'You have all been fitted with implants, so any training you may do yourselves in Virtual Worlds with the aid of the war Macron. Such training can be undertaken within the interactive virtual image simulators in Terminus City. Anyway, many of you with the relevant information and experience can always exchange such data through implants. So any such training will not be a lengthy process and each of you have Macron terminals within your palace apartments on Mars. Anyway, such training can be fun,' he replied.

'When do we start to move our household things?' Cathy asked, with disappointment.

'There is no need for that. Our Martian homes have all that we desire. Anyway, we are not moving on a permanent basis. Think of it more like a second home. We should start from tomorrow onwards. Venusa and Martia can contact their ships tomorrow for a temporary loan of robots. All of the heavy furniture and appliances will be left behind, but you will see for yourselves after our visit. I have arranged for several layout plans to be available.'

'Thank goodness! That means we only move some personal items. And no paintings and sculptors, please!' Cathy replied.

'No Dear, they will be displayed electronically. Terminus City is a lot more beautiful and comfortable than the mansion, with all the latest technologies as used on Eden. Everything was manufactured on Venusa and Martia's ships by clever robots and androids. All that is presently required is the human touch, and I can assure you that it's not as claustrophobic as our beautiful mansion here. They are built on the same scale as palaces on Eden, although not quite as large.'

'Will Terminus be our permanent home?' Cathy inquired.

'We are the rulers of Osmaron. Rulers do not have permanent homes. In future the whole of Osmaron will be our permanent home. Nevertheless, we must be prepared to go where we are needed for the good of all, not only for ourselves. However, we can visit anywhere at any time when we are not busy elsewhere.'

They were satisfied with that answer.

'After the evacuation of Caefon Dome, that dome will be transformed into a tropical forest with many varieties of plants and small animals. Those will include a small lake and stream. In the not too distant future, all of Mars will be converted into a green world like Earth. With the addition of special machines, Mars will eventually acquire a thick carbon dioxide layer within its upper atmosphere. That new addition will maintain a more stable temperature, thus enabling less of the ferocious sand and dust storms we observe at present. Then certain bacteria will generate oxygen and other gases, while some essential elements can be extracted and piped through portals from some of the outer planets. In future, this area of Mars will form a small part of a large underground city complex and Terminus will be just its entry and exit points,' he replied.

After lunch, most of the women were wearing their overcoats in anticipation of another cold adventure on Mars, away from the warm and sunny mansion. However, when they arrived in Terminus, they found themselves within a most comfortable environment, with thick warm carpets laid on every surface within the palace area.

There were beautiful gardens everywhere, with animals and insects that appeared to be as real as life, but all were virtually animated images. They could observe outside streets with people going to and fro about their daily duties and each image-window had its own blinds with its relevant image matched to the other windows on that face of the hexagon. When the blind was shut, that image would simply vanish.

The inner walls were covered with a special material that could be changed to many different wallpaper patterns by simple programming and voice commands.

'It's incredible!' shouted Cathy and the others soon removed their overcoats and decided to see what the place really had to offer and what they could do to improve matters.

Because all of the palace's apartments were built to a similar plan, they chose the most central hex as their standard.

'Each of our council members will have two levels, which will give you a floor area of over twenty thousand square metres for guests and family rooms. You can modify your palace to your own designs as and when you wish and it naturally becomes part of your own wealth. The top two floors numbered A1 and A2 belongs to my family. Jerry and Miranda are below me, but we can always swap palaces if we want, by the mutual agreement of both parties concerned. Anyway, I have decided that everyone, other than myself and Jerry, draw lots and I expect each one of you to be with me in the A-Hexagon. The reason why I have chosen the topmost levels is one of security and believe me, they are all identical,' George said.

Each hex was numbered in an alpha numeric sequence, from top to bottom and began with the letters, A to Z, then, AA to ZZ and finally, AAA to ZZZ. After those letters appeared numbers from 1-99. The 100th level from the top was used for recreation, and so on.

Within the third circle of hexes were their main shopping centres, restaurants, theatres, clubs and other places of entertainment for the benefit of the councillors. That area was secured from other areas of the city.

They were amazed by the quality of everything and even the plastic furniture had the texture of real wood. All was manufactured from the silicates and carbon-based chemicals extracted from the Martian environment, many of which had been separated from Martian soil.

To them, Terminus was so beautiful that it put areas on Eden to shame, even though much of it was projected images.

'Here, you have no problems of security. Even holographic doors and walls may be created to deceive intruders. There are few dangers from the environment and you are all queens and kings of this world. One day it might even become more important than Earth, politically,' he said.

'I think it's wonderful and homely,' Cathy said and this time they all agreed. Jon and his group of six preferred the extra space with direct portal links to Eden and all the main federation worlds. There was also no Terminal Virus or Infilates. The only problem was the lack of real sunlight, but even that aspect was not essential, since every one on Earth tended to use sun-blockers or keep in the shade and well away from the dangerous and harmful ultraviolet radiation. Anyway, all lights were chosen to emit just the correct levels of ultra violet.

'We can grow our own vegetables within the local pressurized transparent domes, and fruit and food plants can be cultivated in Eden Dome after it's repaired, thus making us fully independent from Earth. I have commissioned several larger domes to be built throughout the Martian surface within these plains. Those pressurized transparent domes will make perfect agricultural environments and as Terminus expands most of its population can move to lower levels within the planet's surface. Many of the city parks are already covered with transparent domes,' George said.

'Where does the energy come from to power such an incredible city?' Jerry asked.

'From several powerful fusion generators buried deep within the Martian surface,' George replied.

When they returned to Earth they immediately communicated with Venusa and Martia's ships and most of their removals were already on its way.

Later on that evening George called Andy into his study in the mansion.

'Andy, please get your officers and recruits together, we are all going to Mars to begin the real offensive against the enemy. Your

training camp there has now been superceded by better technology. Our Martian base contains all the necessary facilities in place for our future missions and the Omegron portal links our city there with Caefon in Andromeda. Further, we are to commence training in earnest for a future assault on Caefon within Andromeda, against the Javols. That one will be a very important mission, so I want everyone to be at peak.

'Martia's ship will give you all the necessary weapons for your training. The other important aspects of your mission, I shall explain to you and your specials in a few days. There is more than enough accommodation within the training facility for tens of thousands of your Specials and extra hexes can be built at a moment's notice. However, you will have to take your own supplies for the duration, until the distribution lines become more automatic.

'I would also like you to secure Terminus City with your best young recruits as part of their training. That way, we shall never need to use a permanent human police force. They can be assisted later by android police guards. In the mean time, Chad and Carl can continue with their recruiting and training programs both here and in Europe.

'We visited Terminus today in your absence, and the ladies, including Joan, enjoyed the city complex. We are to randomly draw numbers tomorrow, but they are all more or less the same. Anyway, you can visit A1 and see for yourself when you arrive there.

'Joan can manage your affairs there while you are involved with your specials.

'Everyone is to be evacuated from Caefon Dome to assigned areas within Terminus. That is, after the miners have undergone some form of rehabilitation and given suitable jobs and positions of responsibility. Therefore, training will be essential if these miners are to exist within our culture and conduct themselves in a proper manner. However, this time the whole gang will be involved with minimal assistance from you. You will have too much on your plate at this time.

'Later on, perhaps you can have a well-earned rest on Planet Eden with Joan. Then you can assign your best officer to take

your place. At that time, you will then become Chief Military Councillor of Mars,' George said. Andy was so surprised by his future promotion prospects that he couldn't even have said "thank you". Somehow those words were in his estimation too inadequate and far too little to offer.

'I know how you feel, Pal, so don't you say a word. Anyway, much responsibility goes with the new job, which includes securing the whole of Mars,' he said, while he lifted a computer disc and handed it to Andy.

'This is an update on future requirements, including the predicted flow of recruits from Earth over the next six months,' he said. Andy saluted and left the room.

CHAPTER 36

The United Nations Conference

George had special protection cloaks made for every member of his Gang, including little Clair and they looked quite dignified in the high shoulders and rear high collar. He also got Clair a most beautiful headband from Eden, with a large central ruby that was surrounded by many diamonds.

This item matched the white satin-like cloak that sometimes reflected bright sunlight in many colours. The band looked more like a crown and automatically adjusted to her head. Somehow Clair had changed from the sad little kid to a most informed person, so very soon every one realized she was someone special. They would also ask her for advise and lavish her with presents. Probably the main reason for those changes was due to the respect and love she received from the mansion at that time. Anyway, she was not the same little frail girl she used to be and walked upright with power in her steps.

On the day of the great conference he decided to take Hercules and Clair with him. He spent a little time that evening briefing them on his plans for that visit and his all important speech to the UN. He was never the one for preparing speeches, and preferred to speak from the heart with all such communication being spontaneous.

George expected the United Nations building to be filled with every important leader, worldwide. After all, his changes would directly affect every continent on Earth well into the distant future. He also expected the whole show to be sent out via satellite, and be almost simultaneously viewed by all countries represented.

He arrived without security at the UN building and when he walked into the large auditorium, it was amidst cheers and shouts. After an introduction by the President, he walked up to the rostrum and Clair and Hercules took up positions on either side of him.

'Greetings to everyone on Earth and may unity, peace, happiness and love follow your paths along the road to a better future!' he cried and they happily cheered back in turn. Then he continued.

'This period in our lives signal a most important turning point since the history of our world began. This is the time when every human being has to take stock of his life on Earth and consider his purpose within our galaxy of Osmaron and beyond.

'Mankind's technologies had increased to such an extent that he had begun to threaten all life on Earth. He would shortly have begun to detrimentally affect other life-forms within local systems in a similar manner if he continued with his money making methods, desires and selfish concepts of existence.

'Our Galaxy of Osmaron, known to many as the Milky-Way, is now the domain of the Federation of worlds of which I have made Earth a member. But Earth will only play an active role after she is able to release her shackles of greed and corruption. This is because the members of The Federation follow rigidly certain rules of conscience and respect to all other life. However, I have little doubt that many of you here are quite capable of joining even now.

'My friends, I would dearly love to introduce you to the greater universe, but first, I have to rehabilitate you in line with our own ways and methods of existence. You should realise that many of the most advanced minds within Osmaron never ever die. Like me, they may have as comfortable an existence in the centre of the sun as they can in the harshest and coldest environments of space. They can exist without oxygen, pressure or indeed anything. Without even the existence of matter or even of the laws of this dimension. Yet, we have the power to shift the sun to another position in space, to even move the solar system to another galaxy if it took our fancy and that immense task is performed by a simple thought and moving our heads. However, even power brings with it much responsibility. We are not free to do as we wish for our own self gratification, because our conscience tells us it is wrong to do so. Anyone can use power to destroy and harm, but what constructive purpose can be served

by such ridiculous actions in a universe where everything is possible. Before we move our feet we should consider what life we crush underfoot with each step.

'Within the federation of worlds, all normal tasks, including policing, are carried out by very competent androids and robots. Those were designed and programmed for a specific purpose. Take Hercules here for instance, he is one of our finest androids, made of solid metal and with the ability to melt and reform into any life-form or machine of an equivalent mass. He has the most acute senses required for tracking an enemy and his nuclear weapons can vaporize a large building. His self destruct has a blast value equivalent to a mass of twenty thousand tons of TNT. Once given the order to locate an enemy, he will travel throughout the universe until he locates his prey, God forbid,' George said, but as he spoke Hercules began to undress and transformed into a most ferocious looking Bengal Tiger that roared mercilessly, then he transformed into a Bat-Vulture which resembled a human size griffin, with the most deadly claws, glowing eyes and most fearful features.

By now his audience began to get quite frightened, but Hercules soon reformed into his preferred human form.

'Don't be frightened. These things you have to know, for the technologies within Osmaron are quite advanced and are most formidable.

'Within the federation we prefer people to use their minds. The menial tasks we leave to intelligent automatons. So you see, we require nothing from anyone and least of all money, just the capacity to develop and use our minds and abilities to build beautiful worlds like Eden. However, there is a system of credits that places everyone in the system on the same level from birth. After that time, it's up to the individual to make his mark,' he added. Then he pointed and a large area of the room became a beautiful garden of meditation. A heavenly place that everyone would eternally desire.

'Earth could one day be like such a world, if you truly wanted it.

'Every occurrence in history has been recorded.

'Every incident can be re-created.

'Every life can be reclaimed even from the Sands of Time.

'Every soul, identity or entity can be given a place within the Planes of Gohenna and that is a fact.

'It is my task to plan for this part of our universe over several millennia and I have decided to add Earth, my troubled planet, within my stock taking for the next millennia. This is because I have not given up on you and I sincerely believe, that given a little push, you will follow in the right direction.

'Ultimate power is something that we all dream of having, but even the greatest lords of the Universe, with all their powers, will always seek humility. A true god never says he is God, even when he sees his children make so many mistakes. Although he may at times feel like taking drastic action to resolve the matter once and for all. But then, he thinks like a loving parent, with unconditional love, and does what is good for all his children. Not just mankind on Earth, but everyone.

'Does my philosophy make any sense to you?' he shouted, but then became peaceful as if controlling their minds with his manner of delivery.

'On this world, I think greed and selfishness has predominated for far too many centuries. Those destructive desires and influences have always set you back during your evolution. Like a form of addiction or some uncontrollable desire. Like demons from hell, these ambitions take many over and begin to control them by giving the impression that you, their slaves are in control.

'What if those of you, with a strong desire for gold were placed on a golden planet, would you still enjoy that form of addiction. Wouldn't you need your friends and the basic requirements for your own survival? So isn't friendship and love more important than gold and loneliness?

'I could never quite understand why Earth-bound humans have always tried so hard to accomplish so little by way of attaining true greatness. You exert so much effort through each generation for so little reward. You build and with little concern you destroy, and even within your short lifetimes those items you consider more precious than life itself becomes out of date. You labour to save money in quantities that you are seldom able to spend

yourselves and even your future heirs may squander your hard earned savings with little thought or consideration of your past efforts.

> *So much beauty, yet unseen,*
> *A life too short and yet so keen.*
> *When only dreams can pay the price,*
> *In wanting, as if to throw a dice.*
>
> *With thoughts of God and afterlife,*
> *And with religions a-running rife.*
> *I sometimes shriek at what I find,*
> *when I allow you to freely use your mind.*
>
> *In basic visualization, one could never see,*
> *In simple understanding, one could never be.*
> *In greed sustained till Earth's no more.*
> *Why should your life be one always filled with gore.*
>
> *With greater battles is your future guaranteed?*
> *With your lesser kinds to feed and breed?*
> *Then Earth's population would always be extreme,*
> *Too many greedy fools would always infest the creme.*
>
> *Yet, no worst planet parasite was ever conceived,*
> *To ruin worlds where demons would never lay a seed.*
> *It is time to say goodbye to you my gentle fiends.*
> *Perhaps this universe was never a place for you of reckless minds...*

'What if you could live forever and had little requirement for money or the accumulation of wealth.

'What if the whole universe belonged to you and everyone else, living together within their different cultures and habitats. Couldn't you spend your days instead caring for the Earth, Osmaron and perhaps even the Greater Cosmos?

'With eternity ahead of you and the technologies necessary to choose whatever careers, as and when you required them for *your own benefit and for the benefit of those of your own families and friends. Wouldn't such an existence be more profitable and desirable? Wouldn't such an existence be like Heaven on Earth.*

'If you had a liking to fulfil those desires, then you would be considered an intelligent species most suited to the Cosmos. However, if you were the type with an uncontrollable urge to trample over all others to collect meaningless trophies, in the form of the extinction of innocent life-forms. To collect little nuggets of gold, just because you think they shine brightly or whatever you consider your personal addictions to be, under the banner of supply and demand. To stimulate overpopulation just to generate those demands, in the ever increasing spiral of destruction and carnage, with little care for others; then you would be considered an unwanted predator species of the viral type.

'This universe has no place for such universal predator species, parasites, global pests or planetary virus and perhaps you are better out of it.

'However, I have decided to give you a new beginning and a second chance. I shall replenish and repair your world and heal the sick, and aged.

'Within just six months I shall give you a choice between the Empire of Osmaron and your own addictions.

'Those of you Infilates who wish to partake and once again become free individuals, with the future possibility of a younger body, can have the ability to procure your own offspring. However, you will be taken to Andromeda to begin a new life there. But with the freedom to return to Osmaron and visit Earth in due course.

'Such resettlement is necessary if the population of Earth is to be kept within the five hundred million human population limits required for its sustained survival.

'You will be given your own worlds like Earth, with your own estates in perpetuity. On which you can build your own homes and families,' he added. Then he pointed a finger and the image of Eden faded away and a new one took its place.

'This is Caefon, within Andromeda. I have donated this world which is the size of Earth, to those Infilates and others with a

need for adventure. As you see, it's even more beautiful than Earth at this time. There are no humans or other animals about, just a few fishes in the sea, so it should be a great challenge to anyone, and there are many such worlds within Andromeda.

'I am on your side, you know, but I am also on the side of beauty, order and life. Whatever decisions I take are for the good of all and not just the fortunate few, either by their intelligence or power.

'Knowing that there was little future for mankind on Earth, certain events were set in motion many years ago. For by now you would have completely destroyed this world, which isn't really yours to destroy. You would have destroyed all its innocent life-forms who also have rights by virtue of their own existence. Because of those measures, Earth's human population will drop naturally until it reaches a population of five hundred million.

'If there are no controls, your population will again begin to rise uncontrollably. Therefore, instead of re-seeding the Earth's atmosphere with more Terminal Bacteria, it has been seeded with the Antidote instead. Thus allowing its human population to live normal lives without the need for special drugs. In future, any over population that is above the limits that I have specified, shall be recited elsewhere within Osmaron or Andromeda.

'The alignment of the planets have signalled an irreversible change in your lives. Henceforth, many of you will become very responsible citizens of Osmaron and will use your freedom wisely.

'Trust me on those unanswered questions, for my love for you is eternal.

'Now it's time for me to revitalize your world and its inhabitants,' he said.

Then he looked at Clair and she stretched both hands forward, as if sleep walking but without moving from her position. From the tips of her fingers bluish glows appeared which coiled away towards the windows. Then they divided into numerous paths, to travel out of the building and encircle the Earth. Then he stretched his hands out.

'So be it!' he said, as his fingers formed living flames of energy which had a life of their own. They separated into numerous strands and went through the window and walls, as if those windows and walls were not there, to follow their separate ways upon the Earth.

It was not long before the sky above became a strange crimson and was filled with lightening as the tension built up within its atmosphere.

The process may have taken a full ten minutes, after which time Earth would never have been the same planet again. By that time there were shouts of people in the streets outside the building, either from just plain fear or the wonder of seeing some loved one completely healed.

Wasted muscles began to reform on distorted and damaged bones. Complete legs began to grow from some triggered genetic coding. Deaf ears began to listen to the great turmoil. The blind began to see.

The aged Infilates began to grow new hair as their bodies began to change from over 70 years to under 30.

'The whole world was one in crisis, as people dropped their crutches and other aids, and began to embrace each other in the streets and parks, where they had accumulated to view his speech.

Once more, he stretched his hand outwards and large almost spherical objects formed within the room above their heads. Showing bands of galaxies.

'This is our universe, with all its billions of galaxies and this tiny part here circled contains our three closest galaxies, namely Osmaron, Andromeda and Triangulum. These areas are also where many of you and your families will find yourselves in the future; for they are also our home galaxies,' he said. With those last words he and his two companions walked out of the room and simply faded into nothing while they were being chased through the corridor by reporters, thus leaving them completely shocked by the strange occurrence. On that historical day many on Earth were shocked to their innermost cores and consciousness.

CHAPTER 37

Earth in turmoil

After the United Nation's Conference, the two ships simply vanished from their positions in the sky above the Trade Centre and so did George and his two companions.

The Trade Fair continued for two more days before its contents were disassembled and transported to one of the large hexagons, within the Councillors Complex in Terminus City on Mars.

After that time, many recruitment offices were being opened throughout Earth and recruits of all ages and inclinations were signing on in droves, in the hope of a better life within the greater Osmaron Empire.

Some areas of Solarian Banking were being dismantled and channelled into the new recruitment effort. Many senior members like Professor Khan (Ben), Chad, Carl, Professor Jean-Claud Chairmowich, Jeremy and others, who had been involved in the effort since before George was born, were given their own quarters within Terminus. Many were trained to be administrators of that city and were assisted by the many Macrons. However, all important personnel were to remain on Mars until the remodelling of Earth was completed.

'Hal and John Simmons were completing special anti-Javols project on a distant uninhabited planet. Those newer biological weapons were too dangerous for Earth, even within the most isolated dungeons.

Nevertheless, many still commuted to Sol-Newtown and other areas on Earth to assist in the many programs. The main effort was given to the recruitment and rehabilitation program which also included the Infilates' rehabilitation to Caefon in Andromeda.

George had put forward many questions in his speech to the nations of Earth and many suddenly realised that there was a more creative and better existence than the one they had served for so long.

The Infilates realised they had been given a second chance, to make good their lives and to have their own children. That was something for which many would have given almost anything.

Having seen the powers of their lord, as he was then called, they began to trust in him fully as their leader and saviour. Why should such a powerful figure give a toss for any of them unless he really cared? After all, he had the powers to take whatever he wanted from anyone. Yet, he asked for nothing materially, just love and the abolishment of their old ways of greed and self-indulgence. That was a small price to pay for a future on a beautiful world like Caefon, with contented and happy people, and so they thought.

However, there was still a large part of the population that would never sacrifice their wealth and property without a fight. Those were set in their ways with little hope of redemption and included some of the wealthiest Fertilates and politicians. But they were outnumbered in droves.

The very young, chronologically, which were now the future of Earth, wanted a way out and the majority preferred the idea of being able to explore their part of the universe either as Specials, fighting for a better order within the universe, or as farmers, engineers, artists, scientists, sports and game competitors, and so on within the large Federation of Worlds. The list of careers were almost endless.

Many also wanted to join the new priesthood which used the hexagram as their symbol with George as their leader. They called that new order The Patriarchs of Osmaron or Patrials and the female priestesses they called the Matriarchs of Osmaron or Matrials. That religion was based on Siend Seno's own religion more commonly known as the Senots.

They were to be the real parents of the universe with responsibility for all life. They would give their all to the Cosmos, towards the preservation of life symbolized by the Greater Purpose. By so doing they would educate those intelligent species to control their own environments to their benefit and in line with Osmaron culture. Those evolving on harsh worlds were given extra resources to help them make the leap to better things and less hardship.

The members of The Gang were considered to be such high

priests, once they were ceremoniously given the special satin-white cloaks and Clair was now responsible for all the priestesses or Matrials.

By now, Andy had Mars under tight surveillance with many probes, including defensive and offensive weapons. While Hal and John focussed on the protection of Earth from Javols. But they were never in any danger of attacks from Earth or other members of the Federation. Those were just precautionary measures, in preparation for attacks by Javols and other unknowns. Such preparedness maintained a state of alertness. It also made them aware of future dangers in their galaxy and beyond.

Satellites Gimbal and Eta had also been seeded with the Global Antidote and now had direct portal links with Terminus on Mars and many were being recruited within those two satellites. But their main purpose were as observation posts for Earth during that period of change.

Caefon Dome on Mars was cleared as soon as all of its occupants saw videos of their new apartments within Terminus City and were given the promise of permanent work within the city. The Dome was then used to house many Infilates during their training on Mars before they were returned to their respective cities on Earth, proudly wearing the uniforms and wings of the Osmaron Empire. They would then continue the program of recruitment within their home cities before being dispatched to Caefon in Andromeda.

Many now commuted between Earth and Terminus on a daily basis and Terminus was fully patrolled by Andy's special guards and androids. There were not yet enough resources within Terminus to sustain a population in excess of half a million people, even with supplies from Earth.

Jerry took the lead in organising all political operations on Earth and now had his own special primorphs who followed him and Miranda everywhere they went.

The momentum of change was so great that none of the major countries could prevent the wishes and movement of their people without provoking serious riots in the process. Many such riots existed when the people revolted against their materialistic and unchanging politicians.

Terminus City was soon separated into four sectors or quadrants, with a zero reference line in the north south direction of the planet and that line also corresponded to the Martian zero time datum and its zero line of longitude.

The apartments away from the central area of palaces were limited to just one hundred square metres per apartment. Each was equivalent in size to a large house on Earth when one considered the use of robots and main basement utilities. Larger families were usually given two such units. Furthermore, homes and permanent fixtures, within the federation, were given freely to those who needed them, although certain luxurious items were discounted from their earned credits. However, even babies earned enough credits to maintain a full time nurse and any other requirements during the duration of their growth. Hence, even the poorest was self-sufficient and could increase their credits by getting more involved within the system, and Osmaron was everything to do with involvement.

At present, Terminus had a capacity of over ten million humans, but its resources could only be generated slowly, as and when the larger agricultural domes were built and cultivated.

Venusa and Martia's ships had already had their robots surveying certain areas of the region. George had also ordered some of the giant earth movers and constructor ships from Polok and Lodor, thus releasing those two favourite ships to be his future personal flagships. The new ship, originally called New Vogon, having been since renamed Daisy, was assigned to Clair and her priestesses.

Soon, many super large multi-layered transparent domes would be constructed throughout those regions, to contain wild forests, fruit plantations and natural parks, with every conceivable plant and animal from Earth and elsewhere. Those were to be all interlinked by underground tunnels with automatic sealing locks. However, secured portals were everywhere.

Such large domes would be constructed in several layers and

sections, and nursery and propagation areas were to be isolated from the main growing fields. But they were just a cautionary measure, in case of decompression due to meteoric damage or unforseen high velocity storm damage. Light was by nuclear powered satellites with adjustable reflectors. Such systems converted matter directly into light energy within the relevant spectrum. However, since the processes were similar to those within the Sun, filters were seldom required.

All these processes were just temporary since George intended to reform the Martian atmosphere using numerous robots and androids. Robot ships would collect all the necessary gasses and chemicals from the outer worlds to replenish the Martian atmosphere.

Many of the domes were constructed within a concrete ring several metres thick and over twenty metres tall. However, the height depended on the curvature of the transparent roof, which was intended to completely surround the dome and act as a windshield.

The large ground-based plasma installations would search and destroy any large meteoric wanderers that targeted sensitive areas of the planet, but there was always falling debris from such interactions, although not of too great a problem.

Because the atmosphere of Mars was so thin, most of the invading meteors always ended up on its surface, leaving small craters where they landed. But such occurrences were now extremely rear within a given area, although well within the lifetime of Terminus City. Nevertheless, the orbits of all dangerous meteors were constantly checked and could be altered if they posed an immediate threat.

CHAPTER 38

The special cloak of office

Just two weeks after the United Nations Conference, Donald resigned his position as President of the USA, thus leaving his government in the hands of his Vice President, Stanley Crowe. Then he joined the gang with his wife on Mars. After his arrival, George made him Chief Councillor of the new Terminus State, now a large area of Mars which included Terminus City.

Once they were settled in their new positions of greater responsibilities, George communicated to each in turn, inviting them to their very first inaugural dinner at his Palace Apartments.

'Family and Friends, it's nice to see us all in one place for a change, after the exertion of previous weeks. I invited us here together, because I didn't wish formalities of Council Chambers at this time. I prefer the use of that place for informal matters and to debate the more serious issues facing society as a whole. This get-together here today, mainly concerns the priesthood, for when our temple chambers are completed. However, it is also meant to be a social gathering of our senior family members, where we can discuss the more personal issues of The Gang as a family and iron out any issues we may have. By so doing, we can further improve our relations with each other and modify our positions and responsibilities as necessary within The Greater Purpose.

'In future, I intend to hold one such dinner party every week, just for discussing our own family needs and problems. However, not every one of you are expected to attend each time. Nevertheless, your input will always be appreciated whether here or elsewhere.

'I have chosen today for the presentation of the special cloaks, which have been designed to my specifications and your measurements. I should however remind you, that possession of these special cloaks place you in a position of greatest responsibility to all life within the universe. Being priests and priestesses we should always comply by the rules of membership

that are now listed on the main temple walls.

'You should also know that being chosen allows you the extra privileges to become Supreme Councillors of Osmaron.'

'As I call your names please come forward and accept your gift by saying, **'I accept the responsibilities and honour bestowed upon me by the acceptance of this precious item as a symbol of my dedication to The Greater Purpose'.**

Those of you wishing to abstain may remain seated and explain your reasons for declining afterwards,' he said and began calling their names. After they had accepted the box, they took the oath and went back to their seats.

'It will be very much appreciated if you could wear your special robes at future dinner parties,' he said.

There were no refusals and they all placed their packets on the other table and continue with the dinner.

'I seriously thought it would take me a longer time to get used to Terminus City, having been so attached to the mansion, but I was wrong. Are you all pleased with things as they are?' he asked.

'I think I can speak for my wife and others, when I say, we are very happy and for once in our lives, feel almost completely fulfilled,' Donald said and the others agreed.

'We are now members of the Supreme Council of Osmaron and very soon I expect Lords Malik, Bailor and others to join us in the priesthood, but that's up to them. I now think it's time for you all to apply for specific posts within the council and I have compiled a list of suitable ministries and positions. I have therefore decided to leave the post of Ministry of Science and Ministry of Construction and Shipbuilding out of the list for now.

'The Ministry of Customs and Excise goes to Lord Meron.

'The Ministry of Planetology also goes to his group, with Lord Lennox as its head.

'The Ministry of Shaditry goes to my father, Lord Jeffery Longhurst.

'My mother, Empress Sarah, remains the true empress of Osmaron and will continue as before with her important conservation tasks throughout Osmaron and later Andromeda.

Since she will be excluded from our wars against the Javols, her duty will be to maintain order within Osmaron when we are elsewhere.

'Lord Hal has been nominated chief councillor of all security on Earth.

'Lord John Simmons will be chief councillor in charge of the creation of all bio-weapons and nano-bot soldiers, aided by Lord Chairmowich and others.

'Our Grand Lord Gerra becomes an Honorary member of the Supreme Council and so does Lords Vektron, Patron, Faemon and the few remaining of his people. But there are literally hundreds of ministries, so you will each find something of your liking to control and you can always change ministries or apply for a new one every ten years or so. During a new selection period to be arranged democratically. Ancients, Like Lord Seno and others will come under our Ministry of War'

'As you know, the Cloaks will offer protection and give you great powers with its utility belt - after you have been fully trained in its use - through your implants.

'The Pentagram with its central circle makes it clear to everyone what we stand for. But while using the Cloak in the invisible or transpositional mode, you are unable to breathe or consume any outside matter. Therefore, during long periods of such operations it will be necessary to use your own oxygen capsules with the nasal filters provided. One small capsule contains just enough air for two hours. The single large one holds enough for just over twelve hours constant supply, including reserves and they can be clipped into position in any environment once vectorized. Nevertheless all pockets are bottomless, so any items placed therein will shrink to a much smaller size. However, they will weigh the same in that state, so there are limits.

'You can also carry dehydrated food in the larger belt pockets, if you find yourselves isolated or lost in deep space. Those pockets are also bottomless.

'Never materialise or re-vectorize without your mask, unless you are within a human environment.

'Always re-vector from human to human environments. Because once you re-vector into normally vectored matter you become normal again and all matter including your bodies are affected in a similar manner. However, with practice, even if you found yourself in deep space and gasping for breath, vectorization will be instantly triggered by the safety sensors within the suit. So the chance of temporary death is very remote. It's usually the agony and pain felt that is the problem. You may also program certain parameter thresholds within brain implants. As a matter of fact, many operational sequences can be so programmed.

'If during the process you are not sure, you can alter the revectoring angle slowly from zero, until you sense problems, then remain at zero until you are assisted. If by some unfortunate circumstances you find yourself in a vacuum, your body will literally explode. We would then have to bring you back with the machine and you might not like that trip. Further, your new body will only have memories from the last Psyrotron scan, so be careful. Nevertheless, all those problems can be alleviated once we link our implants to the Cloak's sensors. Then, our implants can make those decisions for us invisibly and in the background. So, you should first link your implants to the Cloaks, which can make the decisions for you when facing unnatural and dangerous situations in unknown places. The response of this automatic process is also much quicker.

'Only I can do it anywhere, even in the middle of Sol, our sun, without the need for implants. But I shall use your methods anyway, because they are more natural. However, very soon all those deficiencies will be circumvented with better technology. I'm sure all our suits will be upgraded many times in the future when we learn their weaknesses, so feedback is essential in making progress.

'We are currently in the process of creating virtual indestructible bodies that can exist anywhere within our universe. Once completed we can download our minds into them during special missions. On completion we can resume our human forms. However these items will not be ready for some time. So we use what we have at this time.

'You can always consult the Macron for more information on any of those topics.

'Once you become used to your cloaks, it becomes part of you and simplifies every aspect of your lives.

'If the Macrons are unable to help, then please talk to Clair, she knows everything worth knowing within the Cosmos on virtually every topic. Because of that particular reason, I have nominated her as Chief Priestess. But she has a long way to go before she becomes an adult. So I would also like you to help and advise her when you can, and I am sure she will return your favours in greater measure in the not too distant future. I have also adopted her as my sister.

'I have already begun to design a self-creating Cloak, but I'm afraid it's still on the drawing board. Now any questions, anyone?' he said.

'Can we visit Earth occasionally to meet family and friends whenever we like?' Anne-Marie asked.

'Cathy and I visited the mansion today and everything over there is quite safe and secure, so please feel free to visit there or my mothers house whenever you need a break from here. You know, it belongs to you as well, so please make use of its facilities. That also includes our new Vogon now Daisy, if foreign planetary trips are necessary. Presently both buildings are tightly secured, but I'm not sure of the local towns and villages.

'Very soon we shall receive over ten giant ships of the realm, with thousands of smaller ones arriving here on Mars. They are to patrol the solar system and are required in preparation for the first of our many struggles against the Javols, on Caefon and elsewhere within Andromeda.

'We are now getting ready for our first assault on the Javols and need to secure Lower Cantor and the Omegron Portal for that purpose. That underground city will in future be used as our main base within Andromeda. Then we can seal the planet off and begin transferring people and animals to the planet's surface, after removing dangerous bacteria and so on.

'Those of you who would like to come along for the ride should make that fact known to Andy. However, that assault must be

very well-planned and will be very messy... on the Javols side that is, so please give us a little time to train you,' George said.

'Please count me and my group in!' Jon Yelled.

'I would like to come along as well!' Cathy shouted.

'And me!' shouted little Clair. But all the others wanted to go as well.

'Yea, I need some more payback since our last encounter on Tyrrel!' Tim shouted and they laughed.

'Everyone can come along, suitably cloaked, but a few of us must first go ahead and put the main power on and I want two Councillors here, to handle things at this end with the battle Macron.

'No robots or androids will be used on this first mission.

'The Omegron Portal has been left on standby mode all those years and the underground city of Lower Cantor must now be a mess after so many years of decay. Anyway, it will only take one of us at a time and we don't know what to expect at the other end, so I shall go first and act if necessary. Then you may follow and observe, while our assault troops and those suitably trained can visit the surface through the self-destruct portable portals that we intend to install on the surface during this mission,' George said, as he turned to Andy.

'If everything is to go like clockwork, I think we have some real training work ahead of us,' he said and Andy smiled.

'Why don't we call uncle Plato, Meron, Mallory and his special females, they might also wish to assist?' Merol said.

'Ok, we'll invite the whole group from Eden and elsewhere to come along as well. They could all do with new cloaks and some training against Javols. Lady Venusa, please send a message to that effect for me,' he said and she nodded her head in acceptance.

They had a lengthy discussion that evening and got many fears and misunderstandings out of the way.

The following day Lord Meron and his group arrived with their trunks for an extended stay, and were each given their own comfortable palace apartments in the central hexagon. They had apparently packed those trunks many days in anticipation of a long awaited call. Later on, Mallory, Roseanne, their children, and Ebony and her group of Amazonians arrived. The latter had assisted Mallory on earth to subdue many criminals and gangs over twenty years before, until they left with him for Polion II. They were probable six of the best women fighters within Solaria.

Then Hal and John arrived, they were both wearing their own designs of Chameleon nano-bot suits. Those suits could transform into the most hideous forms, including invisibility.

That evening they celebrated their new status and their forthcoming first assault against the Javols.

'I have decided to set a day aside for the inauguration of Terminus City and its Mayor. Therefore, invitations will be sent out to mother, father, Grand Lord Gerra, Lords Vektron, Patron, Faemon, Malik, Bailor, and other important people of the realm. It's time we had a real celebration to commemorate the birth of our newest city!' George said, feeling good within himself for the way things were going.

'I'll drink to that!' Donald shouted and the others lifted their champagne glasses in agreement.

CHAPTER 39

A briefing before the first Assault

That day all of the senior officers were assembled within the main military auditorium in Terminus City. That area was inside the towering building with the large winged federation crest on its front parapet, on top of the main entrance. Just above the crest was a flag carrying the imperial colours of the federation in blue, green and orange. That flag included the large red pentagram and white star with a similar winged imperial crest at its centre. Air was made to circulate within that area of the dome so that the flag was always waving at full mast. However during the assaults against the Javols it would be placed at half mast.

Andy was wearing his blue uniform with its many decorations and medals of bravery. Most of those he received from his past operations on Earth with his Specials. He commanded them to stand at attention and George walked in, dressed in the white cloak, but with the hexagram and imperial colours emblazoned on his left breast just below the winged insignia. They all stood at attention until he arrived at the rostrum.

'Please be seated!' he said in a resounding voice, but continued.

'For everything there is a season and for everyone a course of action that will lead to the ultimate and final result of victory. Our present season is about to change from a most desirable summer to the most bleakest of winters, during our struggles against the Javols. But I can assure you all, that at the end of our struggles our final conquest will bring the most beautiful and lasting summer to be experienced by everyone. Many of you have been briefed in the past on the subject of the Javols and of their present savage occupation of Andromeda. So I shall skip most of the specifics on that most deplorable of all life-forms for now. We shall find out the more intricate details about them soon enough when we meet them in combat.

'However, our assault must be two-pronged. Over the next few years we are to infiltrate and slowly take over all habitable worlds within Andromeda and Triangulum for re-colonization.

But first, we are to secure permanent bases within both galaxies, from which we can mobilize sautes and surprise attacks against the enemy. Initially, those assaults will be backed by our Military Macrons here and within a local base within Andromeda. I have therefore decided that we use Lower Cantor within Andromeda for our first base.

'It is a sealed underground city and almost completely inaccessible and impenetrable by Javols. It also gives us full access to the Omegron Portal.

'Our main mission is to clear Caefon of all Javols and their bases. We are to clear the complete planet without the Javols' high command becoming, in any way, suspicious of our presence and actions,' George said. Then he created the image of the planet Caefon with all its continents while showing the positions of deep space probes which had been laid by the Ancients and their more recent maulers.

'Most of these deep space probes are still operational and will give us prior warning of any large scale invasion forces and clusters of Javols. Those we link with our primary systems on arrival.

'The long-term plan is to lay Anti Javol Disruptor Mines, normally called Mine-Probes, about such worlds within a radius of ten light years or so. These mine-probes are themselves mobile. Once programmed, they will remain dormant and concealed at their programmed positions in space until they sense our enemies.

'We expect Caefon and most planets within the outer regions of Andromeda to be mainly unpopulated by Javols. Therefore, we begin from the centres of the main outer region and move inwards towards the centre. That process of occupation is not a fast one and may take us several years to complete. But as we clear a world, we mine the space around it and occupy it with our people from Earth. Then we fit our large automatic Plasma Bases and arm our military, who initially will be our trained Infilates. However, they will not be in any great danger, for our present weapons are very effective against the Javols, who are not as advanced as we are, technologically.

'They must never be able to copy and use our own weapons

against us, hence, every one of our weapons will be booby-trapped against Javols and that factor is automatically included during their manufacture.

'Javols now use many habitable worlds for the breeding of fish, crustaceans and larger animals. Those also include human types that they prefer for their food, so there are other variables in the equation and many of those primal species, despite their lifelong persecution, may be spies and Javol's sympathizers. Some may even be disguised Javols. Therefore, you must consider anyone other than our own specials, with their identification signal, to be the enemy. Further, Javols may appear like pillars, boulders, rocks and even trees. However, the old types of Javols cannot imitate many colours like green, yellow, red and such like; just more neutral colours like browns and greys. They could imitate a dead tree or a stump, but not a living tree with green leaves. Even so there is great range in neutral shades, so beware.

'Whoever or whatever we capture that we think is not a Javol, will be placed within portals and deported to an isolation prison for interrogation by androids. If they are Javol, their molecules will be disrupted by the portal and they will die on arrival.

'We do not take live Javols!

'In any event, Javols will not be expecting such sudden attacks without a previous warning, as they are not yet acquainted with inter-dimensional drives, vectorization or even portal technology.

'Our weapons, like the Plasma Beam and the Gravitron, will vaporize and disrupt thousands with each blast. However, you should also be aware of their potential to act quickly and turn a situation around almost immediately in their favour. Furthermore, un-disrupted pieces of Javols can rejoin to form complete Javols, so beware.

'Many of their occupied planets might also be mined and can only be neutralized by our large ships. Hence, those worlds will have to be thoroughly scanned before they are occupied by permanent settlers.

'They must never be allowed to communicate with their local bases or MasterMind. With that in mind, we have designed a very elaborate and complex scheme, with the use of LPD driven Javol Duplication Mines that are programmed to take the place of a

Javol of standard form after its destruction.

'Note, I mentioned the words standard form. That is the form they prefer while in their habitats below ground, but they can also occupy several other forms, being microid in construction. You will find that they adopt different forms for different occupations. For instance, they will change into the most fearful forms when fighting or preying on an innocent civilization.

'First, the enemy must be made to transmit certain signals, including its own personal identification code and its recent instructions from its local base to MasterMind. That problem we are able to overcome when our probe transmits certain Subliminals to the Javol, with all the necessary instructions that the Javol is not aware of, until it's too late. It is then induced by those same instructions, to transform and by so doing disintegrates into powder.

'That mind-probe then becomes that Javol to all intents and purpose. After that operation is completed, the mine-probe also becomes our spy and relays all information received from the Javol's local bases to our Military Macrons.

'Thousands of such probes have been manufactured and programmed for Caefon. After our arrival, we build our own ammunitions and probe factories there and begin mass production for the local systems.

'Before we have to set special mines in orbit, small groups of our Specials are to secure certain areas and disable their main local base transmitters and storage ships, if they exist in those areas.

'This effort will greatly rely on stealth if we are to duplicate their operations and prevent others from becoming suspicious of our actions.

'Individual Javols might not be very clever, but when grouped together, they become a formidable fore to work against. Each of their highly specialised minds come into use as a single entity. You must always remember that they have at their disposal the memories and experiences of all their previous generations. They can also link up and become one giant Javol.

'They never forget, just specialise within the confines of their MasterMind. Local Javols, who are part of a group might also be *aware of a companion's death, as the identification link or carrier is abruptly disconnected at death. Each will have to be isolated and their carriers found and replaced before it is terminated naturally from its group by their own termination code. However, that aspect is not to be considered a great problem if you use your radiation guns or Mazons. Those are capable of receiving that information for feedback purposes, once a Javol is targeted. It is then able to retransmit that signal with its disconnection codes before the Subliminals are sent to the target.*

'On your utility belts are sensors and other warning devices that feed directly into your sealed helmets and implants. Therefore, you will always be aware of primal life-forms and Javols in your own vicinity.

'You must never underestimate a Javol.

'The order of the day is to hate and kill all Javols without mercy. They are not normal life and will show you no mercy. They are also quite clever at deception, so whenever they appear you exterminate them like vermin, for that is what they are.

'They can quickly transform into most life-forms of an equivalent mass. Those include humans and a wide range of predators and herbivores, so beware.

'The first part of our mission is to secure Lower Cantor and to turn the power on. We then take the Omegron Portal off standby, then clear and secure that area while assembling our larger defensive weapons.

'During this time, I shall visit the surface and access their positions and strengths in that area. Then we can plan for the next stage of our mission, which is to locate a hidden area for use as a temporary surface base.

'We might still be able to use the elevators to the upper town and museum, or where it used to be. However, with some luck that area might still be under rubble or even be overgrown by trees. In which case, we can clear a small area to fit our tents and screen generators, while ensuring they are completely hidden from view. That part of the surface was previously destroyed by Shadite Plato for good reason.

'Many of you will have screen generators fitted to your special suits, so please use them in order to become invisible. But you will have to become visible in order to use your weapons. Without special cloaks your screen generators do not prevent you from being harmed, so take note.

'Once that area is selected, you are to install a portable portal in order to get other items and specials onto the surface, as and when they are needed. Then we begin to release several mines in the area, before proceeding to take out all local installations and replace their main transceivers with ours.

'The areas of our camps must show no signs of our occupation, hence, we take extra portals and plant them at other locations which we use as secondary bases. By so doing, our tracks are minimized and ground sheets may be laid whenever necessary, to mask shoe-prints, etcetera. We cannot afford to leave any clues behind. Use LPDs whenever possible for mobility. They are also included in our cloaks.

'When a Javol is killed, it stinks to high heavens and just that smell can alert other Javols down wind of the corpse or pile of sludge, so you will need to use disintegrating nets. They serve a dual purpose. The net will induce them to escape through its course mesh. In so doing, they will attempt to transform into a suitable escape form, which will cause them to fall apart like Humpty-Dumpty. The net will then disintegrate, along with the Javol's remains.

'Each net capsule contains twelve nets and your utility belts contain four such capsules. Those capsules you insert within the upper chamber of your Mazon Gun. Do not confuse them with the oxygen ones, which are always kept at the rear of your belt and are coded differently. So spend some time getting used to your equipment and relevant colours and codes.

'This is all you need to know for now and I have prepared a chapter on the topic which is available through your seniors.

'You may now please ask relevant questions,' George said.

'Does our duplicating mines smell as fowl as the Javols they replace,' Cathy asked.

'That's a very perceptive question. The answer is yes, but only after the change. At that time special perfume chemicals are released... and by the way, no perfumes are to be used by anyone on any of our missions,' he said and they smiled.

'What if we suddenly came face to face with one of them, Sire?' a senior asked.

'You always shoot first and ask questions later. If it's one of ours or a primal life-form, there would not be much damage done, because our personal small weapons are destructively optimised for Javols only.

'If they are that close to you, there is a good chance that they have been unable to communicate with the others. Then they will begin to form the necessary tools to kill you, so always shoot before they transform into more effective killers. That way, they will disintegrate even without a net. But if they have already formed their tools, you will have to shoot and then net them. So you use your Mazon Gun and say a little prayer. But you should have been able to sense their presence through your sensors before then or even smelled their presence, like dead fish. Further, after transformation they are able to spray deadly microid dust, which can take a human body apart, so be always aware of the dangers,' he replied.

'My Lord, what if one of us are captured?' another asked.

'You pretend to be a native of the planet. Perhaps one that lived hidden within its caves and developed your own technologies... or confuse them in whatever way you can. Even pretend to be insane by hopping about like a mad hatter, while sending us your location. Those actions will confuse them for a time.

'The whole idea is to delay their decision making system so that they are unable to communicate with their bases while we neutralise their transceivers. Then we come and rescue you. After that, we have to terminate all local bases and Javols, just to be on the safe side. Then we have to clean the whole planet as soon as we can and pray to God that no one had escaped to warn the others.

'We are to have all mine-probes in place before we conduct complete sweeps. That process is necessary if we are to intercept those trying to escape.

'Here on Mars, we are shortly to receive over one hundred giant battle cruisers and several thousand smaller frigates that

are specifically designed for that purpose. Those special ships have been fitted with torpedo tubes for the laying of mines and missiles for that very purpose. However, the large ships will take a few hours to arrive within Andromeda and the smaller ones about fifteen minutes. So their trips will have to be planned and synchronized in advance of our operations. That is, if their presence is to coincide with any major action at that end. Our War Macrons will coordinate such attacks,' he said and continued in general.

'From tomorrow, we commence the Javols simulated wars for real with our Battle Macrons. Every possible scenario will be fought, time and time again, until they become second nature to your being.

'Those virtual images and games are as realistic as life, but unlike the Javols, they do not fight back in a harmful manner,' he said and left Andy to continue the briefing.

The Gang spent the following weeks training with the other soldiers in the virtual image chambers and when Andy was satisfied with their competence, he gave them each a set of recruits to train. Having passed all relevant tests, they were then made captains and commanders, in order to gain the respect of their warriors.

The Martian Space force only included humans and was now over five thousand strong and the Martian Specials were double that amount. Those considered unsuitable for both forces were placed in the group called recruits under ten separate grades, and there they remained until they were promoted or reclassified.

Several large constructor ships soon arrived on Mars and began to clear a large area some twenty miles south of Terminus City. That area would be the first major airbase of the Osmaron Empire and was to be constructed before the arrival of the main fleet.

CHAPTER 40

Evil Dracma goes to Triangulum

The Javols' high command Hexolyte Demons, Dracma and Lupher, had become very apprehensive and tense, after they became aware of certain permanent changes within the fifth dimension. They realised they would have to quickly find a new method of communication, if they were to maintain the necessary levels of security and order among all those thousands of billions of Javols throughout Andromeda and elsewhere.

Lupher had fed most of his calculated data into their computer MasterMind, which he himself had constructed several millennia before. He had constantly updated and improved the system and its programming during the intervening 3000 years period of the Javol's conquest of Andromeda.

That massive computer called MasterMind had grown to an incredible size and now covered a large part of Endoh's world, including its moons.

So far, no solutions had been found to the problem of the fifth, but Lupher soon came up with an idea for a containment vessel that could take him or his brother to Triangulum. While there, it was hoped they would find advanced minds and technologies to assist them in their conquest of the universe without the rapacious and unrelenting Javols.

That trip would have taken under fifty Earth years to cover and there was little room for error, by way of delays in transit if they were to continue their existence in this universe. They had to take into consideration the small seepage of fifth, ninth and other higher order energies which could not be regenerated within its confines. Such a ship would be built more like a coffin, but to keep them alive during the trip.

Although their present hybrid form seemed to contain their beings well, while they were close to the galactic centre, its usefulness could have been less effective when their demonically possessed Javol bodies moved away from that location. Further, such losses of their life-force could have been even worse out in deep space between the galaxies, with less gravity and stellar energies than was normal, and those extreme conditions could further assist those losses.

'I think you should go to Triangulum and search for Father Dracos's cave, while I remain here to handle these pathetic idiotic Javols. In the mean time, I might find a solution to our communication problem and perhaps you can, with a little luck, find the father's cave and make us each a special insulating cloak and a faster ship. Then if you have some extra time on your hands, you could get us an android fleet of ships. I know, it has been a very long time since, but we are not primals and have always built our equipment to last.'

'Much too long!' Dracma replied, while ripping off a leg from a previously sacrificed Timit woman. It was greenish with splatters of congealed blood spots throughout. He took the flesh off the bone, swallowed in one gulp and threw the bone towards a large corner pile. Then he drank a mug of her still warm blood.

'Nice vintage. Much more delicious when we starve them for a month!' he shouted and burped loudly.

'You will have to do it, my worst brother. This is to do with our survival in an infested rat-hole, with no easy way of escape. These idiotic Javols are not even able to use basic pentagrams and have destroyed all the ancient portals. Anything will be a lot better than remaining in this place for another three thousand centars, twiddling our claws with these idiots about,' Lupher said. He was currently munching on the semi-frozen brains of one of his fattest Timit. These are nice and crunchy, he advised. So Dracma did likewise. Then he topped it with a pint of vintage blood from a large refrigerated container. Lupher then did likewise.

'That really hit the spot. Nice vintage!' Lupher burped noisily.

'No, Brother. Why should I take the risk on such a hazardous venture while you remain here relaxing in starlight with your personal computer? I shall not! If I go, you also must follow,' Dracma said in a most insistent and adamant tone of voice.

'But, Brother, there is no other way. If I design such a special ship for two, it will take even longer to get there. Thus reducing both our chances of survival and what will these idiots do in my absence, even if I reprogrammed MasterMind as best I could. Events are changing about us, even as I speak and I now sense a great threat to us both. So I must hold this end, being the technical expert, while you the sadistic politician and cunning diplomat, go and conquer some clever minds to work for us. These Praille, Thoraxi and Trace have little knowledge or concepts of such advanced technologies and we are unable to deal with them directly.'

'I am still not convinced!'

'On your arrival, simply find an advanced species and worm your way into their political system by your special skills of deception and overwhelming charm. Get androids to build you a fleet of super-fast ships, then you can send me equipment and instructions for building one of the larger portals so that I may return and we can begin conquering the universe and have some more enjoyable and disgusting fun together,' Lupher said. He finished munching the brain and took another leg from the table. He removed all flesh with his almost razor-sharp teeth and began munching at the bone to get at the marrow.

'Do I have a choice in the matter?' Dracma asked, still in a determined frame of mind. He was showing a disappointing frown on his crinkled face with a reduced glow in his eyes.

'That's settled, then!'

'I only wished we could send one of those idiots from here, but I am afraid, it would multiply and eat all our expectations from underneath us, while we wait here for no purpose. And how can we give a god's job of work to a primal sibling,' Dracma replied. Then without saying another word Lupher took the advantage.

'It's nice to know you agree and I shall make it up to you in due course, Brother. You just wait and see,' Lupher replied.

'When will the ship be ready?' Dracma asked.

'All... ready, Brother. I had it made a month ago, but it had to be fully tested,' Lupher replied.

'How could you test it without one of us in it?' Dracma queried, still not fully trusting his brother.

'You should have a little faith in me, Brother. There are many things I learnt while imprisoned within Aron's tank, during my lengthy meditations. One of the first things I became aware of, was the almost insignificant seepage of elemental life energies from all those prisoners. I soon realised that I could hold more of mine by following certain procedures and to also suck and absorb others in passing. By so doing, I could have remained there to eternity, but when the idiots, Javols, arrived they ruined everything, even my current meditation. By then, I was even stronger than when I entered the tank aeons before. I might have become a predator of both body and spirit, eh brother,' Lupher said, with a deliberate grin.

'You are telling me that you can sense elemental seepage and have become a spiritual vampire among other things?' Dracma asked.

'Yes, Brother, I think both, and I am telling you that the little special ship is lined with a similar substance that I was able to analyse during my long stay in Aron's tank. Almost that same material was used to coat Aron's tanks. Therefore, you should not worry unduly, Brother. Anyway, what shall I gain by your demise. One less person to communicate with, which just leaves me to talk to myself. With little chance of leaving this place in the foreseeable future. You know, I always preferred intelligent company, it's just fools that I dislike,' Lupher replied.

'Ok, Brother, I am convinced. Make it as comfortable as possible. I don't want to be bored on my long trip, so please get me some of the special Timit women from the Pronkii cluster. They seem to have a higher torture threshold and repair quickly. With a little luck and suitable hibernation quarters, ten might last the trip if I ration myself,' Dracma said.

'Consider it done, Brother and we can have a special feast with many Timit sacrifices before you leave,' Lupher replied.

Dracma selected a slave from the group of the three remaining women. She went forward chanting.

'May I visit my glorious lord in paradise this day!' she said.

Dracma took her in hand and rung her neck like a chicken, then decapitated her. Then he drank her flow of warm blood till the final drop.

'That's better!' he burped.

In another month the evil Dracma was on his way to galaxy Triangulum, but would take just under fifty years to complete the journey if everything went as planned.

Lupher, still quite apprehensive and nervous, decided to arm his troops as best he could and gave orders to the MasterMind to analyse all unusual occurrences within the galaxy of Andromeda.

Javols were then sent out to scout the outer galactic perimeter in expectation of another invasion. But Lupher had sadly underestimated the technologies of his foe. Their means of invasion were not from that direction and their invaders were already within Andromeda and preparing for their first planetary conquest.

CHAPTER 41

Caefon in Andromeda

While on Mars, George entered the Admin Dome dressed in his special white cloak. He was followed by Cathy and several members of The Gang, including Mallory and a few of the Ancients.

'Please wait here until my return. This task should not take very long,' he said to Cathy and the others, as he walked unto the conveyor that would take him to the Omegron Portal.

'He thought into the system and the portal went off standby and into transmit mode. During that mode of operation the conveyor changed direction, taking him towards the portal instead.

Most portals could only be operated in the simplex mode or in a single direction for added security. That meant they had to be reprogrammed for a change in direction and the Omegron Portal was no exception to that rule.

Part of the portal's funnel, on the transmitter side, formed into a staircase which led unto a secondary horizontal membrane that glistened like an oil patch, with many rainbow colours radiating from within that area. That was the transmitter side and the Martian one had never been used before for that direction of travel.

Although he was aware of his great powers, he couldn't prevent his human feelings of danger in the course he was about to take.

He could in all probability have transmitted himself to Andromeda by thought, but didn't want to create too great a disturbance in the fifth. He would also have had to locate the underground world of Lower Cantor on his arrival, which sounded more like irrelevant hard work and inefficient time wasting while others were waiting. Furthermore, he had to test the system for the others, if they were to follow afterwards.

George had to freely fall through that scintillating area and preferred to use it in its present mode of operation.

He stepped onto the membrane and found himself falling into darkness. Suddenly he hit a soft surface and a small light came on to indicate his surroundings. He could observe several signs and symbols that were written in hieroglyph, which were the Ancients' form of sunolingua and read the information.

"**Receiving Port One**"... "**Sealed Exit Area**", it said in bold red and he suddenly realised he was within the receiving chamber of the Andromedan Portal within Lower Cantor.

He very quickly got up and went towards the exit. He released the latch and opened the curved door which formed part of the spherical chamber. As soon as he got out, he began to smell and scan the area for signs of Javol's, but although the air was quite stale and rank, it was just breathable and there were no signs of his adversaries anywhere.

He walked up the main thoroughfare of the underworld of Lower Cantor and moved in the direction of the control station. He continued his journey amidst the accumulation of rubbish and dead leaves that were being constantly shuffled to and fro by the moving air currents.

All the beautiful forests were now dead. Due to the lack of circulating water and artificial solar energy since the many decades of neglect when the powerful solar lamps were turned off to save energy. Their leaves were being blown about everywhere and their rotting mass must have given the area that pungent smell of decay.

'What a waste,' he thought and kept moving.

The ventilators were also off and would remain that way until the planet was secured. Any difference in air temperature or circulating air currents coming from the museum area might have alerted the Javols above, or so he thought. Natural decay had taken its toll, which was further accelerated by moving debris and he could faintly observe small black beatles chewing on the dead leaves further accelerating the process of decay.

'Not too much damage has been done. Just a little biological to the small forest,' he murmured.

After walking another fifteen minutes, he stopped at the rectangular black building marked "**Power Station**". Then he walked towards it and thought into the electronically coded lock. It released and he continued into the main, but less critical control area.

Those fusion power stations were built on several levels underneath the main control room. The master switches, including the self-destruct code entry panel, were housed within another room that required a much higher grade one security clearance. He knew that the unit would automatically enter its self-destruct mode if it detected a Javol, or anyone attempting to abuse the system in any way. He concentrated all his efforts on that lock and the very solid vault door opened to reveal a mass of blocks and blinking lights, which became alive as they sensed his presence.

'I give the code "**No Javols**". Please switch to main power and return to normal activities, but keep the main ventilation off until specifically requested,' he said in the ancient tongue and suddenly the main lights came on and the power-station whirred into activity. The bright sun-lamps began to glow, showering the large underworld and dead forest with light.

Suddenly the sky projectors flickered into operation and once again the place resembled the surface of Caefon in late autumn, with a horizon that went off to near infinity in all directions that were in view.

'Now to power-up this portal from standby and check the elevators,' he said to himself.

He went back down the street, this time using the suit to propel him along at great speed. Then he went into the transmitter side of the large portal and selected another code which gave him access to another panel within its strange fields. Yet another thought and there was a bright flicker of light that reduced to a deep bluish glow.

'The other one on Mars should now be operating in dual mode and at full power. Javols will not be able to get within a mile of this place if they wish to remain alive,' he said again to himself. Then he walked in the direction of the main station, this time in bright artificial daylight. On arrival, he was surprised to find two android guards sitting as if in hibernation, but still guarding the elevators. They sluggishly got to their feet as he approached.

'I am a friend and I am human. Have you any new information to report since the city was cleared, my faithful friends?' he asked and the closest one spoke in a metallic voice.

'No, Master. We have not sensed anything out of the ordinary,' he said.

'You may now go and recharge your batteries, then check the city thoroughly, reporting any changes in status before resuming your station at the elevators,' he said. They hurriedly left to follow his instructions.

He entered number one of the main surface elevators, pushed a few buttons and it whirred into action. In just five minutes he was at the small upper underground town. It was a mile above the surface of the city, but still about a mile beneath the planet's surface.

On arrival he went towards the main laboratory, then towards the recreation complex and local buildings. But here again, the air was stale and rank.

Finally, he decided to take a stroll towards the small forest, then towards the small lake. He went past the fountain, now blocked with dead leaves.

The small lake had since evaporated and was almost completely filled with rubbish and dead leaves. He sighed in sadness as he viewed the area.

'Don't you worry. The filtration unit is now on, so the cleaning robots should soon be here?' he said. 'You have better days yet to come. I wonder what Jon and his pals would think if they were here with me at this moment in time?'

He assessed everything as best he could before entering the same elevator, but this time programming it for a slower speed towards the surface. At least, that way he could stop it almost immediately if he sensed any debris in its path. He knew that the upper station would have been thoroughly isolated by those carefully placed explosions. They were triggered by Plato just after the evacuation, but even so, one could never be absolutely sure of such things.

After several minutes, the elevator came to an abrupt stop within the uppermost station and the door opened in complete darkness. He removed a small torch from his utility belt and began searching the area just in front of him, but it was completely filled with rubble. All he could see was a mass of concrete and metal girders.

'This area will have to be cleared with plasma torches. I wonder how thick...?' he murmured to himself. He vectored his body and found himself walking through the solid wall. By altering the angle of phasure of his suit, he could sense the density of the material through which he was travelling. To him, it was like swimming through an ocean of matter, although there were no convection or circulating currents to take one along some other unwanted path. His LPDs automatically adjusted to his rate and direction of progress. But one always tended to settle on a surface or the interface between two different materials of different densities. When he needed oxygen, he simply placed the filter over his face and breathed his own air. That was until he found himself within the atmosphere again.

'Travelling this way is easier than I thought,' he murmured.

It was truly an incredible experience and he knew that he would be rejected by solid matter if the suit failed. But any real danger was only possible if a normal person was pulled within the middle of a star. That could happen when the cloak wasn't used with its special helmet. The helmet and suit combination could keep a normal person alive, even within that environment, or in deep space for many hours. Being able to utilize energy from many different sources.

As he went through the debris, he searched for density changes, keeping his feet on the surface while searching for a suitable pathway.

'No wonder the Javols could not find the elevator. Plato and his friends did too good a job in destroying this section,' he again murmured.

He soon found a small channel through the debris which was not as dense as the others. It opened out into a large concealed room within the lowest level of the museum. On entry, he revectored to become normal again and walked up the staircase amidst the smaller rubble. Then he entered the next level of the surface city museum which was covered by creeping plants.

'What a beautiful hideout,' he said to himself. He went through two more damaged rooms of the museum before he found himself in bright daylight. It was presently showing through the thinner layers of creepers that were now directly above his head. He vectored again and walked through the building, but there were no Javols anywhere. Neither could he had sensed their local presence. He was sure there would be some form of their installations or farms on Caefon, but he was also certain that Lower Cantor would never be discovered by them before his main assault.

Everything in that part of the city of Cantor had been destroyed by explosives and the ruins were extensive and overgrown by green and purple weed and vine everywhere. He viewed the area of desolation and realized not a single human remained on Caefon. It was once a world with billions of beautiful families and children laughing and playing, now it was completely dead. He observed the scene of desolation and vowed he would do everything in his powers to prevent the same happening to Earth and other beautiful worlds like Eden.

He walked towards a large green and violet meadow, now at the beginning of summer and used his senses to scan an area of over twenty kilometres in every direction, but there was still no sign of Javols.

'We'll need to get our mine-probes up here as soon as possible in order to thoroughly scan this world, its moons and outer worlds. If the whole place is clean, we can commence the Infilate evacuation from Earth in a few weeks time. In the mean while, I can despatch some androids to assist the local robots and have Lower Cantor cleaned and refurbished more quickly,' he said again to himself.

He walked towards the elevator through the debris and this time took it back to the lower city. Then he strode towards the portal, entered the other cubicle marked red for transmission and was back on Mars and moving down the second conveyor in the other direction.

The whole trip had taken him the best part of two hours and Andy, Meron, Jon, Cathy and the others were still there patiently awaiting his return.

'Sorry for the delay, but I had to check and secure several things including our surface base. I have found no sign of Javols within a twenty-kilometre radius from the museum. Lower Cantor is now up and running and the Omegron Portal is on full power and fully tested.' Jon and his colleagues were pleased with that knowledge.

'The planet is in beautiful summer violet and green, but there are creeping plants growing wildly within and above the museum which also works in our favour. The elevator is in perfect working order, but the main surface entrance to the museum is completely blocked and can only be cleared by plasma torches. I intend to despatch several androids to the city within the week to clear and maintain it until we arrive. Unfortunately, there are decaying leaves everywhere, due to the dead forests within both sections, which may take more than a week to clear.'

'The numerous robots will begin tidying up once powered up,' Jon replied.

'I have left the ventilation off, but we can switch it on at night for short random periods when we are there. Assuming Javols are not in the area.'

'Desalination plants can replenish for now. They should be more than enough for a few thousand soldiers,' Lira said.

'I shall have a Javol's sensor rigged within the museum for scanning the local area. Friends, things are looking very good!' he said, as Cathy grabbed his hand and pulled him towards the local portal.

'You must be hungry, Darling!'

'Very!' he replied.

'Why did it take you so long?' she asked, showing great concern.

'The elevator was slow and I decided to walk most of the way instead, to slowly observe the environment and feel the place for myself. I could not send anyone in until I was fully satisfied that everything was perfectly safe.'

'Sorry, Darling, I got worried!'

'You know what I mean,' he replied and she agreed.

CHAPTER 42

First Assault plans

George spent the following few days advising The Gang and getting plans ready for the first assault mission to planet Caefon within Andromeda.

Finally, the large Martian base had been completed and they took the private underground train to the central part of the base. While on route they found the environment quite busy with many new venues operated by miners and Fertilates alike. All those outlets operated on similar principles to Eden, where money had been replaced by credits. Such transactions could be completed by giving a simple name or ID number. Since no one was dishonest, strict checks were not required.

George had to visit a few stalls on route to say hello to its many holders and get their response to the new environment. They showed the greatest respect and offered him many presents, which he declined to accept. It took his party the best part of three hours to make the journey, with many stops on route, but the experience made a pleasant change from travelling through portals and reminded them of similar facilities currently in use on Earth.

The train had the imperial hexagram printed on every side and was acknowledged by all as the imperial coaches. Regarding the Martian base, George and his entourage were to inspect and open its dual facilities that were designed for humans and androids alike. The place also contained a large cafeteria, briefing rooms and toilets for the human members of the fleet.

That military environment was designed for action personnel and included many fast reaction competitions and anti-Javol games within self-training areas. But there was also a large medical unit just in case of emergencies.

George, Cathy and the others entered and George gave another speech to the troops, about the defence of Osmaron and their great future in the Imperial Fleet and they cheered him. Then he cut the three-coloured ribbon and the large base was officially opened.

Terminus City was divided into quadrants, the military and the scientists were each assigned their own quarter of the city, with higher than normal security. The other two quarters towards the west of the datum line became the free Martian city. That part was free for all with very affordable rented accommodation.

After the base was completed, the giant constructing and excavating ships went to another local area and commenced building the massive agricultural domes.

Soon after the completion of the base, numerous ships of the fleet arrived. They numbered one hundred and forty-four giant battle cruisers and one thousand and twenty-four smaller seek-and-destroy fighters. Those could also act as drones, without any pilots.

All ships were designed with dual controls for special androids and humans alike, but implants could be used directly without manual controls.

George could not be more pleased with the way his plans were unfolding. He would often call them together in one of the private ministerial chambers, for an update and a general discussion of important matters of state.

Venusa was now his second in command within his own Ministry of War, and he was soon accepted as their emperor and head of all other ministries. Not that they had much choice in the matter. George was too overwhelming for anyone to circumvent.

Cathy was given her own area as minister for the promotion and assistance of young intelligent life-forms and Miranda was made minister for sports. She would set standards and organize Olympian competitions for all within the Osmaron Empire. But many positions were not yet assigned.

'Venusa, please call The Gang together in private chamber number one. I would like to brief them on our future mission to Caefon. Make it for three p.m. today, thank you,' George said.

By three p.m. they had all arrived including Anne-Marie with her two children Julie and Johnny. Their nanny had gone to Earth on a shopping mission for the family.

'Friends, I have received your requests for ministerial positions and have abided by those requests as best I could, but a few of the important ones have been duplicated, so I have made recommendations. Those letters, I have sealed and addressed to you personally,' he said.

An android soon came along and began handing the letters to each member in turn.

'Your ministries will only be finalised after you are happy with your new positions. There is no reason why two senior members cannot share the same office on a fifty-one, forty-nine basis. That is providing, there is one senior member who is responsible. That position of seniority can be rotated on a yearly basis. You may consult each other on this subject freely, but I would like this matter resolved as soon as possible. Then we can each settle down to more specific work. My main reason for calling you here today is to discuss our future mission on Caefon and how I would like our group to partake in this program.

'As usual, Venusa and Martia will handle the Imperial War Room at this end and both sisters have been made my Ministers for War and Propaganda, respectively.

'Andy has been selected as Minister for the Military, its training and maintenance in and out of war. In times of war his efforts are to be coordinated with the war and propaganda ministries, aided by his father Mallory.

'Pamela has been chosen as our Minister of Publicity. Those are my permanent selections for now, as they are urgently required for our future military campaigns.

'With the exception of Councillor Andy Colman, Venusa, Martia and myself; all other members may be present as official observers and soldiers on our forthcoming mission.

'It will be a two-pronged attack and the first is to include myself and eleven others in our ship Micol while others follow in Daisy. Daisy can hold up to 101 passengers. Those will include our best Specials and their Commanders. They will be held in reserve, in case we are overwhelmed. Our task is to scan that solar system for traces of their bases and intercept their transmissions.

'Once we have pinpointed their positions, we call several of our frigates to lay the necessary mine-probes and all bases concerned will be neutralized.

'After that task has been performed satisfactorily, Andy's

troops, now situated on Caefon, will be signalled and surface mine-probes will be released. During the following period several bases will be placed at strategic positions throughout Caefon and portable portals installed. Then the larger ammunitions will be transposed to those locations.

'Lower Cantor has now been fortified against all possible future eventualities and the surface museum base is now in position.

'Those of you who cannot come with me in Micol or Daisy will go to Lower Cantor via portal. For security reasons, I would like the location of Lower Cantor to be kept a secret from all non military personnel. Only the most senior members of staff should be told on a need-to-know basis. In future, both parts of the Omegron portal here and in Andromeda are to be considered Martian. Therefore, Lower Cantor will be considered Martian territory.

'The future inhabitants on the surface should never know of the underground city's existence. All others may think it a Martian underground world and I have given orders to modify the portal entry and exit points with the necessary Osmaron signs.

'The central elevators at Lower Cantor will also be made inoperable, with all transport limited to portals. All air circulation with the outside will be confined to oxygenation equipment linked to the local sea, with internal air purifiers. We take no chances on this our first mission against the enemy.

'To all intents and purpose, Lower Cantor will be on Martian territory and it will always remain that way in the future until I say otherwise. I now have to think of the future security of that world and others in the area, not to mention all our people back here.

'After the old museum is rebuilt, that area of Cantor will become our main Osmaron Embassy with all the necessary facilities.

'The moment Caefon has been secured, we shall erect a large monument to all its dead. Then we are to build a temple on the same site. At that time the rehabilitation and re-colonization of Caefon will truly begin and a beautiful city shall be built where Cantor once stood.

'The Infilate immigrants are a hard working lot and can grow our food for us in exchange for equipment and technology.

'There will always be several consignments of our troops in that system and robot ships and probes will secure the system with their main bases and observatories on Caefon's moons and outer planets. That way, any future invasions will be intercepted well before the ground-based Plasma Beams are activated.

'Caefon will be tightly screened and controlled during this period of adjustment.

'To recap, the operation will be conducted in the following four phases:

'One - We are to check the stellar system for Javol bases and installations.

'Two - Andy and his group are also to do likewise on the surface, after we have given them the go-ahead.

'Three - We then target and substitute those bases in sequence depending on their numbers and Andy does likewise after we have secured the local space.

'Four - We then tightly secure all areas and begin to build impenetrable underground fortresses almost equidistantly throughout the planet, to be manned by androids.

'During all this time, many frigates will be docked here, fully laden and waiting for our signal and destination coordinates. If there are just a few Javols' bases, we might be able to take them out ourselves with the few mine-probes we take along, and with a little assistance from our ground base. If not, we signal the frigates and call in the troops.

'During this time it is imperative that all the Javols' farming installations are maintained, but with their Javols replaced by our probes.

'I also think our media people should be involved here as well. Pamela and her team can plan some programs relating to the Great City Terminus and the successful wars fought in Andromeda against the Javols for the Osmaron Empire. That way, Earth should give us her sympathies.

'The ship *Micol* will save all visual images of our exploits and Pamela can detach a team of her finest war reporters to Caefon.

'That is all I have to say for now, so please ask your questions?' George said and sat in his special chair.

'My Lord, how long will this operation last?' asked Tim Chiang.

'If everything goes to plan, within one shift, which is six point eight hours on Caefon and one third of its day-period. By then, it should be all over and when we are finished, the Javols will be non-the-wiser of our conquest,' he replied.

'Could we be attacked by them in Micol or Daisy?' Cathy asked.

'No. We can freely transpose away from them or make them detect our image imprint at a different location in space to where we are situated. Daisy contains the latest technologies for killing Javols. Her hull radiates a killing wave which includes subliminals. The waves will disrupt their bonds and turn them into useless dust. She can take out swarms that way. I can assure you, it's an unequalled fight. We also have thousands of John's nano-bot soldiers waiting patiently for action under Trego and other commanders. Those will enter the frame only if we are overwhelmed. Then there are Titans and others waiting in the wind. They are the worst and carry a most deadly anti-Javols virus.'

'That's nice to know!' Cathy replied with an air of uncertainty.

'Since the destruction of Caefon, we have advanced by leaps and bounds, while they have only advanced a little because of their singular specialised way of thinking. A true scientist must be highly creative and gain knowledge in many fields in order to invent a unique product. Having eaten all the real minds within Andromeda they have little chance of any real advancement, unless they are able to copy our technologies and they are very capable in that way. However, this is only the taking of Caefon and the real battle has not yet begun,' he replied, turning to Venusa.

'If there are to be no more questions... we shall get ready to leave tomorrow at noon. We should arrive at our destination early in the morning. That time corresponds to our position in space directly above the museum. Please have a good night's rest!' he said, and they excused themselves from the meeting and followed him out of the large ministerial chamber.

CHAPTER 43

As free as a bird

Early that morning George entered the ship, Micol, through a local portal. He had since fitted one on Micol for his and Cathy's convenience. In many ways that addition was better than the glimmering staircase, which was noticeable by all and sundry. Micol was parked on the top of A1 building, just above his palace. There George stood wearing the black cloak of Aron. That cloak he always wore in times of war because it brought out the very worst in him and today of all days he wanted to be at his most evil. The cloak appeared red hot and shimmered in the Martian atmosphere.

He had since learnt its different modes of operations and found he could use it through his implants without endangering anyone. Although it changed him into Jull, with his fighting attributes and skills, a small part of his mind was George which allowed him a modicum of self-control. Nevertheless, there he impatiently sat, waiting for the others to arrive.

Since George had the small portal fitted on Micol, Aron's casket had been installed within his special bunk. For added safety, the canopy above that bunk could only be opened with his own special code through his brain implant. Further, with the portal installed, Micol was given strict orders not to release his stairs or allow entry to anyone without his express permission. However those facilities could only be used when he was within range of similar identical portals, so the stairs were necessary on occasion.

Just before their departure time, which was equivalent to twelve p.m. in Terminus City, the others began to enter the ship, until they were all present.

Those that were accompanying him were, Cathy, Jon, Lira, Merol, Jerry, Miranda, Meron, Plato, Arel, Jonathon and Clair. Others followed in Daisy, also parked locally. The ship Daisy had her own inter-galactic portals that could also be used locally. Also onboard Micol were a few mine-probes in case of emergencies. However, seeing his new glowing form and strangeness, they were perplexed, but brave.

'We have all been briefed, so let's do it, Micol,' Jull said, as he glanced at his fragile looking human companions wearing their special white cloaks.

'Little one!' he said, staring at Clair with that penetrating look.
'Come here!' and they all shivered, including little Clair.
'Yes, my brother?' she replied, in her little coarse voice.
'Do you know who you really are?' he asked, in that powerful voice.
'Am I not your sister, Corra, from the distant past?' she replied.
'Ah, my girl. You know! You know!' he said, as he lifted her up and looked at her small figure.
'But your body is so tiny and frail in this period of your existence. Do not dismay, you are still at the beginning of your growth cycle. Yet, you were fully grown when we defeated Hexolytes and we did them well together.
'Your Eternal Cloak awaits you at Father's Cave, you know. Perhaps we might visit there later, if it still exist,' he said, as he began to put her down.
'Yes, brother Jull,' she said, as if trying to humour him. Then she rejoined the others, still shaking slightly from her ordeal.
'How long will our trip take, Micol?' he asked.

'Two point six hours in Earth time, following a standard route, Great One,' Micol replied showing utter humility, as if his very survival depended on it.

'In that case, let me cut a whey through space for you,' he said.
He started waving his hands in front of him and began churning the space as if it was milk. As he waved in a circular manner, the air beyond his fingers glistened like the surface of a still stream. As he waved even more, the glistening surface rippled and through the ripples they could see the faint outline of a distant sphere with two smaller ones close by. He waved even more, saying; **'through the currents of space and time let the causal threads form, grow and enmesh. Let them grow and enmesh,'**

he said and as he continued his chanting, the world began to get larger, until the sphere occupied the complete rippling field and then continued to increase until details of the old museum could clearly be seen, as if just a few metres away.

'We are over two hours early, so please vector your suits, hold hands and follow me to the lower world you call Lower Cantor,' he said and they all took a small pill each, clipped on their oxygen units, held hands and floated out of Micol, now completely screened from detection.

They floated downwards through matter and the museum, then the upper town, to finally land in the main underground city. There they stood for a while observing the dead forests and buildings through their special visual sensors.

Many androids and robots could be seen throughout the underground city. They were clearing and transporting rubbish to the oxygen assisted incinerators. Some of Andy's troops could also be seen close to the portal. They were assembling weapons and erecting tents for temporary accommodation for the task ahead, while the androids carried on their tasked undisturbed. Even Trego with his nano-bot troupes could be observed in rank and file. They were determined to kill Javols.

They searched through the lower city, flying through the air and buildings like birds, and they liked the feeling, for it turned them into little gods with the ability to observe everything from on high, although they could not be observed by anyone. Then they flew upwards to the little town, looked through the large laboratory, the recreation facility and then a quick stroll to the little lake just beyond the dead forest. That was where Jon, Lira and his companions had spent the longest few days of their lives many decades before their arrival in Osmaron.

Finally, they observed the base within the damaged and overgrown museum. When they were finished, they still had over an hour to spare.

'Now, you have seen the real powers of your cloaks when they are used properly and without my help, and oxygen was not even required after the tablets were taken. But the tablets will just last one hour and you can always use your oxygen face-mask or helmets in more extreme environments,' he said.

They were completely stunned and confused by his powers over everything and soon went back onboard Micol.

'**We must now visit the moons and check the local system through the fifth. I shall monitor all local communications through the fifth. Micol may do likewise while scanning their surfaces for concealed bases. Then we visit Meron's planet and the outer worlds...**' he said, but before he completed his statement, Micol interrupted.

'Warning! A globe of several Javols approach. They are about two-point-six light years away. Their trajectory places them on a course outside of our present coordinates. My sensors also detect a large supply ship,' Micol said.

'**They are not moving towards Caefon, just adjacent to this system, on their way towards another world at the galactic perimeter. Perhaps taking food supplies to one of their outermost posts. They must be aware of my presence in the fifth through the Hexolytes they freed and are now taking steps to prevent an invasion like the previously failed one.**

'**They have been given a false sense of security and power, and are trying to prevent an invasion from without, not knowing that this one is to be from within and is already here.**

'**Oh... how childish is their reasoning. For I can destroy them now by a single thought back into the cosmic dust from whence they came, but alas, I must allow our plans to follow a set course of action.**

'**We must allow them to go about their useless processes for now. We shall serve them later,**' he said, with utter disgust for any of their kind. But he and Micol continued scanning the local environment for signs of a particular type of order, symbolized by the Javols' type of installations.

CHAPTER 44

No prisoners are taken

It took the Javols' sphere and their supply ship several minutes to pass the system, yet George and his group still had over half an hour to spare, so they decided to check the two local moons.

'I have since detected no H-wave signals from the whole of this system. Yet, I shall polarize and jam all transmissions towards the galactic centre. There will be no undercurrents, so we shall not be detected and any scheduled Javols will not break their current assignments unless they receive a countermanding order from a more senior base or directly from their Master Mind,' Jull said.

'Master, all fifth-order transmissions have been neutralized within detectable range,' Micol confirmed, as he checked the current status of the fifth-order vectors within that part of the galaxy.

'I have detected a main base and storage installation. It's on the cold world called Meron's Planet and it's a very large installation, possibly manned by several hundred Javols. There are also two smaller bases, one on each of the darker sides of our local moons. They usually prefer the cold for preserving their biological food stores and can hibernate well away from the threat of their enemies. But those safety measures will not save them this time. They have dug their own graves by so doing.

'That large storage facility might also mean they have a farming installation somewhere on Caefon. Perhaps on its more agricultural continent called Feltwol,' Jull added.

He sent a thought to the Martian war Macron and twenty frigates were on their way. It would take them over fifteen minutes to get to their present position using their advanced dimensional drives.

'Now we wait for our ships to appear before we have some

fun and kill some Javols,' Jull said, with that most dreadful glare in his eyes, to even instil fear in Javols. Nevertheless he wanted his gang to gain first hand knowledge in killing Javols hand-to-hand. That way they could train others in their different and more effective fighting styles.

Within seventeen minutes the android driven ships had arrived and materialized in the vicinity, although still with energized neutral screens to avoid detection.

'We have to entice them away from their temporary induced hibernation, then we register their identification numbers and schedules before they are killed. Then our mine-probes take their places,' Jull said as if experienced at such matters.

A timed flare was fired from one of the frigates to simulate a falling meteor. After ignition, it burned like a bright star, flooding the area with light and heat for several seconds, and with certain additional explosive effects. Then they waited until the top iris shutter of the Javols' hideout was released and one Javol came out of the hexagonal tower to investigate.

Soon there was another, until seven were out of the structure, suspiciously searching for clues in an attempt to deduce what had occurred. They also attempted to transmit information to other local bases, but instead were asked for their identification codes and other information. Then they were asked how many were left inside, in their own unique frequencies which they immediately released to their supposed head base.

Suddenly the entrance to their den was blocked by seven lookalike Javols, weapons and nets were fired, and before long they were struggling to escape the nets. As they transform into a more malleable substance to escape, they fell back into blobs of dead microid matter which triggered the nets and they began to glow, becoming white hot, then bluish and finally to vaporize the brilliant mass of Javol's cells into billions of individual atoms.

The new imposter Javols entered the lower chambers with more spare mind-probes. Eight more Javols were killed and replaced. The fifteen new mind-probe duplicate Javols simply continued the specialized programs of their predecessors. Although more

Javols were expected at such a large installation, there were no more. Those fifteen were obviously the minimum required to maintain that facility. Their duplicates would now continue as their replacements and go into hibernation until required by the federation.

'**There may be many such installations and bases throughout Andromeda.**

'**Hibernation prevents them from using up their food stores and other energy resources and yet, they retain the ability to revive themselves and can react almost instantly when threatened.**

'**They are truly the most unique survivors in every sense of the word.**

'**Our work is done here. We may now return to the moons and continue our search there. Payback is sweet,**' Jull said.

Two more hexagonal structures were found on the dark sides of each moon with their entrances constructed in the same manner, with iris type shutters.

'**Here we do likewise with the special flares,**' he said. More flares were released, but before they hit the moons' surfaces they exploded into different colours. Thus, giving a fireworks display in the rarefied and near vacuum of the moon's environments.

One of the basses was occupied by five Javols. The base on the smaller moon had been abandoned many years before. They both made good bases for the Osmaron Empire; for even Javols would not suspect their enemy's basses beneath their own or within their own areas.

'**We can now scan Caefon's continents for their other farms and bases, if any,**' he instructed and Micol began his search. Soon they were surprised by what they saw as a large human village were displayed on Micol's screen with many large grazing animals that were not too unlike Asian buffaloes. They were not native to Caefon and neither were the greenish Timit humans with sharp fang-like teeth and clawed hands. To their further astonishment, they observed several Javols hovering over the fields and issuing instructions to their senior male Timit human slave-masters, who were wearing half helmets on their heads and a whip in one hand.

The women in that field were harvesting a berry-like fruit that could only be used for their own consumption. Perhaps full of the necessary proteins and carbohydrates for the previous carnivorous human population, who for obvious reasons were not allowed to consume the grazing animals, which were used for some other purpose. Ever so often the whip would be snapped at one of the women and they would grown and screech a little, but speed their rate of harvesting.

'Those greenish humans are not from this system and are obviously used by them for farming the herbivores,' Jull added.

'Brother, they were taken from the Timit world within the Pronkii Globular cluster and they are known as Timit Humans. They were one of the last human types to be invaded within Andromeda and were discovered just before their MasterMind decided to save and harvest a few of those life-forms that were useful to them and didn't pose any threat. The Timits are virtual savages, but intelligent enough for such basic tasks. They are also preferred by their seniors as a delicacy, because of their high pain threshold, high amusement value and powers of rejuvenation,' Clair said.

'How appropriate,' Lord Meron replied, now feeling a little more confident in Jull's presence, but choosing his words very carefully and not wishing to offend the War Lord in any way.

'There must be several hundred Javols within this installation and the Timit humans might have access to their transmitters, so we should also keep an eye on them,' Cathy said.

'Not if the Javol's issuing the instructions are replaced first in the chain of command. Admittedly, the process may take a little longer than usual, but the more we take over that way, the easier our task becomes,' Jull replied. Then he relayed instructions to one of the frigates, which arrived almost immediately, but shielded from view. It released a neutrally screened mine-probe not far from an isolated Javol. The Mind Probe would automatically have changed its form and colour to that of the local Javol.

That probe soon pretended to be a Javol in trouble and wondered into some trees, making sure it was observed by the commanding Javol in question, who soon followed to investigate. But shortly afterwards, a Javol rose from the trees and went towards another. It issued an instruction for help and both went to the same place. Once again only one lifted out of the trees to be quickly joined by a second imposter and so it went on until all the commanding Javols were replaced.

'Taking them out is a lot easier than I thought and they are not in the least prepared for us,' Cathy said.

'Since the arrival of our antiquated maulers, they must have assumed our technologies to be beneath them. Anyway, they have always been an arrogant species and think us primals to be incapable of any opposing technologies,' Meron said.

How very wrong they were, to have made such assumptions!' Jull commented with a sense of sarcasm.

CHAPTER 45

The main assault

After all the Javols' airborne guards had been replaced, the large installation and base were to be visited and neutralized. Both facilities contained underground links to each other, but without defensive systems.

'This one we take ourselves, but with mine-probes standing by, just in case we need them at a moment's notice to replace those we kill. Daisy's Specials will assist later,' Jull said. They floated out of Micol towards the large installation below. As they surveyed the uppermost floors of the partly submerged building, they could observe many Javols going about their daily duties. They tended to get more numerous at the lower levels, so they decided to visit the lowest level to investigate and were shocked by their incredible numbers. There were Javols of all types and they were orderly in their operations.

'We work downwards from the top until we get to the neck of their home enclosures or dens. Then I flush them out, while those of you further up pick them off one by one. Let us pray their numbers do not overwhelm us before they are duplicated and attempt to escape. For this job we shall require many mind probes through the locally installed portals. But we shall have to kill most of them,' Jull said.

They separated into groups of two. Cathy and Clair went towards the left wing of the building, with Clair following behind. Hal, now in his special Chameleon suit followed John in a similar outfit. They were hell-bent on making their name in killing those pests, as they called them.

Suddenly, Cathy found herself in a darkened room with a single Javol in front of her and instantly revectored in order to fire her weapon. But to her surprise two more Javols came up from behind and surrounded her. There she remained stunned by fright as they move closer. She had not yet fired her net on the first one and they were brandishing their weapons ready for the kill.

Luckily for her, they were equally surprised. They were not yet ready to use their poisonous dust which they usually sprayed at their primal victims.

She quickly took hold of herself, gave a strong thought through her implant, and suddenly faded from view and floated towards the ceiling. All three Javols lounged into her previous position, crashing into each other as they did.

They were surprised by the strange manifestation and hid themselves in the dark, waiting patiently for a recurrence of whatever it was. They sent several waves of instructions to local Javols, but they were out of range of aural and visual communication. Within their bases they tended to use visual and audible means to communicate and that type could not penetrate their thick insulated wall enclosures to arouse their companions.

Cathy had just recovered from her initial fright from that close encounter when little Clair arrived on the scene.

'I just took out a couple. They are nasty and are very tricky customers, so be careful. Would you like me to take them out for you?' little Clair asked, full of confidence in her killing methods.

'No. I know where they are hiding and I would like to settle this score myself. I can shoot and net them as they follow me down the corridor, but you can be my second if things go wrong,' Cathy replied, bravely.

Suddenly, she landed back unto the floor and proceeded towards the corridor. Then she unvectored, while Clair remained invisible and followed along the ceiling with her weapons at ready.

The moment the Javols saw their human prey they immediately gave chase. Each with their own array of specialized tools as if prepared for a delicious treat. Those tools were efficient at taking people and things apart and they could modify them at will, even during the dissection of their prey. She made sure that she was at least five metres from the closest one before she stopped in her tracks, took aim and fired, but apparently nothing happened. She fired number two net but thought she had missed as the first Javol crashed into the side wall. There it remained with a slight change to a more reddish colour, firing its strange poisonous dust with no effect. The others soon moved forward and did likewise.

The first Javol had been caught and struggled to free itself from number one net, but nothing happened. She nervously fired number three and number four nets. Then she fired pulses of energy again and again at the two following before she vectored and floated up to the ceiling. She was followed by the poisonous mist, which passed through her invisible vectored body and stuck to the ceiling.

They were all struggling within the nets, trying to rip them apart with their special tools, but the super strong and highly elastic mesh held and tightened its hold even more firmly about the Javols' bodies. Then they gave up the struggle and decided to change their body's shape in order to escape through the course mesh. But the moment they began to grow outwards, their body extrusions suddenly stopped and collapsed back unto the central lifeless blob or mass of cells, now engulfed by the net.

After a few more seconds the nets began to glow and very soon there were three blinding flashes and they were no more. A signal was transmitted and three new, but friendly lookalike Javols, arrived to take their places. Clair then floated down to join Cathy who was observing what little remains were left while contemplating the sadness of her first kill.

'It's a pity we can't kill them without revectoring each time and they take so long to die. We have to learn to switch to either mode of translation in case we find ourselves in immediate danger.'

'We can make the process easier if we time it through our implants. Although plasmas are quicker, they create more smoke and heat. Also parts of Javols can rejoin. This is the safest way!' Clair advised.

'It gets a lot easier after your first kill. Then you know what to expect the next time around and it soon becomes second nature. Our implants are then programmed with the process of that kill. The more we kill, the more experience we gain, so let's do so more killing.' Cathy replied.

'Now, let's get out of this place. It probably stinks to high heavens,' Clair said, as they continued searching. Both were still wearing oxygen masks and fully vectored.

'I wonder if we were able to get their identification codes in time?' Cathy asked through implants.

'We don't have enough mind-probes for all of them. Anyway we can program a single probe with several, so we kill as many as we can. All their ID codes will be in their base computer,' Clair replied.

'Anyway, I suppose they can't transmit a thing while trying so desperately to escape and they can always be given dud codes, until we extract their data from the master computer,' Cathy replied. Although codes were received those were not replaced with mind-probes. Soon it was decided to only replace their seniors and a few lowly Javols with such probes.

'Anyway, let's stick with each other for now my little sister. You can watch my back and I yours!' Cathy said and they continued to kill five more Javols before continuing to the next lower level.

'In case you are worried, we have been able to get their identification codes and other particulars from most of the outside guards we killed. According to what my brother has received, there are thousands of them in this place. It's one of their main stations in this sector.'

'I know the process is supposed to be automatic with the nets, but I received no updates to say it was done,' Cathy replied.

'When there are so many in one place, information is always freely available within the group. Else they would be constantly falling over each other in the process of chasing each others assignments, even with their advanced computers. That way, there is more freedom for each individual within their group.'

'Nice to know! And all in one place, giving more meat for the grinder!' Cathy replied.

'We kill them freely. So don't worry on that score. Anyway their base computers also store a lot of that sort of information, so we can kill them without too many worries on that score, and the probes can download their information directly from our implants, when we are ready,' Clair said.

By that time many portable portals had been fitted and most of the upper floors had been duplicated with mine-probe lookalikes. They had continued to complete the killing on those levels while the team progressed to the lowest levels. The new mind-probes were also relaying confusing information to Javols, making them go to wrong places. At that time the Javols in that base were utterly confused like cats chasing mice.

'Come on people, let's move it. Place a servo tripod at this end and point the weapon over there. Don't worry about our people, weapons are only optimised for Javols,' Jon barked to a few soldiers as they entered that part of the enclosure.

Hal and John journeyed up a long corridor towards the Javols base. That one contained their officer types. Their colours were different for identification. As they entered they fired one of their special weapons and all those Javols became infected. Most began to vibrate as the virus took effect and began overheating until they literally fell apart.

'I never realized our bug was so efficient against these vermin!' John exclaimed through implants.

'Could be these later types are more susceptible. This gives us a great edge!' Hal replied.

They soon removed their plasmas and vaporised their remains.

'Good thing we can't smell the stench in here!' John said.

'And there was none!' Hal replied, as he fired at the last pile of remains.

After they cleared that area they returned to join George at the lower levels with plasmas in hand. They decided the virus alternative would only be used if overwhelmed. Anyway, they wanted to gain more intricate knowledge of Javols for training purposes.

CHAPTER 46

The Javols' den

After Clair and Cathy had cleared their area and killed many more Javols, Cathy got the knack of the process and did not make any more mistakes. They returned to Micol to recharge their weapons and collect more oxygen capsules, but found the ship to be on its own and feeling left out.

'They are now fighting many within the lower levels. Their underground den is extensive and Lords Jull, Meron and Plato have gone to its lowest levels in order to flush them out into the hands of their comrades who are waiting at the higher levels.

'Lord Meron has been hurt by their poisonous weapons,' Micol said.

'Micol, why don't you link with my implants, then you can experience as I do and advise when you can,' Cathy said and he was thrilled that he could now partake in the destruction of his enemies.

'Let's go and do some more damage! They will need us!' Little Clair shouted and immediately vanished, followed by Cathy.

'You mean payback with extreme prejudice!' Cathy replied.

'Is that what you call it?' Clair was focussed and determined as the female matriarch Cora would be. After all, she was really the sister of Jull.

Having collected several items, they drifted out of the ship through the upper floors of the building with weapons in hand.

Apparently, Meron was nipped on his left arm and although there was little blood, the wound was highly infected by their deadly poisons. He had since been moved to a quiet corner, but nothing could be done while the battle raged. Neither could he had used his implants in order to vectorize and become invisible again. The pain was too great.

The excruciating pain which penetrated his whole system seemed to overcome his natural will to do anything, even with his implants. Jull was actively trying to vaporize as many of the opposition as possible, so Meron was visible and vulnerable to all, but so were all those actively fighting the battle, excluding War Lord, Jull.

There were thousands of Javols in that area. It was like being in a cavern of massive devilish gargoyles. As they came up and were netted, more were inching forward while their dying companions struggled with their nets all over the upper levels. Their superiors used every possible type of deceit to gain access, but their human enemies completely ignored their pleas. The Javols had attempted every type of Andromedan language in a desperate attempt to communicate with their alien enemies, but in vain.

The whole process was slow and tedious, so Jull sent instructions to the ship Daisy, then hovering above the installation. Very soon a large plasma gun was erected on tripods just beyond the neck of the cave. It pointed away from the group and towards the entrance. It was controlled by Andy and several of his Specials.

On arrival, Clair went up to Lord Meron's rigid body and placed her hand on his forehead in order to suppress his overwhelming pain.

'Now, Meron, you can vector your cloak,' she commanded and he vanished from view. Then she and Cathy took him back unto the ship, Micol, to administer a special antidote to the Javol's poisons.

He soon recovered.

'For a while... I thought I was on my second visit to Gohenna,' Meron said and the two ladies were happy to see his smiling face again. But he was with friends and knew that any damage during combat would have been put right after the battle was over. He had a small gash on his suit where he received the poisonous jab.

'Don't worry, the suit is self repairing and will be as one when you get to your feet. Use your small puncture kit in your utility belt to repair your under garments if need be,' Cathy said.

After he had applied the special chemicals and materials to the under garments and they were as one, he got up, shrugged his shoulders defiantly and the cloak radiantly repaired itself.

'We must now return to the fight, with greater determination and vigour!' Lord Meron insisted and once again they were on their way. He had observed the loss of his world years before and was not going to be out of the picture on the day of taking it back.

'Yea! Now it's payback time with extreme prejudice!' Little Clair yelled and soon disappeared from their midst. Meron's wounds made her more determined.

Now in the thick of things, Jull sent a signal to Andy. Soon Andy, Mallory, Ebony and the other members of the group were on their way, including several Specials with more weapons and supplies.

Three more Plasma Guns were set to automatic at the mouth of the den, while the other comrades were at fixed positions down the vast corridor. There they remained while picking off stray escapees as many attempted to gain their freedom. But they had to get through eight enthusiastic members of The Gang. Mallory and his six female warriors, each equally positioned through the main corridor and close to the Javols' escape hatches to the upper levels. The remaining three assisted Jull with the Plasma Guns at the mouth of the den.

'Hal and John were hovering above one of the entrances targeting them as they ascended. Tregor and his nightmare warriors were held in reserve. He was soon asked to take position over the base and vaporize all Javols that got that far.

'Guys, it's time for more serious action. We take no prisoners!' he shouted to his warriors and took positions.

By this time, the complete area was filled with a dense mist of plasma residue and evaporating Javols. It smelt like sulphur and gunpowder. During that fight they were more dependant on their special sensors and implants.

'Behind you!' Arel shouted, as Miranda fired her weapon and the net with quick reflex action. It was second nature to those trained women while using implants in Virtual Mode. In that mode they were several times faster than Javols and so were their communication.

There was now a constant stream of Javols leaving the den. The three plasma guns needed time to recharge after several releases, therefore many came flying out of the mouth of the cave during those periods. It was wide enough to allow seven Javols to escape at once.

It was just a matter of taking pot shot as several of the batlike gargoyles darted out of the circular horizontal hole in the ground. Yet, because of that reason they were able to contain them. Nevertheless the process was almost endless, as several thousand Javols remained within the den.

Jull, understanding the extent of the problem, instantly ordered another large plasma gun for himself and floated downwards into the massive den.

'Now you vermin can take a little of your own medicine for a change,' he uttered. Those words were in their own language and they leaped towards him, jeering in their vilest colloquialism. But by that time he was way up in the high ceiling close to their exit and getting ready to spray them with super heated plasma.

'Here!... Here!...Here!...' he shouted. He randomly appeared about the ceiling, confusing them away from their main exit and inducing them to go after him instead. As he fired, so did that area of the den melt into molten Javols and liquid rock, and they began to scatter from fear.

'Here I am, you suckers! Come and get me!' he yelled. Yet again they plunged upwards where he was expected to be, only to be vaporized by the black figure several metres away. Suddenly he began to spray the whole place, until the gun was exhausted and needed time to recharge. He then went back above the den to get a new gun. By that time there was a complete regiment within the corridor, but mine-probes were kept well away in case they confused the troops and diverted fire power towards them instead, for they looked exactly like the Javol's and took their most natural forms.

Although they could not be damaged by the smaller weapons, their presence would only add to the confusion, so they were restricted to the uppermost floors while the battle raged within the lower levels.

Andy, Tim and the others were now assisting in the clean up process along the large corridor. They allowed nothing to survive. Even structures like pillars and boulders were fired upon to ensure they were not Javols.

Daisy and the twenty small ships above constantly transferred supplies and mine-probes via their portable portals. Those they had installed at the onset at the upper floors, but at the higher levels in the Javols base.

Jull and his Gang had fought continuously for over five hours and were now quite exhausted. The moment the new gang members arrived, they learned the game after their first kill and took their positions, giving the others time to leave the polluted area and take some rest and special nutrient pills.

Jull got himself yet another larger plasma gun and floated back into the den with similar antics as before. He used that plasma weapon until the walls within that area ran with molten rock and metal. When he was finished, he stood into that main area and surveyed their bits along with the destruction. There was now just a single Javol left remaining in a corner. That one was vibrating in fear and unable to do anything because of its inflicted wounds.

'There was one...And then there was none,' Jull said, as he blasted its remains into molten metal and floated upwards to join his friends.

The large corridor above the den was now uncomfortably hot from the convection currents coming from the lower den. He gave orders to fit three weapons in the corridor and left that installation for the mine-probes and Andy's specials to seal off.

'No Javols must escape from this world to warn the others and we need several more replacements for this place, even if we program each probe to do the tasks of fifty Javols,' he said. Then he transmitted another signal for some more frigates to lay mines throughout the system and it was done.

Subsequently, they would build their own bases below the Javols' one and with portals for easy access. That way, they could always control the Javols' command computers and keep an eye on their future plans in the area, when more appeared from their central command.

During that assault only warriors with Implants were used, so that any dead could be brought back.

As they searched through the Javol's den later that day, they had several surprises.

The stench of that place was beyond human endurance and there were several chambers within the smaller caves in the den. Many had chains and shackles fitted to the walls with pools of fatty human remains and dried blood splattered on those surfaces.

There were also several young Timit women that had been flayed, brutalized and tortured to death, all hanging from shackles and some chained to the cave walls. Those images were sickening to watch and brought home the evil ways of Javols.

Every gang member wore facials in case of poisonous dust, unpleasant surprises and smells.

The numbers of Javols killed that day were just over seven thousand and it would have taken them a little while to replace them by several hundred mind-probes. But that had to be done if their efforts were to remain anonymous.

At the end of their real first battle against the Javols, they hugged and kissed each other and even Jull smiled at them in appreciation for a job well done. For now they had proven themselves in battle and deserved his respect. The many wounded were soon healed and made whole by their very advanced brand of technology.

The green Timit humans on the meadows and farms had no knowledge of the battle or even that they were under new masters. They would remain that way for now until he had a thorough knowledge of their part in the Javol's plans.

When they arrived back at Terminus City later that day, there were already celebrations in all four sections of the city. Pamela had relayed information to Earth about the great successful battle in Andromeda, to capture the planet Caefon.

Meron, Jon and the other Caefonites were pleased with their efforts on that momentous day. In over three thousand years, only now were they able to fight back in earnest and on equal terms. The Ancients had finally regained their world Caefon after so many years. Their current success was now a lot more encouraging, even with the fearful Jull the Patriarch Warrior there to keep an eye on the battle and guarantee their success.

They soon realized how formidable their enemies the Javols

really were and knew their chances of survival even with the special cloaks would have been close to nil if Jull was not there.

During the battle no one died, but several were wounded from Javols' poisonous dust and special tools, molten rock and falling debris. However, the special cloaks held their own and reduced all such damage to a minimum.

CHAPTER 47

The magic wand

After their glorious successes on Caefon in Andromeda, further improvements were made to their microid suits and weapons, particularly in those areas susceptible to Javols' attack.

Once again, George called them together on the eve of their first successful battle to yet another of his unscheduled dinner parties.

'Let us drink a toast to a job well done and the first real conquest to the Warrior Patriarchs of Osmaron. May all our future battles be as completely successful and as quickly resolved as our first,' he said and they all drank to future success.

'I have called you here today to discuss certain immediate plans and a course of action that we might need to take regarding Earth's future. This is meant to be a free discussion between member councillors, so I would also like to hear your views. After that, we may take a vote. I have decided to release the recording of the Javol's destruction of Caefon throughout Earth, to be backed by a campaign of "The Warriors of Osmaron" versus "The Evil Javols of Andromeda". Our present successes are to be reenforced by constant articles of future successes and drawbacks as and when they occur. We shall also introduce game machines, so that they can get practice at shooting Javols. I think this is important if we are to win over the young to our side before we change the political system there.

'Pamela is to plan one of her unique programs with the help of her contacts throughout the mass media, internationally. It will be done in such a manner that in just weeks, many of Earth's population will want to join the fight. By so doing they will be absorbed within the greater plan, for the common-good,' he said.

'I think it's a brilliant plan. We are now able to kill two birds with one stone... to get them on our side to fight against a common enemy and by so doing, significantly reduce Earth's population and in the process absorb them all within the Empire,' Jerry said, enthusiastically.

'And I have several ideas in mind if dollar money is not a

problem,' Pamela replied.

'Money will never be a problem and you can have some of your colleagues' assistance, including myself; before they are assigned to their own ministries. As Jerry has indicated, I need to get Earth on the move to fight our common threat and in the process get them interested in resettlement away from Earth for now. At the appropriate time they will be enticed into becoming good citizens of the Empire. Thus giving us time and space to rebuild our home planet and clean its environments. When we are through, there will be no more countries on Earth, just protectorates like on Eden, with a few beautiful cities and no polluting technologies. Anyway, many will prefer to return to new palaces on a better world after the Javols' defeat.

'Industries can be sited on the Moon or elsewhere and Earth can always trade with other members of the federation for much of her technological requirements. Anyway, that is my father's department.

'You may discuss further relevant questions on this topic with Lady Pamela.

'Now, there is also the matter of Jerry and Miranda's forthcoming wedding and we need to select one week's holiday for the City of Terminus, in commemoration of our first victory against the Javols. During which time I am to say a few words to the population with Donald and the Mayor at my side.

'Finally, there is the memorial ceremony on Caefon. Which I think should be concluded before we commence the rehabilitation and resettlement of Infilates and others over there.

'I am looking forward to the time when we are freely able to visit our colonies within Andromeda and beyond. In future Caefon and Earth shall be considered as one world. This is because of their twinning by our Grand Lord Gerra.

'At that time we may build beautiful palaces on our other home world, Caefon, if we wish, as we shall on Earth in the near future.

'We all know that we are able to live anywhere within the universe, but I think it's a lot better when we are among friends that we love and trust,' he said.

'When can we visit Lori III and Tarran?' Cathy asked.

'After our celebrations here, we can take Venusa's ship for

another trip. But only after the evacuation program has been set in motion. Then we can access their needs and assist wherever we can,' he said.

'When do we expect Empress Sarah and your father to join us?' Bawaki asked.

'Mother and the other family members are to join us before the memorial ceremony. Mother has her own tasks of keeping this galaxy of Osmaron free of our enemies while we are away fighting. She, Lord Seno and his people are to secure Osmaron.

'Malik and his family and Bailor will also be visiting during this period, so we have lots of work to do before the holiday begins. They have also learnt of our present victory and would like to share in the celebrations,' George replied.

'We would like to get married on Earth, if possible,' Miranda said.

'In that case, the wedding can take place after the Ancients' memorial ceremony on Caefon. Why not use the Mansion for that occasion. It now belongs to us all.

'I have already issued instructions to craftsmen and engineers for building the monument on Caefon. Mother and others can also visit Caefon for that purpose.

'I have scheduled this building process for two weeks, so all we need to know is a date for the wedding after that time. I am sure Miranda will set a date to coincide with the week after that period. Nevertheless, I would like us to build a significant monument in that area after the Javols' are gone. It will be one of the most spectacular, incredible and unique construction in the whole of the galaxy, so we shall have much to consider on that score,' he replied.

'In that case, I would like our wedding to be on the next Saturday after the memorial. That gives us more than enough time to prepare,' Miranda said.

They all agreed and when they finished dinner an android entered the room holding a black box with hexagrams on each face.

'This was meant to be a surprise,' George said, while opening the box and removing a long white stick that resembled a wand.

'These are your batons of office, but they are more like wands. Each is tuned to your individual implant codes and can be used as part of your dress, or as a self defence device against Javols and primal life-forms.

They can only be operated through your implants and are only to be used in emergencies. They are designed to go with your cloaks and add the extra touch of seniority when utility belts are not required. Because of those reasons, they are always kept on your person and slide into your small side pocket,' he said and continued handing them out with instructions.

The site of the monument was cleared and a small citadel built and made ready, while Lower Cantor was being completed. Soon many screened robotic construction units were dispatched throughout the system to build the new bases and erect the defensive weapons in shielded and screened bunkers.

The whole system was to be tightly secured and monitored. That job had to be completed before the resettlement of Caefon and the commencement of the real Battle for Andromeda. But before then, Triangulum would be visited in order to be secured and screened from the first wandering Javols.

CHAPTER 48

Ceremonies and celebrations

Miranda had meticulously organised and prepared every aspect of her wedding. She was assisted by Cathy and other members of The Gang, and the mansion was having a quick facelift for the forthcoming wedding celebrations which were to be held on Earth.

Ulysses and Hercules were back together at the mansion. They always shared their experiences with each other and when they were not actively involved in manor security, were having a few rounds of golf.

The ancient video of the Javols' previous destruction of Caefon, three thousand years ago, was shown over the mass media of Earth during peak viewing. The gore pictures had taken everyone by complete surprise and was backed by the most sensational videos of their recent conquest of Caefon. Suddenly its people were aware of a most dangerous threat to humanity everywhere and wanted to join the greater struggle with the promise of intergalactic adventure. They soon forgot about their mundane problems and wanted to take on their enemies for the future survival of Osmaron.

After that time, there were endless queues at recruitment offices and George had to quickly modify his plans and increase accommodation facilities on Earth and on Terminus to absorb the extra recruits.

He had also decided to give all Infilates complete freedom throughout the system once they had been rehabilitated into the Osmaron Empire and had taken their oaths of allegiance.

He gave instructions for a large cleaning and rejuvenation installation to be built within the training area on Terminus for the purpose of education and training. After their transformation, it would be up to them to score extra points within the greater empire for services rendered.

The day of the memorial ceremony soon presented itself, as the building of the temple came to completion on Caefon in Andromeda.

George and others had arranged for several garlands of flowers to be plucked from the fields of Caefon and they were spread throughout the temple. The monument or Wonder was not yet constructed.

The temple was central with several alters. Its walls and floor were of a pinkish marble material with beautifully painted glass windows that had been imported from Earth and elsewhere for that purpose. Several of the walls and ceilings portrayed beautiful images of the ancient Caefon, well before the Javols came into existence and the place resembled a large cathedral on Earth, but without statues. Those would be added later.

Meron took the ceremony at the monument before proceeding to the nearby temple to pray for the souls of all those lost families and other life-forms in Andromeda. Then they knelt and had a moment of silent prayer. Finally, George and Clair went to the altar, placed the golden hexagram with cross upon it and said a few religious words.

It was a very solemn moment and all past memories came flooding back into the Ancients' minds and the women couldn't hold back the tears.

When it was all over, they took the temple's portal to Lower Cantor for lunch within one of its buildings. That one had been refurbished and prepared for the occasion.

Knowledge of Jerry and Miranda's wedding had been kept a secret from the media. Even so, everyone of importance within the organisation was invited, including Grand Lord Gerra.

The Grand Lord wanted to visit and complement George on his recent successes. So did Lords Vektron and Patron who had initiated the three thousand year plan that sacrificed Caefon in the process. Lord Seno and the others on Orban also wanted to be involved after watching the ceremony. It was their original world as much as any other and they were concerned for its future survival. So Lord Seno decided to assist in planning another great monument along with the building of a new city of Cantor.

Jerry and Miranda's wedding would be the first conducted by

George as high priest of his new religion and he was dressed in a special robe. Clair followed as high priestess. She was the first to be escorted to her own makeshift throne by several of her own age of young female followers. They were holding her long white gown away from the marble floor.

Miranda was dressed in a standard beautiful wedding dress and Jerry in grey suit with black bow-tie and hat to match. All the other participants were in best dress for the occasion.

When they were all sat in the large room prepared for the service, the music began to play and Donald escorted his son Jerry towards the makeshift alter. With Miranda's father just behind, escorting his daughter to stand next to her future husband.

George took the proceedings in much the same way as a Christian marriage ceremony and when they took their vows, the rings were exchanged to seal their commitment. Then they kissed passionately.

When the ceremony was over, most of the councillors went to change in more relaxed clothes for the reception. The main reception was held in another larger room within the mansion. However, the ships, Daisy and Micol, were also decorated and made available for the occasion.

Everyone of importance was there, less reporters, and the Grand Lord, Vektron and Patron were also among the guests, posing as normal human visitors. But that did not stop George and Clair from recognising them.

'Ah, gentlemen, there you are. I thought you might have been too busy to visit us at this time. However, you have greatly honoured us with your presence,' George said, while bowing gently.

'It is a fine religion, and a fine ceremony was given,' replied the Grand lord.

'Religion has always been an important ingredient in the human psyche. It instils hope in those suffering, with a promise of a better future, even after primal existence. But it also gives the masses a common conscience which makes them better citizens and much easier to control by way of laws. However, such programming must begin at an early age in order that they take firm rooting,' George replied, but the Grand Lord knew

The Chronicles of Galaxy Osmaron series

The Chronicles of Osmaron series point a way to one of our possible futures. In this future, technology is more advanced. But our real problems come from a local galaxy, where another human species have accidentally created the ideal nano-bot type soldier. They are truly unique in the sense that they are almost indestructible, can copy and replicate almost anything, can live for ever, can reproduce their own kind and require living organisms like us for food. At least that was the unintended nano-bot type demon that came out of the mould after their second and final experiment.

Those nano-bot Javols went on to destroy all major animal life, including their creators, within Andromeda and are presently on their way to our Milky Way galaxy (Osmaron). The most advanced in our galaxy, who are non-human, decide to fight back for the survival of all naturally evolving life, but have to first inform lesser civilizations like us of the impending danger.

Before we can confront the demon Javols, we must first advance our technologies to Class 5. This is about 100,000 years more advanced than Earth's present levels. During this period Earth undergoes many changes due to Global Warming and human overpopulation, but manages to survive the onslaught.

Wars will rage, but apparently ubiquitous humans will always find ways to survive and win the day.

www.ingramcontent.com/pod-product-compliance
Lightning Source LLC
Chambersburg PA
CBHW020353080526
44584CB00014B/1004

everything there was to know of all religions so Lord Vektron changed the topic.

'We have observed your progress in these few months, and quite frankly, we were impressed. If that progress continues in a similar vein... very soon we shall have very little to do ourselves,' Lord Vektron intimated.

'I would willingly like us all to work together for the common good of our universe. We should never forget that we are all committed to a common cause and by working together we can never pull against ourselves or duplicate our efforts within the Greater Purpose.

'Why don't we form a special ministry within the Osmaron Empire through which our mutual efforts may be channelled. Please think about what I have said and I would like you both to visit Terminus with us and spend a little time during our city celebrations,' George replied.

Clair and Cathy soon came along to greet them at the bar. Then Clair took George aside.

'My brother, I have sensed the infidel Dracma on his way to Triangulum. He will get there in under half a century. He intends to build a super fleet, return to Andromeda and assist his brother Lupher to take over the universe,' Clair said, looking a little worried by that knowledge.

'Let them be for now, my dear. We can always find them again if we wish,' George replied. He ordered another drink for Clair before rejoining Cathy and the others at the bar.

People on Earth still remembered George Peterson as their saviour. Nevertheless, he didn't wish to confuse or distort that image in ways detrimental to his long term goals, by appearing prematurely anywhere on the planet before certain events had run their course.

In his opinion, that past image impression could only be reenforced by the correct type of publicity. Therefore, they left the mansion as soon as the wedding celebrations were completed.

The following day, Terminus City was inaugurated. It was formally named and given provisional status as the main training city of Osmaron.

Donald led the ceremony and re-nominated Mayor Rochet, who

was the existing mayor of Caefon Dome with Donald as the president of Mars. Mayor Rochet was presented with the golden mace of office and took the oath gracefully.

After that part of the ceremony was over, George gave a speech to his citizens and when he finished, the real celebrations commenced.

Sarah, Lumak, Grand Lord Gerra, Vektron, Patron, Malik, Bailor and many senior members were given the grand tour of Terminus. They were shown all its technologies that made the city a complete human environment within the Martian plains and they were amazed by its uniqueness. That same city, could also have been programmed into virtually any alien environment by the touch of a button, except for atmospheric gases and necessary physical structures, but those could also have been added in time.

Sarah and Lumak decided to consider it their second home while Earth was being prepared.

The leaders of Osmaron and Earth were finally being brought together for the great war against the Javols within Andromeda and elsewhere, and now they had the weapons and cunning to complete the conflict in their favour and against all invaders of Osmaron.

Epilogue

Numerous swarms of rapacious Nano-bot Javols are currently on their way to our galaxy. They will arrive within 50 years. They are so numerous that they will blacken the skies of most worlds. Their sole purpose is to dominate and rear us like cattle for their own sustenance. On arrival they will be hungry and starving and will feed on all life until many come close to extinction.

Only George Peterson, in the form of Jull the warrior Patriarch, with his new breed of soldiers and weapons, will hopefully save the day. During that most vicious conflict many will die and he must ensure we have a fighting chance.

By the time of their arrival the human population of Earth will be reduced to just 500 million. This new situation will give Earth enough time to rebuild her forests and wild life. However during that time the whole governing structure of Earth will be replaced by powerful Headrons, Macrons and their policing androids. They will ensure that Earth never returns to the days of selfish and capitalist mankind in the form of Infilates.

Never again will mankind be given free reign to destroy a beautiful world in the name of greed. The days of Infilates are truly over.

George has quite a political fight on his hands with Earth's governments. Will he win that day?

A NEW SOCIETY ON EARTH

In the interim period, before the new Solarian empire, there will be a new society on Earth with no financial Banks.

No more manufactured money, in the form of notes and coins. Only his new credits and cards for transactions.

All cities and towns will contain recycling depots for everything. Those are run by Freetimers.

Every individual will work just 6 months in each year for full salary. Therefore double the people will be employed.

Every individual gives two months in each year freely to their local communities, for assisting the elderly, and the environment. During that time their community allows them travelling expenses and food, plus a uniform. After that time they can be promoted to a higher officer grade (Grade One or higher). Grade One officers in any profession are given a special Credit Card for 5% discount on all transactions within their community. Grade Two Officers get 7.5% discount, etcetera. Higher grade officers are given greater discounts and are elected to run their communities. Since recycling depots are run by Freetimers all recycled goods are cheap.

During this two month period of community help, workers are called Freetimers. All Freetimers are compelled to wear uniforms during this time.

The last four months of each year belongs to the individual, for holidays and such like.

George's new society is very efficient and valued by all.